Believers Church
Bible Commentary

Elmer A. Martens and Willard M. Swartley, Editors

BELIEVERS CHURCH BIBLE COMMENTARY

Old Testament
Genesis, by Eugene F. Roop
Exodus, by Waldemar Janzen
Judges, by Terry L. Brensinger
Ruth, Jonah, Esther, by Eugene F. Roop
Jeremiah, by Elmer A. Martens
Ezekiel, by Millard C. Lind
Daniel, by Paul M. Lederach
Hosea, Amos, by Allen R. Guenther

New Testament
Matthew, by Richard B. Gardner
Mark, by Timothy J. Geddert
Acts, by Chalmer E. Faw
2 Corinthians, by V. George Shillington
Ephesians, by Thomas R. Yoder Neufeld
Colossians, Philemon, by Ernest D. Martin
1-2 Thessalonians, by Jacob W. Elias
1-2 Peter, Jude, by Erland Waltner and J. Daryl Charles
Revelation, by John R. Yeatts

Old Testament Editors
Elmer A. Martens and Allen R. Guenther (for *Jeremiah*), Mennonite Brethren Biblical Seminary, Fresno, California

New Testament Editors
Willard M. Swartley and Howard H. Charles (for *Matthew*), Associated Mennonite Biblical Seminary, Elkhart, Indiana

Editorial Council
David Baker, Brethren Church
Lydia Harder, Mennonite Church Canada
Estella B. Horning, Church of the Brethren
Robert B. Ives, Brethren in Christ Church
Gordon H. Matties, Mennonite Brethren Church
Paul M. Zehr (chair), Mennonite Church USA

Believers Church Bible Commentary

Ruth, Jonah, Esther

Eugene F. Roop

HERALD PRESS
Scottdale, Pennsylvania
Waterloo, Ontario

Library of Congress Cataloging-in-Publication Data

Roop, Eugene F., 1942-
  Ruth, Jonah, Esther / by Eugene F. Roop.
    p. cm. — (Believers church Bible commentary)
  Includes bibliographical references and index.
  ISBN 0-8361-9199-4 (Kivar-bound squareback : alk. paper)
  1. Bible. O.T. Ruth—Commentaries. 2. Bible. O.T.
Jonah—Commentaries. 3. Bible. O.T. Esther—Commentaries. I. Title.
II. Series.
  BS1315.53 .R66 2002
  222'.3507—dc21   2002001690

The paper used in this publication is recycled and meets the minimum requirements of American National Standard for Information Sciences—Permanence of Paper for Printed Library Materials, ANSI Z39.48-1984.

Bible text is mostly from *New Revised Standard Version Bible,* copyright 1989 by the Division of Christian Education of the National Council of the Churches of Christ in the USA, and used by permission. Abbreviations listed on page 6 identify other versions briefly compared.

No part of this publication may be reproduced, stored in a retrieval system, or transmitted in any form or by any means, electronic, mechanical, photocopying, recording, or otherwise, without the prior permission of the publisher or a license permitting restricted copying. Such licenses are issued on behalf of Herald Press by Copyright Clearance Center, Inc., 222 Rosewood Drive, Danvers, MA 01923; phone 978-750-8400; fax 978-750-4470; www.copyright.com.

BELIEVERS CHURCH BIBLE COMMENTARY: RUTH, JONAH, ESTHER
  Copyright © 2002 by Herald Press, Scottdale, Pa. 15683
  Released simultaneously in Canada by Herald Press,
Waterloo, Ont. N2L 6H7. All rights reserved
Library of Congress Control Number: 2002001690
International Standard Book Number: 0-8361-9199-4
Printed in the United States of America
Cover and map by Merrill R. Miller

11 10 09 08 07 06 05 04 03 02 10 9 8 7 6 5 4 3 2 1

To order or request information, please call 1-800-759-4447 (individuals); 1-800-245-7894 (trade). Website: www.mph.org

To my grandchildren,
Matthew and John Roop,
Eric Yager

Abbreviations/Symbols

//	parallel to
*	The Text in Biblical Context, TBC
+	The Text in the Life of the Church, TLC
AT	Alpha Text, a Greek version of Esther
cf.	compare
EFR	Scripture translated by Eugene F. Roop
e.g.	for example
esp.	especially
Heb.	Hebrew text
JB	*Jerusalem Bible, The*
KJV	*King James Version*
lit.	literally
LXX	Septuagint, the OT in Greek
MT	Masoretic Text of the OT
NASB	New American Standard Bible
NIV	New International Version
NJB	*New Jerusalem Bible, The*
notes	Explanatory Notes
NRSV	*New Revised Standard Version* (see © page)
NT	New Testament
OT	Old Testament
[Short Story]	Typical reference to Essays in an appendix
Tanak	Acronym for Heb. OT: Torah/Law/Pentateuch, Nebi'im/Prophets, and Ketubim/Writings
TBC	The Text in Biblical Context, after section of notes
TLC	The Text in the Life of the Church, after TBC

Contents

Series Foreword 11
Author's Preface 13

Ruth: A Story of Famine, Friendship, and Fertility

Overview 16
The Consummate Short Story 16
Where Does Ruth Belong? 18
A Glance at the Whole 19
Meaning and Message 20
An Outline of the Major Units 23
How to Read Ruth 24
**1. Introduction: Famine, Displacement,
   and Death, 1:1-5** 26
   * Famine in the Land (Text in Biblical Context) 30
   + People Living at Risk (Text in Life of the Church) ... 31
2. The Story of Two Widows, 1:6—4:12 33
Episode 1: Return to Bethlehem, 1:6-22 34
   * Naomi and Job 40
   + Complaint Against God 41
Episode 2: Going for Grain, 2:1-23 43
   * The Poor in the Biblical Tradition 53

   + God Who Blesses 54
Episode 3: Seeking Security, 3:1-18 56
   * The Childless Widow 64
   + Beyond Assistance to Security 66
Episode 4: Agreement at the Gate, 4:1-12 68
   * The Unrecorded World of Women 75
   + The Person of Substance 76
3. Conclusion and Coda, 4:13-22 79
Birth and Naming of a Son, 4:13-17 82
Genealogy of Perez, 4:18-22 85
   * The Women in the Genealogy 86
   + Good and Faithful Servant 87
Outline of Ruth 90

Jonah: A Story for All

Overview 94
Jonah as Understood in the Past 94
What Manner of Narrative? 97
Message and Meaning 98
A Glance at the Whole 99
An Outline of the Major Units 100
1. The Unfulfilled Prophetic Mission, 1:1—2:11 103
The Commissioning of Jonah, 1:1-3 104
   * Commissioning of the Prophet 109
   + Reluctant Response 110
The Drama at Sea, 1:4—2:10 112
   On the Sea, 1:4-16 113
   * Foreigners Acknowledge God 120
   + God and Nature 121
   Under the Sea, 1:17—2:10 122
   * Psalm of Thanksgiving 128
   + Jonah: Saint or Sinner? 129
2. The Unfulfilled Prophet, 3:1—4:11 131
The Recommissioning of Jonah, 3:1-3a 132
   * Commissioning the Prophet—Again 134
   + Human Freedom and Divine Persistence 135
The Drama on Land, 3:3b—4:11 137
   In the City, 3:3b-10 138
   * The Sign of Jonah 144
   + Divine Freedom and the Promise of Forgiveness 146

Outside the City, 4:1-11 147
* The Concluding Question 154
\+ The Mystery of Divine Compassion 155
Outline of Jonah 157

Esther: The Orphan Queen

Overview 160
The Orphan Queen 160
Controversy and Concerns 161
Different Versions of Esther 162
A Festival Novella 164
Meaning and Message 165
A Glance at the Whole 168
An Outline of the Major Units 169
Scene 1: Tension in the Royal Court, 1:1—3:6 173
Episode 1: Conflict in the Royal Family, 1:1—2:20 174
    Deposing of Vashti, 1:1-22 174
    * Israel in the Persian Empire 179
    \+ The Fabric of Society 180
    Selection of Esther, 2:1-20 182
    * From Insignificance to Importance 188
    \+ Heroes of Faith 189
Episode 2: Conflict Among the Royal Courtiers, 2:21—3:6 191
    Conspiracy Against the King, 2:21-23 192
    Conflict Between Courtiers, 3:1-6 194
    * Choosing Disobedience 196
    \+ Mixed Motives 197
Scene 2: Action and Counteraction, 3:7—7:10 199
Episode 1: Haman Versus Mordecai, 3:7—4:17 200
    The Plot of Haman, 3:7-15 201
    Response of Mordecai, 4:1-17 204
    * Women in Danger 207
    \+ For Such a Time as This 208
Episode 2: Esther's First Intervention, 5:1-14 211
    * The Dangerous Banquet 215
    \+ Obsessions 216
Episode 3: Royal Decree Honoring Mordecai, 6:1-13 ... 218
    * Irony and Divine Intervention 222
    \+ A Haughty Spirit 224
Episode 4: Esther's Second Intervention, 6:14—7:10 ... 226

* Proverbs and Esther 231
+ Capital Punishment 232
Scene 3: Resolution and Celebration, 8:1—9:32 235
Resolution of the Crisis, 8:1-17 236
  * Leadership in a Foreign Land 240
  + Self-Protective Leadership 242
Institution of Purim, 9:1-32 244
Epilogue: Ahasuerus and Mordecai, 10:1-3................... 251
  * Listening to Rage and Terror.. 253
  + Living in the World 255
Outline of Esther 257

Essays
  Characteristics of Hebrew Narrative 260
  Character Types in Hebrew Narrative................................ 263
  Comedy: Humor, Irony, and Satire..................................... 263
  The Diaspora 265
  The Interpreting Community of Faith 266
  Jonah and Historical Analysis 267
  Khesed: Uncommon and Faithful Action 268
  Kinship Marriage 269
  Moab 270
  Narrative Structure 271
  Narrator.. 272
  Nineveh 273
  Novella 275
  The Persian Empire 275
  Poetry 276
  Purim.. 277
  Questions... 278
  Redeemer/Go'el 279
  Short Story 280
  Twelve Prophets 281
  Village Farming 282
Map of the Ancient Near East for Ruth, Jonah, Esther 284
Bibliography.. 285
Selected Resources 295
Index of Ancient Sources 297
The Author... 303

Series Foreword

The Believers Church Bible Commentary Series makes available a new tool for basic Bible study. It is published for all who seek more fully to understand the original message of Scripture and its meaning for today—Sunday school teachers, members of Bible study groups, students, pastors, and others. The series is based on the conviction that God is still speaking to all who will listen, and that the Holy Spirit makes the Word a living and authoritative guide for all who want to know and do God's will.

The desire to help as wide a range of readers as possible has determined the approach of the writers. Since no blocks of biblical text are provided, readers may continue to use the translation with which they are most familiar. The writers of the series use the *New Revised Standard Version*, the *Revised Standard Version*, the *New International Version*, and the *New American Standard Bible* on a comparative basis. They indicate which text they follow most closely, and where they make their own translations. The writers have not worked alone, but in consultation with select counselors, the series' editors, and the Editorial Council.

Every volume illuminates the Scriptures; provides necessary theological, sociological, and ethical meanings; and, in general, makes "the rough places plain." Critical issues are not avoided, but neither are they moved into the foreground as debates among scholars. Each section offers explanatory notes, followed by focused articles, "The Text in Biblical Context" and "The Text in the Life of the Church."

The writers have done the basic work for each commentary, but not operating alone, since "no . . . scripture is a matter of one's own interpretation" (2 Pet. 1:20; cf. 1 Cor. 14:29). While writing, they have consulted with select counselors, worked with the editors for the series, and received feedback from another biblical scholar. In addition, the Editorial Council, representing six believers church bodies, reads the manuscripts carefully, gives churchly responses, and suggests changes. The writer considers all this counsel and processes it into the manuscript, which the Editorial Council finally approves for publication. Thus these commentaries combine the individual writers' own good work and the church's voice. As such, they represent a hermeneutical community's efforts in interpreting the biblical text, as led by the Spirit.

The term *believers church* has often been used in the history of the church. Since the sixteenth century, it has frequently been applied to the Anabaptists and later the Mennonites, as well as to the Church of the Brethren and similar groups. As a descriptive term, it includes more than Mennonites and Brethren. *Believers church* now represents specific theological understandings, such as believers baptism, commitment to the Rule of Christ in Matthew 18:15-20 as crucial for church membership, belief in the power of love in all relationships, and willingness to follow Christ in the way of the cross. The writers chosen for the series stand in this tradition.

Believers church people have always been known for their emphasis on obedience to the simple meaning of Scripture. Because of this, they do not have a long history of deep historical-critical biblical scholarship. This series attempts to be faithful to the Scriptures while also taking archaeology and current biblical studies seriously. Hence, at many points the writers will not differ greatly from interpretations found in many other good commentaries. Yet these writers share basic convictions about Christ, the church and its mission, God and history, human nature, the Christian life, and other doctrines. These presuppositions do shape a writer's interpretation of Scripture. Thus this series, like all other commentaries, stands within a specific historical church tradition.

Many in this stream of the church have expressed a need for help in Bible study. This is justification enough to produce the Believers Church Bible Commentary. Nevertheless, the Holy Spirit is not bound to any tradition. May this series be an instrument in breaking down walls between Christians in North America and around the world, bringing new joy in obedience through a fuller understanding of the Word.

—*The Editorial Council*

Author's Preface

In the past two decades, the Christian church in North America has come to recognize anew the importance of narrative, of story. Stories not only report events and entertain readers; as Christians in many other cultures have understood better than we, *story* also defines and renews community and personal identity. We are connected to the past and directed into the future by the stories we remember and retell.

The life of each individual and every congregation has meaning, purpose and direction as it is incorporated into the Great Story of the Christian church, grounded always and forever in the Bible. We realize the defining power of narrative as we teach the biblical stories to our children and recast them in drama and song for worship. We recognize the transforming power of biblical narrative as we share these stories with folks whose lives are haunted by a dreary and depressing story or controlled by a violent, destructive narrative.

The biblical stories of Ruth, Jonah, and Esther are among those most prized by children and adults. Children imaginatively accompany Jonah on the stormy sea, shivering with him inside the great fish. Adults weep with Naomi as she returns to Bethlehem, grieving the loss of spouse and children. Then they watch with amazement as this foreign woman, through ingenuity and risk, transforms one family and also all generations to follow. With each retelling, we stand with Esther almost paralyzed in the face of those with evil design who seek to destroy the community of faith.

These three biblical narratives belong together not because they follow in sequence in the Bible or because they tell stories from the same era. Instead, Ruth, Jonah, and Esther share a single genre, a kind of literature we know from all cultures and times—the short story.

The form of a short story is distinguished from the biblical genre of saga and Gospel by its brevity, simple plot, and limited number of characters. These three short stories stand alone as self-contained entities. Other narratives that might be considered short stories are incorporated into other books and sagas, such as the story of Joseph and the stories associated with Daniel.

The purpose of this commentary, set within the believers church tradition, is to open Ruth, Jonah, and Esther to the community of faith, study, and prayer. Heaven forbid that this commentary replace a reading of the narratives themselves. Indeed, the identity-defining and transforming power of Ruth, Jonah, and Esther are released only by reading the stories in their entirety. I hope this commentary can function as a catalyst for increased understanding and appreciation, as well as a stimulus for community discussion and discernment. Indeed, this commentary grew out of the study of these stories in congregational discussion and seminary study. It is intended to give back to those settings some of what they have given me, and in so doing promote an increase of faith, hope, and love.

Countless people had a hand in completing this commentary, and I risk inexcusable omissions by listing names. Nevertheless, the series Old Testament editor, Elmer Martens, read the manuscript many times, and Herald Press editor, S. David Garber, carefully reviewed it. Also, Elmer Dyck, Jay Marshall, Donna Ritchey Martin, and the editorial council of the Believers Church Bible Commentary took extra time to read and comment on parts or the whole. I thank the faculty, staff, and trustees of Bethany Theological Seminary, who provided encouragement, opportunity, and the impetus to write. In the seminary president's office, Sandy Powell and Margie Mullins provided direct and indirect assistance in preparing this manuscript for publication.

Finally, I thank the students in both the graduate and academy programs of Bethany Theological Seminary for their perceptive comments, questions, and papers, all of which contributed to the commentary. This book is dedicated to the saints of the past and present who have taught me the Bible, and also to the generations to come. Most especially, this book is dedicated to my grandchildren and all other children and grandchildren who are just beginning to learn the biblical stories. The best books remain for them to write, the most profound interpretations for them to voice, the most faithful service for them to render—through Jesus Christ our Lord.

—*Eugene F. Roop*
  Bethany Theological Seminary
  Richmond, Indiana

Ruth

Ruth: A Story of Famine, Friendship, and Fertility

OVERVIEW
The Consummate Short Story
No biblical narrative has charmed and enthralled readers through the ages more than the story of Ruth. J. W. von Goethe (1749-1832), the great German writer, characterized Ruth as one of the most beautiful short stories handed on to us in all of epic and idyllic literature (Heinemann: 342-3). The pastoral scene in the small village of Bethlehem awakens all the senses of its readers: the sights and sounds of village life, the smell of the grain field in the midst of harvest, the taste of freshly baked bread, the touch of a man and woman in the dark of the night.

The power of this brief narrative to provide models for responsible community life continues to impress lay readers and scholars alike. Phyllis Trible (1978:166, 196) finds in the aging Naomi and the youthful Ruth a paradigm for radicality, women making their way in a man's world. Lief Hongisto sees Naomi as a heroic figure who maintains her faith in the face of misfortune. Marjory Bankson discovers in the relationship between these two women an example of the seasons for all friendships. Kathleen Farmer experiences this as a drama of redemption, for Naomi, but also for those able to walk with Naomi through the story (1998:892-893). Most heroic of all, however, is Ruth, whose actions and words model steadfast love: "a woman of great strength and determination," "a woman worth more than seven sons of Israel" (Fewell/Gunn, 1990:105).

Likely some of Ruth's power to charm comes from its pastoral character. It reads as a story without a villain, life without evil. Although village peasants in Bethlehem have lived through times of distress, in Ruth even the most dangerous elements, famine and widowhood, are resolved without physical violence and terror. In that way Ruth cannot be equated with other epic and folk literature, which customarily includes intense conflict and the struggle of good against evil (Milne).

Most biblical stories from *the days when the judges ruled* tell of life far more violent and dangerous (Ruth 1:1). We read of deadly conflict between Deborah and the Canaanite prince Sisera (Judg. 4–5), the exploits of Samson among the Philistines (Judg. 14–16), and the raging revenge of the Levite against Gibeah (Judg. 19–21). Thus the violence in the stories of Judges only serves to highlight the relative serenity of life in Bethlehem.

Life in Naomi's Judean village can be difficult, but the people are responsive to the needs of others—with some prodding. The narrative seems to illustrate the familiar phrase: "We know that all things work together for good for those who love God, who are called according to his purpose" (Rom. 8:28; NRSV footnote: "God makes" this happen). How different that sounds from Joseph's final speech to his brothers: "As for you, you meant evil against me, but God meant it for good" (Gen. 50:20, NASB). Even though both short stories have happy endings, the world of Ruth seems far less dangerous and politicized than that of Joseph.

Yet hiding within the idyllic world of kind villagers, charming landowners, and harvest festivals, readers find a real world, one less than ideal. Nor can the characters in Ruth be reduced to ideal types: the heroic mother, the benevolent landlord, and the faithful foreigner. The pain is real for Naomi, a mother whose world has been turned from pleasant to bitter (1:20). The anxiety is intense for Boaz, a pillar of society startled from sleep by a woman at his side (3:8).

The social dividing wall seems impenetrable for Ruth, a woman who is seldom addressed without mention of her ethnic identity, a Moabite. Israelite tradition carries a memory about the Moabites as conceived through incest (Gen. 19) and banished forever from God's sight because of their indifference to Israel's needs (Deut. 23:3). Ruth is hailed but perhaps never completely accepted (Ruth 4:14-17; Fewell/Gunn, 1990:105).

Where Does Ruth Belong?

The book of Ruth has had almost as much trouble finding its place in the biblical canon as the heroine did to find her place in Bethlehem. In most English Bibles, Ruth appears after Judges and before 1 Samuel (as in NRSV, NIV). That location was established by the Septuagint, the Greek translation of the Hebrew Bible. For some time scholars assumed the Septuagint order represented an alternate Jewish ordering to the one found in the traditional Hebrew scrolls. Now it appears that the Septuagint, as we have received it, represents an ordering of the canon established in Christian rather than Jewish circles (Beckwith: 181-222).

Another tradition places Ruth in the third section of the Hebrew canon, the Writings (cf. English version of Tanak—an acronym for Torah/Law/Pentateuch, Nebi'im/Prophets, and *K*etubim/Writings) *[Twelve Prophets]*. Although the order of the Writings was somewhat fluid, Ruth came to be grouped together with four other books as the five Festival scrolls (Megilloth). Each of these scrolls was read at a different Jewish festival: Song of Songs at Passover, Ruth at Feast of Weeks/Pentecost, Lamentations at the commemoration of Jerusalem's fall, Ecclesiastes at Tabernacles, and Esther at Purim. Some Hebrew manuscripts list the Festival Scrolls in the calendar order of the festivals (so Tanak). Other Hebrew texts use a more chronological order for these five stories. Such an ordering places Ruth first, since it tells about the time *when the judges ruled* (1:1).

As is true of most biblical short stories *[Short Story—see essay at back of book]*, we know little about the origin of the book of Ruth. The narrator informs the reader that Ruth is a story of olden times, when judges ruled, perhaps at a time when customs in the legal court of the village elders were different (4:7). Some scholars believe the narrator looks back from the tenth or ninth century B.C., when people wanted to know more about the ancestors of David and Solomon (Campbell, 1975:23-8; Hubbard, 1988a: 23-35). Others think it comes from an even later time, after the Jews return from exile in Babylon (after 538 B.C.; Gray: 366-70).

Many scholars have concluded that a later retelling of the story supplemented the original narrative by adding the genealogy to the end, to further emphasize this as a story about David's ancestry (e.g., Murphy: 87). Others think this conclusion came with the original story, insisting that the family genealogy at the end is fundamental to the purpose of the narrative (Nielsen, 1997:27).

Not unexpectedly for a Hebrew short story, the narrator or author remains anonymous *[Narrator]*. Not only do we not know the exact

Ruth Overview   19

time of composition, we do not know who might have been the first storyteller/author. The short story of Ruth stands alongside Esther as a narrative about women. But Ruth distinguishes itself even from Esther as portraying the life of women in the village, not in the palace. In Ruth and Naomi, we see women in their world, women against their world, and women transforming their world (Trible, 1978:196).

A story so much about women might well be a story by a woman (Hubbard, 1988a: 24). Perhaps one day we will find her among the wise women who told stories to pass on the tradition and also to influence the course of events (Campbell, 1975:22-23; Brenner, 1985:33-66), or among other women who confidently made their way in the social world of ancient Israel (Gottwald, 1985:557).

A Glance at the Whole

A few weighty words play key roles in this narrative *[Characteristics of Hebrew Narrative]*. Some key words help guide the course of the story through particular episodes or scenes. In that connection, we will look at *return* in chapter 1 and *glean* in chapter 2. Other words, especially the word "redeem," play an important role throughout the entire story. We need to take a look at those as we begin our study.

The basic plot line of the story moves within contrasting images, represented by specific words *[Short Story]*. The introduction of Ruth describes a world of famine and death (1:1, 3). The narrative moves quickly to reestablish fertility in the field (1:6). Only gradually, however, does that benefit the two widows (2:17-18). The plot tension is fully resolved when death has been replaced with birth (4:13-17). That hopeful event waits until the concluding scene. The movement from famine to fertility, and from death to birth, provides this marvelous narrative with a simple plot, one that deserves to be designated as an idyll.

The focus of Ruth, however, lies less in its plot action than in its people. The simple plot functions as a vehicle for important reflection on the way people relate to one another. Hence, the reader should not be surprised to find that dialogue dominates the narrative *[Characteristics of Hebrew Narrative]*. In fact, direct speech is found in fifty-five out of the eighty-five verses (Sasson, 1987:320).

In her first speech, Naomi (1:8) introduces a word that the early rabbis recognized as one key to this story: *"May the LORD deal kindly (khesed) with you, as you have dealt with the dead and with me"* (1:8). In many ways the narrative of Ruth is the story of *khesed*. "Steadfast love," the most common translation of *khesed* in the NRSV, may still best call to our imagination the action of *khesed* in ancient Israel *[Khesed]*. Yet an even better way to come to understand *khesed* is to follow Ruth through her story.

Khesed presupposes an emergency situation: danger, distress, death. *Khesed* also calls for someone to act, someone who can intervene to promote life in the emergency. Finally, *khesed* happens only if the available helper chooses to intervene. The narrative opens with Naomi thanking Orpah and Ruth as ones who did *khesed*, who acted to enhance life for one in danger or distress. Boaz also refers to Ruth as one who does *khesed* not just once, but twice (3:10). In addition, Naomi praises God as one who has acted in *khesed*.

God and Ruth are not the only characters who have opportunity for intervening to enhance life in this emergency. The analysis of the story (below) will explore how and why Naomi and Boaz act. Action prompted by motives of survival or self-interest does not make the individual a bad person or even a negative character in this short story.

Meaning and Message

A short story as remarkable and evocative as Ruth is bound to summon a variety of interpretative responses. So it has been throughout the generations.

The narrative of Ruth has frequently been read as a statement in affirmation of resident aliens, non-Israelites who live in Israel. This interpretation of Ruth has often been connected with the era of Nehemiah and Ezra, the fifth century B.C. Some biblical literature of that era urges separation from resident foreigners, seeing them as a danger to purity of faith (e.g., Ezra 9–10). Interpreters have proposed that the story may have originated in that era, and then they understand Ruth as protest literature, objecting to the "anti-alien" impulse of certain fifth-century groups.

Other interpreters relate the role of Ruth's status as a resident alien not to a specific historical era, but to the long-standing affirmation of fairness and justice grounded in Israel's own history. Israel's legal texts refer to Israel's own experience of oppression in calling for fair treatment of the foreigner, stranger, alien, sojourner: "You shall not wrong or oppress a resident alien, for you were aliens in the land of Egypt" (Exod. 22:21). As such, the narrative becomes an illustration that such strangers may prove to be "angels in our midst" (cf. Gen. 18:1-8; 19:1-3; Heb. 13:2).

Still others focus less on the general status of the resident alien and more on Ruth's Moabite ancestry. The hostility between Israel and Moab appears frequently throughout the history of ancient Israel as recorded in the Bible. According to Genesis 19, Moab is the son born from the incestuous relationship between Lot and his eldest daughter: "[Lot's] firstborn [daughter] bore a son, and named him Moab; he is the ancestor of the Moabites to this day" (19:37).

Numbers 21–25 records several conflicts between Moab and Israel during Israel's sojourn in the wilderness, including intermarriage, which the narrative condemns as seducing Israel to worship foreign gods (Num. 25). Read against the background of Israel and Moab, Ruth helps to dismantle walls of hostility that divide and destroy the community, regardless of how convincingly such hostility can be justified.

Others read Ruth as a key component in the story of David. Some speculate that, as David rose to leadership in Israel, some Israelites objected because of David's "tainted" foreign ancestry. If so, Ruth provides a positive interpretation of David's ancestry. David's grandfather Obed is born because God brings fertility to the marriage of Boaz, an important man in Bethlehem, and Ruth, a Moabite widow.

Many interpreters recognize the importance of specific, frequently repeated words as carrying and evoking meaning in this narrative. Kathleen Farmer points to the word "redemption" (*ga'al* and its derivatives) as a lens through which to interpret the narrative. On one level the story narrates the restoration of property to its original owners. But at a deeper level Naomi is redeemed by the baby whose "conception was said to be given by God" (1998:892). This will be a story of redemption for the readers (first of all Israel) as one is persuaded that the redemptive efforts made by God on behalf of Naomi signal God's ongoing redemptive activity in the world.

Most readers are familiar with the interpretation of Ruth as a narrative illustration of *khesed,* uncommon and faithful action, loyalty, and compassion (Sakenfeld, 1999:11-14). All three of the main characters, Boaz, Naomi, and especially Ruth, embody this virtue. The story begins with Ruth choosing love and loyalty over common sense, insisting that she accompany Naomi on her journey of sorrow back to Bethlehem. Blessed with enough food through the determination of Ruth, Naomi returns Ruth's *khesed* by designing a plan to *seek some security* for her daughter-in-law (3:1). The narrative concludes with Boaz finessing the legal system to keep faith with Ruth and Naomi.

As generation after generation of readers listen to the story, they recognize Ruth as one of the genuinely heroic figures in the biblical tradition. Ruth's astonishing loyalty to her mother-in-law, her determination to be noticed in the grainfields by a man who can help, her willingness to risk everything on the threshing floor—such qualities show that by all measures, Ruth is an uncommon woman. This heroic figure has arisen in Israel not as the daughter of a founding family, but coming as the child of a despised people: a Moabite who has lost husband and homeland. Boaz says it correctly: Ruth is truly *a worthy woman* (3:11).

We stop too soon, however, if we experience this only as a story of uncommon people or important virtues. Though the story only occasionally acknowledges the LORD by name, it does display the unseen hand of Providence (as in 1:6). God's active presence is expressed explicitly in fertility (4:13). The theology of the narrative connects directly with the crisis of the plot expressed in the introduction: famine in the fields and death in the family (1:1-5). Elsewhere God is invoked, but there is no dramatic divine rescue of the destitute widows (1:8-9; 2:12, 20; 4:11-12).

The narrative seems a most common one in which the characters act and react not to a divine directive or intervention, but in response to the drama of their lives. Yet most readers sense a Presence beneath and beyond the observable events. Discerned in the drama only through hints and happenstance, one "sees" Good that exceeds the virtue of the people, and Hope that surpasses the possibilities inherent in their circumstances. Surprisingly, Ruth arrives at the field of one who notices her. Happily, a risky plot of intrigue and entrapment succeeds. Fortuitously, a relative defers to Boaz when offered the chance to redeem the land and marry Ruth.

In this story God opens up the future not by dramatic intervention, but by hidden participation. Claus Westermann (1978) has identified this way of expriencing God's work as the theology of blessing. Indeed, one finds in Ruth frequent reference to blessing by God, even using the form of benediction (as in 1:8-9, 17; 2:12, 19-20; 4:11-12). Such an experience of God portrays life as an ongoing drama: God nudges, lures, and opens a redemptive future in the midst of the everyday joys and sorrows of human history.

The story of Ruth, like most biblical narratives, cannot be reduced to a single message or meaning. The narrative presents itself as an evocative book that impacts the reader anew each time it is read. Each generation hears the story with new ears and finds new meaning. That is how it should be.

Even so, the story does not make itself available for any and every interpretation. In reading Ruth, we should expect to have some of our most entrenched convictions challenged as well as our deepest needs met. If we find only confirmation for what we already do and believe, we likely have not listened closely. For that reason the church has long affirmed the importance of reading the Bible in community

Ruth Overview 23

[Interpreting Community]. Almost certainly another person has heard the story differently, perhaps quite differently. In our conversation together about its meaning and message, the story of Ruth can embody its theology of blessing—employing the common agency of conversation to transform us into ever more faithful disciples of the storyteller from Nazareth, Jesus Christ.

An Outline of the Major Units

The story line of Ruth follows the lives of two women who by misfortune are widows, without husband or heir. Their story unfolds in a series of four episodes. One or the other of the widows initiates the action in each of the first three episodes. In the first (1:6-22), Naomi embarks on a return move to Bethlehem. Naomi's dialogue with her daughters-in-law and her arrival in Bethlehem constitute the two central moments in the episode.

The second episode (2:1-23) finds Ruth determined to obtain food by gleaning in the fields throughout the barley harvest. She succeeds both because of her efforts in the fields and because of a chance meeting with Boaz.

Naomi initiates the action in the third episode (3:1-18). She decides to *seek some security* for Ruth. While the dialogue at the beginning and end of this episode is initiated by Naomi, those conversations function as prelude and postlude to the meeting on the threshing floor, where Ruth takes charge of the action.

At Naomi's suggestion (3:18), the women step aside in the final episode to make room for Boaz (4:1-12). Apparently neither Ruth nor Naomi attend the judicial hearing. Because of the decision at that council, however, Ruth and Naomi receive family and security in Bethlehem.

Framing these four episodes is an introduction (or exposition) and conclusion (1:1-5; 4:13-17). The short story ends with a coda or afterword, the genealogy of Perez (4:18-22). Here are the parts in outline form:

Introduction: Famine, Displacement, and Death, 1:1-5

The Story of Two Widows, 1:6—4:12
    1:6-22   Episode 1: Return to Bethlehem
    2:1-23   Episode 2: Going for Grain
    3:1-18   Episode 3: Seeking Security
    4:1-12   Episode 4: Agreement at the Gate

Conclusion: Birth and Naming of a Son, 4:13-17

Coda: Genealogy of Perez, 4:18-22

How to Read Ruth

Before looking in detail at the various parts of the story, take time to read the whole narrative, preferably perusing it more than once. With each reading, experience life in Bethlehem from the perspective of different characters in the drama: Ruth, Naomi, and Boaz. You may find it easier to identify with one or another. Try not to idealize any of them. If you assume that they are real people and not just ideal types, you may discover ways in which they enhance life for themselves, maybe even at the expense of another.

While reading the narrative, use all your senses, not just your mind. Ruth is a sense-filled story, with fields to see and newly mown grain stalks to smell, with food to taste and people to touch, as well as conversation to overhear.

Part 1
Introduction

Ruth 1:1-5

Ruth 1:1-5

Famine, Displacement, and Death

PREVIEW

In the journalistic style of a reporter, the narrator introduces us to a family from Bethlehem decimated by one disaster after another *[Narrator]*. We read, in the matter-of-fact form of a chronicle, the account of this family struck first with famine, which forces a move to a foreign land. This leads to the death of all the male members of the family. The introduction provides the general setting in time and place: in the days of the judges, in Bethlehem, and in the country of Moab. Initially, we are not given names for the family members. They are simply a man, his wife, and two sons (1:1).

This introduction gives the reader brief but crucial background information, including the tension that drives the plot. Hence, it fulfills all the functions of an exposition for a biblical short story, providing a setting for its meaning. Nevertheless, as common in biblical narrative, this introduction leaves much detail to the reader's imagination *[Characteristics of Hebrew Narrative]*. We must decide for ourselves the cause of the famine in Bethlehem and the deaths in Moab. We know nothing of the living conditions of this Judahite family in Moab, not even the exact place of its residence (1:2-5).

In spite of the sparse detail and chronicle style, the movement of the narration impresses on the reader the magnitude of the disaster. The introduction opens with a *man* along with *his wife and two sons* (1:1). It concludes with a *woman* with no husband and no sons (1:5a).

What has begun in family has ended in widowhood. No one who has lived through that process can miss the poignancy of the disaster, regardless of the reportorial style of this introductory unit.

OUTLINE

This introduction names the two main characters of the short story, but that happens almost as a by-product of the account of the disasters. At this point, the narrator does not tell us that the story will concern Naomi and Ruth. Instead, the exposition opens with one summary sentence about an unnamed family (1:1), and concludes it with a second one concerning an unnamed widow (1:5b). In between, the narrator reports the death of all the male family members (1:2-5a).

Opening Statement: The Family, 1:1

A Report of Death in the Family, 1:2-5a

Concluding Statement: The Woman, 1:5b

EXPLANATORY NOTES
Opening Statement: The Family 1:1

The narrator recounts a story about a past time. The opening words of the narrative, *And it happened (wayehi),* appear frequently at the beginning of biblical narratives (cf. Josh., Judg., and esp. Esther). Yet most translations omit that Hebrew word, beginning instead with the notation of time *(In the days,* NRSV, NIV; but see NASB, *Now it came about).*

The narrator sets the story in time designated by era rather than year, in the period of the *judges,* approximately 1200-1020 B.C. Archaeology has provided us a great deal of information about the everyday life of Israel in that era. The history of the era, however, is less clear. The lack of historical knowledge does not hurt our study of this narrative because its story features the everyday life of the common people, not the drama of international politics.

Although we do not know the exact time when Ruth was written ("Where Does Ruth Belong?" in Overview), the narrator reflects village life that has persisted for many centuries in the hill country of Canaan. The village people engage in family farming in fields located around the houses that makes up a town *[Village Farming].* They cultivate hardy grains, ones that can be adequately watered by spring rains or modest irrigation. These grainfields, along with olive trees and grapevines, are supplemented by domesticated animals, mostly sheep and goats.

Village size and life is directly dependent on the availability of water. As rainfall varies according to the season, the older children of the village often take the herds some distance away in search of adequate pasture. A dry spell may reduce available water, forcing some village families to move in order to survive. A prolonged drought may even dry up the well, so that the village is abandoned, only to be resettled when water again became available, perhaps decades or even centuries later.

The peasants have helped themselves by building flat narrow terraces for farming on hillsides and digging cisterns to catch available rainfall. In the fairly arid hill country of central and southern Canaan, however, peasant farmers have never taken water for granted. In this story, ironically, famine strikes in *Bethlehem*, a name that translates as "the house of bread (or food)." The narrator does not tell us the exact cause of this famine. The brief notes in 1:1 and 1:6 evoke a picture of a family forced to pack up what belongings it can and set out in search of a new place to live.

Bethlehem in Judah distinguishes this village in south-central Canaan from an obscure northern village of Bethelehem, west of the Sea of Galilee (Josh. 19:15). Bethlehem of Judah is located about ten kilometers (six miles) south of Jerusalem. We find the village mentioned in a fourteenth century B.C. letter discovered in Egypt, one of a library of documents that detail some of the interaction between Egypt and city states in Canaan (Baly: 106-7).

Bethlehem occupies a central place in the narrative traditions from the era of the *judges* and early Hebrew monarchy. According to Judges 19–21, a Levite took a woman from Bethlehem as a secondary wife. She escaped from him and returned to her home. The priest pursued and reclaimed her. While they traveled back through the territory of Benjamin, the Levite decided to ask for hospitality in the village of Gibeah. Instead of hospitality, he was victimized by violence. The Levite's vengeful response touched off a tribal feud that nearly annihilated the Benjaminites. On a more positive note, tradition about Bethlehem identified it as the home village of David and the place where Samuel anointed him king (1 Sam. 16:1-13; 17:12).

Perhaps memory of both traditions has functioned for the earliest listeners as context for the narrative of Ruth. The story of the vengeful priest contrasts dramatically with the peaceful people of the village of Bethlehem, the home not of the priest, but of the abused woman. Explicitly, the narrator declares that the story of Ruth, Naomi, and Boaz is an account of David's people (4:17).

This Bethlehemite family chooses to move to Moab. The narrator does not tell us why Moab. A trip across the Jordan River at the north end of the Dead Sea and then up out of the valley to the plateau would bring the family to the edge of Moab. Either the tableland to the southeast (Campbell, 1975:50) or the hills immediately to the northeast (Gray: 384-5) might provide the family a haven from the famine that afflicts their Judean village.

In the memory of ancient Israel, Moab carried an overwhelmingly negative image *[Moab]*. According to Hebrew tradition (Gen. 19:36-37), Moab was born as a child of incest. None of the biblical stories about Moab are kind to Israel's eastern neighbor. Instead, they berate Moab as a perverse and pagan country, governed by foolish and fat rulers. In the mind of early listeners to this story, therefore, a flight from Bethlehem (the house of food) in search of food in Moab involves this family in a shameful migration, one that only compounds the irony and the anguish of the family.

A Report of Death in the Family 1:2-5a

Now we are introduced to the family by name. For an Israelite, the name Elimelech would most likely have been heard as "My God is king." Naomi herself identified the meaning of her name as "pleasant" or "delightful" (1:20). Naomi notes the irony of that name in light of the disaster that has befallen the family *[Comedy, Irony, and Satire]*. Famine and death, however, have also made irony of Elimelech's name: where is "my God, the king"?

Many have proposed symbolic meanings for the names of the other characters named in the introduction: Mahlon, Chilion, Orpah, and Ruth. Some think that the names Mahlon and Chilion allude to "sickness and destruction" (Craghan: 204). But those suggestions, plus others made for Ruth and Orpah, seem to come more from their respective roles in the story than from language study.

This introduction seems to take *Ephrathites* as the name of an ethnic group living in Bethlehem. In a genealogical list 1 Chronicles 2:19-20 names Ephrath as the second wife of Caleb, perhaps suggesting her as the ancestor of those who settled in Bethlehem. Other biblical texts use the name Bethlehem and Ephrath(ah) interchangeably (Gen. 35:16, 19; Mic. 5:2; and even Ruth 4:11).

The family has fled to the country of Moab to sojourn there (1:1). They become resident aliens. Resident aliens are always at considerable risk (Sasson, 1989:16). The frequent laws and admonitions in the biblical texts concerning sojourners or aliens call attention to their vulnerability in a social and economic system controlled by native residents. We should not picture the family's move to Moab as a temporary displacement. In keeping with their intention to remain, the two sons marry Moabite women.

Sometime after settling in Moab (we are not told how long), Naomi's husband, Elimelech, dies (1:3). Later Naomi's sons, Mahlon and Chilion, die childless after perhaps ten years of marriage (1:5a). The narrator does not tell us the cause for any of these deaths. Interpretative tradition, Jewish and Christian, has presumed that the death of these men is a matter of divine retribution: Elimelech for taking his family to such a disreputable country, and Mahlon and Chilion for marrying foreign women. But the narrator does not explain the deaths or criticize the deceased. For the women, it does not matter why their husbands have died. They are gone.

Concluding Statement: The Woman 1:5b

This chronicle of a Bethlehemite family has begun with a husband, wife, and two sons. At the end, there is but one from the refugee family, a widow. Her sons have married, but they have died childless. That has left three women as widows and childless.

There is no easy way for a childless widow to fulfill her basic human needs (Rayburn: 163-5). If the deceased husband has brothers, a kinship marriage might be arranged, providing a son (or more) for the widow and thus a place in the husband's family [Kinship Marriage]. This narrative suggests that younger widows can return to their parental homes and remarry (1:8). In terms of the husband's property, practice varies according to location and time. Numbers 27:8-11 does not include the wife of the deceased in the order of inheritance. But other evidence suggests that the deceased husband's property can pass to the wife (e.g., Ruth 4:3). Many widows, however, have no respectable way to earn a living. They are forced to rely on charity or worse, perhaps slavery or prostitution.

Naomi thus finds herself in triple jeopardy—a woman, without family, and in a foreign land.

THE TEXT IN BIBLICAL CONTEXT
Famine in the Land

In biblical narratives, the words *there was a famine in the land* immediately signal danger (Ruth 1:1; Gen. 12:10; 26:1; 42:5; 2 Sam. 21:1; 1 Kings 18:2; 2 Kings 6:25). In these narratives, famine threatens death, creates refugees, and sometimes results in scenes of unspeakable horror. Narratives about famine tell of the families of

Abraham and Isaac being driven from home to become refugees in a foreign land (Gen. 12:1-20; 26:1-11). Both of these men obtained food for their families, but neither expected a friendly or gracious reception in the foreign land. Both Abraham and Isaac endangered their wives in an attempt to insure their own safety. Hurt by famine, Jacob tried to negotiate for food from Egypt, using his sons as messengers. He did obtain food, but in so doing he endangered the lives of all his sons, especially the youngest.

In the days of David, a famine caused the people to search for someone to blame, someone who had angered God enough to bring such a drought (2 Sam. 21:1-14). Blame fell on Saul, by that time dead; so the people executed his sons in hopes of appeasing God. Not till a daughter of Saul had cared for the bodies of her brothers did God respond to their petitions and let fertility return to the land (2 Sam. 21:14). Famine in the days of Ahab and Elijah resulted in the massacre of the prophets of Baal because they were unsuccessful in ending the drought (1 Kings 18:1-40). Famine in Samaria, caused by a Syrian siege, resulted in cannibalism (2 Kings 6:24-30).

It is easy for those with enough food to criticize the actions of those driven by hunger. The hungry sometimes seize food for themselves and their family, at the expense, or even the death, of former friends. On the edge of starvation, they may appear as wild animals until hunger robs them of all energy. Then emptiness replaces the fury in their eyes. Every age has witnessed the desperation that drives the hungry from place to place and leaves a family with few survivors.

The relative tranquility of this story can be contrasted with the violence that marks other stories about the *days when judges ruled* (1:1). Nevertheless, no story can be called idyllic, Goethe notwithstanding, when it begins with the statement *There was a famine in the land*. We know that from the Bible and from our own age.

THE TEXT IN THE LIFE OF THE CHURCH
People Living at Risk

This five-verse chronicle of the life of a Bethlehemite family reminds us of troubles that can strike without warning or explanation in any time or place. Famine finds victims in every age. Drought claims countless men, women, and children more frequently in lands where and when water is less available than in North America. In our cities and villages, malnutrition caused by economic deprivation silently claims victims, often children and elderly.

We like to think that the young, the widow, and the alien are less at risk in our own time than might have been the case in the ancient world. Nevertheless, even now death, unemployment, and abuse can render anyone suddenly homeless, a refugee in one's own land. Poverty among the dispossessed still pushes the widow, the orphan, and the elderly out to the edge of society, even if the threat of starvation may be less acute than in the past. To live as a resident alien renders one invisible or an irritant—threatened with discrimination and deportation. The life of the widowed foreigner still has more problems than possibilities.

The threat to life and limb for the *woman left without [children] and her husband* (1:5b) has been a central concern in the believers church tradition. The urge to respond to those displaced or at risk comes naturally to the faith community, as in Mennonite and Brethren service programs, Heifer Project International, CROP, Mennonite Central Committee, Mennonite Disaster Service, and Church World Service. Indeed, the commitment of government agencies to respond to emergencies owes much to the witness of our ancestors in our church denominations.

Besides sending food and clothing around the world, our church parents, grandparents, and great-grandparents energetically resettled international refugees and compassionately aided those who lost family and security. In the 1940s, the efforts of the Brethren Service Commission to assist detained Japanese-Americans show such assistance extended even to those many defined as "the enemy." However, evidence suggests that the church has been more responsive to widows and orphans far away in "Moab" than to the malnourished and homeless nearby.

All the disasters of the past, as well as some new ones, continue to leave people without means of life support and in "foreign" lands. Our complex international economy and global society have created new groups of "widows." In our day, the situation of "Naomi" may be every bit as tenuous as *in the days when the judges ruled.*

Part 2

The Story of Two Widows

Ruth 1:6—4:12

Ruth 1:6-22

Episode 1
Return to Bethlehem

PREVIEW

The first episode in this story follows the widows as they leave Moab to return to Bethlehem in Judah, the village from which the family originally departed (1:1). The story shifts from the chronicle style of the introduction (1:1-5) to the genuinely narrative style of Hebrew literature *[Characteristics of Hebrew Narrative]*. As common with Hebrew literature, the episode focuses around speeches by the main characters. In this first episode, we learn to know the women from their own words. As such, the women become characters who shape the direction of the story line, rather than simply ones to whom things happened (cf. the introduction in 1:1-5).

Another element characteristic of Hebrew narrative appears in this unit. We find an oft-repeated key word that functions like glue, holding together and carrying the story line. The key term in Ruth 1:6-22 is *return (šub)*. This word appears already in the first verse of the episode: *Then she arose, she and her daughters-in-law, to* **return** *from the country of Moab* (1:6, EFR). The unit concludes with repeating that same word twice: *So Naomi* **returned** *along with Ruth the Moabite, her daughter-in-law, who* **returned** *with her from the country of Moab* (1:22, EFR). Besides marking the beginning and the end of the episode, *return* is used a total of twelve times in the unit.

Certainly *return* accurately describes the journey of Naomi. But the word carries more importance than that. The central dialogue in the episode (1:8-14) is grounded in the word *return*. Naomi directs her daughters-in-law to return to their mothers' homes (1:8). However, the two women refuse to use *return* in that way. Instead, they announce that they will *return* with their mother-in-law (1:10). After twice more directing them to return to their homes (1:11-12), Orpah agrees to such a return (1:14-15). Ruth refuses and instead *returns* to a place where she has never been (1:22).

In this episode, the repetition and importance of the word *return* makes it key not only in its direct role, but also as a signal of the direction for the plot. Fertility has returned to the village of Bethlehem (1:6). And life will eventually return to the family (4:13-15).

The heart of the episode is found in the central dialogue (1:8-18), a dialogue that Naomi intends to be a farewell scene between her and her two daughters-in-law. The importance of this dialogue is not surprising and fits the predominance of dialogue in Hebrew narrative in general and in Ruth in particular *[Characteristics of Hebrew Narrative]*. The return journey is accomplished with the arrival in Bethlehem, bittersweet though it may be (1:19-20).

OUTLINE
The Journey to Judah, 1:6-18
    1:6-7   Preparations and Departure
    1:8-18   Farewell Dialogue

The Arrival in Bethlehem, 1:19-21
    1:19   Reception in Bethlehem
    1:20-21   Response by Naomi

Concluding Summary, 1:22

EXPLANATORY NOTES
The Journey to Judah 1:6-18

1:6-7 Preparations and Departure

The death of the men has made this a woman's story. One woman, Naomi, decides to take charge of her life and return to Judah. Her decision is prompted by the information that the LORD has *considered* (NRSV) his people and *come to [their] aid* (NIV), restoring fertility to their field (1:6). The Hebrew word *paqad* (often translated *visit*, as in KJV) encompasses the process of God looking, considering, deciding, and acting—a total process that no single English word can capture. This divine visit can result in punishment (e.g., Exod. 20:5; 32:34). This time, however, God has restored fertility (cf. Hannah in 1 Sam. 2:21). The narrator does not tell us what Naomi expects to find for herself, but simply that Bethlehem is once again the "House of Bread."

As the women begin the journey from Moab to Judah, the narrator does not speak of the women by name. *She,* the older woman, starts on this journey with *her two daughters-in-law.* The preparations for the journey appear quick and silent. Ruth 1:6-7 seems so repetitive and redundant that some interpreters have thought verse 7 an addition (Jouon: 35). Yet the silent departure of these women refugees reinforces the pain. They leave the land that has claimed their husbands, journeying toward a land from whose famine the family has fled.

1:8-18 Farewell Dialogue

Suddenly the silence is broken. Naomi speaks and directs her daughters-in-law to *return* in a different direction, not going with her to Judah (1:7), but each to her *mother's house.* We don't know why the narrative says their *mother's house.* Perhaps it emphasizes the absence of men in their lives (Laffey: 555). More likely, it reflects the central role of mother in the ancient household (Meyers, 1993:110-4). Kathleen Farmer suggests that used in this way, the phrase, *mother's house,* is the equivalent of encouraging the two young women to find new husbands; hopefully providing the *security* (1:9) they lacked (1998:903).

Naomi's speech of instruction introduces *khesed,* a heavily freighted word that will be important in the whole narrative (Overview) *[Khesed].* As a parting benediction, Naomi asks that God be as steadfastly loyal and compassionate to the two young widows as the two have been to Naomi and to the dead family members (1:8). To reinforce and extend her petition, Naomi requests that God grant them security, a husband, and a home (1:9). In fact, Naomi prays that God will provide her two daughters-in-law all that she herself has lost.

This benediction functions as more than a simple farewell. It closes the relationship, freeing the women from any further responsibility to Naomi (Sakenfeld, 1985:34). No note of disloyalty accompanies such a benediction. The opposite actually seems to be the case. Naomi directs her loyal daughters-in-law to leave her and return home. A kiss from Naomi and tears are intended to close this tender farewell moment (1:9).

Instead of the expected compliance, however, the two women

refuse to leave (1:10). The two provide no reason for their decision. Playing off the key word *return* (Heb.: *šub*), they say they will return not to their mother's house, as Naomi has directed, but *with you to your people* (1:10). The reader may share with Naomi the surprise of that response and the strength of the women's resolve. These young women will not be controlled by their mother-in-law (Trible, 1978:171).

The dialogue becomes more intense as Naomi responds with equal resolve (1:11-13). With command and question, Naomi demands that the two women return in the direction she has instructed. Neither of Naomi's questions require an answer *[Questions]*. The first one, *"Why will you go with me?"* simply expresses emotion, annoyance (Hyman, 1983:17-25). The second question, *"Do I still have sons . . .?"* allows for only one answer: "No!"

In this speech, Naomi's stance toward the two women seems to have changed. Notice how she addresses them as *my daughters* (1:11-12). This manner of address may indicate an intimacy and closeness in their relationship. Or it may signal that Naomi continues in the role of a "mother" admonishing a daughter. The tone of Naomi's speech betrays impatience, if not anger.

Naomi further reinforces her admonition with a hypothetical case. After stating directly that she is too old to have a man, Naomi imagines the quickest possible scenario for her to provide men for Orpah and Ruth to marry:

"If I thought there was hope for me,
  And if I were to have a man tonight,
    And if I were to give birth to sons . . ." (1:12, EFR)

Naomi concludes with questions that are at least rhetorical and perhaps accusatory: *"Would you then wait . . . ? Would you then refrain . . . ?"* (1:13). Naomi answers her own question: *"No, my daughters!"* In a painful summary, Naomi finally gives voice to the complaint that lies hidden beneath her admonition to the two women: *"The hand of the LORD has turned against me"* (1:13; Sasson, 1989:27).

With the end of Naomi's speech, the narrator moves us a step back to observe the response of the women *[Narrator]*. Naomi has tried to direct the actions of her daughters-in-law with her initial instructions and kiss (1:9). This time the two young women make their own decision and in their own name (1:14; Trible, 1978:171). After tears, Orpah kisses her mother-in-law. This is presumably a kiss of farewell, though we have only Naomi's subsequent speech to tell us that Orpah does *return* (1:15), echoing Naomi's act of returning (Campbell, 1975:79).

Orpah's obedience has lost her a further place in the story (Bal, 1987:74). In our imagination, we may see Orpah as a solitary figure, walking back the road the three have just traveled. Many interpreters condemn Orpah, but not the narrator. She obediently does as she is instructed. Her decision may be as much a decision to care for the family as Ruth's decision to stay with Naomi. Orpah chooses to attend to the needs of her family of origin rather than her family by marriage. Tradition has not preserved Orpah's story. However, countless women live her story, even to our day.

Ruth clings to her mother-in-law (1:14). Whether we picture Ruth as seizing Naomi or simply standing obstinately, Ruth's response amounts to disobedience. Naomi tries once more to insist that Ruth return the direction Naomi wants (1:15), as Orpah is returning where she belongs. *"Return!"* Naomi commands.

Ruth finally breaks her silence to reinforce her resolve with her words (1:16-17). In a powerful and familiar speech that the NRSV appropriately puts in poetic form, Ruth ties her destiny to that of Naomi in life and in death (1:16). Ruth concludes her declaration with an oath, inviting unspecified curses if she does not carry through on her promise even after death (1:17). Explaining Ruth's promise only serves to erode its impact. It is enough to read her words and realize that Ruth ties her own future to a woman, who by her own admission, has no future.

There is nothing left for Naomi to say (1:18). Some feel that Naomi's is an angry silence, that she prefers to be rid of Ruth, this young Moabite widow who can only aggravate her problems. One can sense Naomi turning away from Ruth, either in irritation or preoccupation with her own problems (Hubbard, 1988a: 121).

The Arrival in Bethlehem 1:19-21

1:19 Reception in Bethlehem

The narrator provides only one sentence as transition from the farewell scene at the journey's beginning, to the arrival in Bethlehem. We know nothing of the trip except that *the two of them went on* (1:19a). Silence about the journey seems to echo silence between the two women.

The heated argument followed by somber silence on the journey from Moab is broken by the stir in Bethlehem at the arrival of the women. The *whole town* hums with the news. But we are not told the nature of the stirring. Even when the town speaks through its women, *"Is this Naomi?"* we cannot be sure whether they are delighted, surprised, puzzled, or maybe aghast (1:19b).

1:20-21 Response by Naomi

Naomi immediately directs the corporate mood to correspond with her personal feelings. Upon hearing her name pronounced by others, Naomi is struck by the contrast between the meaning of *Naomi* and her lot in life (1:20-21). Her name, meaning "Pleasant," "Delightful," or even "Happy," can only be heard as stinging irony. She chooses another name, *Mara,* "Bitter" (1:20), one that expresses the humiliating shame of her story (1:21). By divine decision, her life has moved from full to empty. Like Job, Jeremiah, and many poets of the Psalms, Naomi expresses her anger when she feels betrayed by God. The name *Naomi* does not reflect her present, nor does it appear to anticipate her future (Bal, 1993:50).

Naomi's bitter speech completely ignores the presence of Ruth. Neither Naomi nor the women acknowledge Ruth's *return* (1:22). Ruth has disappeared except in the *they* of the narrator (1:19). Does Ruth's presence make a difference? The flow of the narrative suggests that this time will be different. The pattern of Naomi and her family has been to leave when trouble comes, to try another place or people. Ruth has broken that pattern. Rather than making the more reasonable choice of separating herself from trouble, as did her mother-in-law and sister-in-law, Ruth has bonded herself inseparably to the one in trouble.

Concluding Summary 1:22

The narrator ends the episode of the return on the same note as its beginning: *Naomi returned* (1:22; cf. 1:6). We are told little about Naomi (and Ruth) living in Bethlehem. Later we learn that Elimelech, Naomi's late husband, has owned a field near Bethlehem. However, we do not know if that benefits Naomi on her return. Typically, the houses are grouped together in the village, with the fields outside the town. Some speculate that there is a house in Bethlehem to which Naomi can return even after more than a decade. Those details, however, are left to the reader. The narrator keeps us focused more on the people than the place.

Even though Naomi may be ignoring Ruth's presence, the narrator has not lost sight of her: *and with her, Ruth, the Moabite, her daughter-in-law, returned from the country of Moab* (1:22, EFR).

Interpreters have long noted with surprise that the narrator has pointedly used the word *return* in connection with Ruth (Hubbard, 1988a: 128-9). Return *(šub)* in reference to a journey means to go back to a previous point of departure. In translation, it is easy to avoid the problem; one can say that Ruth accompanies the returning Naomi.

The narrator, however, may want us to notice something else in the unusual grammatical construction. Naomi feels herself returning empty. She cannot realize the importance of Ruth, who so commits herself to go wherever Naomi goes, that Ruth can return to a place where she has never been. Ruth's *return* stands as a note of hope unnoticed in the pain of Naomi's shame and loss (Bush: 96).

The narrator slips in yet a second note of hope. The widows return at the beginning of the barley harvest. This April-May harvest may provide enough grain for everyone, including the poor, the widow, and the alien. That takes us to the next episode.

THE TEXT IN BIBLICAL CONTEXT
Naomi and Job

Interpreters have often noted that this narrative opens with a situation similar to that in Job. The opening of Job provides us with considerably more information about the cause of the disaster and Job's response (1:1-22). Several times the narrator of Job transports the reader from earth to the divine court and back to earth again *[Narrator]*. This movement gives us more information than even Job knows about the events that have robbed him of family and fortune. In Ruth, we likely know less than Naomi does about what has destroyed her husband and children. We have been given only a chronicle of events that left a childless widow living in a foreign land.

In Job, the suffering is unwarranted, but explained, albeit only to the reader, never to Job. As onlookers who know what is going on, we listen in Job to a discussion among the characters. The ignorance of Job's friends creates misunderstanding and increases anger. In Ruth, Naomi's suffering remains unexplained. We share her bewilderment and her anger. Like Job, she attributes her tragedy to divine decision. In the biblical narratives, famine often presumes a divine agent, and so does unexpected and unexplained death.

God does not blame Job. The opening scene repeatedly identifies Job as blameless (Job 1). We cannot tell about Naomi. We know nothing about Naomi's life that might explain and justify the downhill spiral of her life. Interpretive tradition suggests that Elimelech's death is punishment for taking his family to Moab, and attributes the death of Mahlon and Chilion to their marriage with foreign women. Even so, that leaves Naomi as a confused and innocent victim. The irritation Naomi expresses toward her daughters-in-law and her complaint against God likely come from the bewildering rage of one whose life has been devastated without explanation or warrant.

Reuven Hammer (300-5) suggests that the narratives of Job and Ruth represent two of the Bible's responses to inexplicable suffering. The two narratives take different paths as they come to terms with unexplained disaster. Job engages in debate with his friends about the cause and the role of God in such situations. The book of Job demands that we face tough questions about God. The pain of unexplained suffering will not be alleviated by repeating familiar theological doctrine or even announcing God's compassionate presence with the sufferer. The victim wants to confront God.

Naomi knows the rage and despair of Job. Nevertheless, the narrative of Ruth represents a different response, one that does not engage in theological inquiry, but responds to the pain of the victim (Hammer: 303). In the face of disaster, and lacking all the desired answers, the community has at least one thing it can provide—companionship and aid for the sufferer. Naomi's community does respond, thanks in large part to a Moabite woman who defies convention and disobeys her mother-in-law.

THE TEXT IN THE LIFE OF THE CHURCH
Complaint Against God

Naomi's accusation that God has abused and mistreated her (1:21) strikes many contemporary readers as unfair if not unfaithful. The church currently encourages worshipers to address God with praise and thanks, not with complaint and accusation. We have taken the Pauline admonition to rejoice even in suffering (Col. 1:24; 1 Thess. 5:16) to mean that any complaint against God constitutes a sign of disloyalty. Hence, among most Christians, prayer can include praise and thanksgiving, confession and petition, but rarely complaint and lament.

Such a stance inclines us to admonish Naomi for something the worshiping community in ancient Israel and the early church would accept as normal in a tragic situation. The faith tradition has taught Naomi to trust God's protection and care. She has expected God to honor justice and not allow the innocent to be sent back empty. When the opposite has happened, Naomi voices a traditional statement of complaint: *"The LORD has dealt harshly with me, and the Almighty has brought calamity upon me"* (1:21).

Over a third of all the canonical psalms belong to the genre of complaint or lament. We seldom read the lament psalms and even less frequently use them in public worship. The best-known complaint psalm to most Christians is the one quoted by Jesus on the cross: "My God, my God, why have you forsaken me?" (Ps. 22:1; Mark 15:34). In Psalm 22, the one afflicted not only complains about treatment by God (22:1-21), but also about mistreatment by "evildoers" (22:16-18) and about the shame of the situation (22:6-7).

Our biblical ancestors of faith took the divine promise of love and care so seriously that they would cry out to God when they experienced divine neglect. They found that God was not only big enough to handle their anger, but that God often would respond to their complaint with the love and care they had come to expect.

As a victim of unexplained and seemingly undeserved suffering, Naomi appropriately complains about God's treatment of her. Thus far, Naomi does not see that, in Ruth, God has answered her complaint even before she voices it.

As a people who have been denied the right to complain about God, we find ourselves in a difficult position. Unwarranted suffering makes us as angry, as it did our forebears in the faith. Like them, we need to attribute unexplained disaster to some cause. Often we blame our suffering on our own sin, on the evil of others, or on a vague sense of misfortune. We refuse to entertain the notion that God should be held accountable for not preventing the disaster. With such thinking, we limit God's active presence to walking with us or comforting us, even at those times when we want explanation and accountability.

If we reclaim Naomi's dialogue with God, we may well find ourselves in a much more intense and satisfying conversation with God in the midst life's most anguishing moments. Such conversation might do more to handle our rage and heal our spirit than the present stance, which refuses to presume on God's promises.

Ruth 2:1-23

Episode 2
Going for Grain

PREVIEW

Naomi complains that she is returning to Bethlehem empty (1:21). According to the introduction (1:1-5), her emptiness involves a lack of food and the death of her husband and sons. This second episode (2:1-23) takes up the problem of food. The narrator has already told us that Bethlehem has food (1:6). Naomi and Ruth arrive in Bethlehem precisely at the moment when food will be most plentiful, the beginning of the grain harvest (1:22; cf. 2:23). However, we do not know the extent to which this widow and her Moabite daughter-in-law will have access to that food.

In our own time, we recognize that the matter of availability of food and access to food are two separate issues. While the narrative introduction has begun with the problem of the availability of food (1:1), with this episode the crisis shifts. Will a widow and an alien have access to enough of the available food? From earliest times, the religious and legal tradition of ancient Israel has insisted that the widow, the orphan, and the alien are to be cared for (Exod. 22:22-24; Deut. 10:17-19). As is the case even today, a law often is needed to remedy lax practice. Perhaps to remedy Israel's neglect, these rules help to ensure food and shelter for widows and aliens.

In the first episode, the oft-repeated word "return" *(šub)* has carried the narrative along, emphasizing not only the direction of

Naomi's journey, but also movement in the story as a whole (cf. Ruth 1:6-22, Preview). This second episode also contains such a frequently repeated and important verb, *glean (laqat)*. *Glean* is used in the opening scene between Ruth and Naomi (2:2), in the closing words of the narrator (2:23), and ten more times in between.

This narrative features the practice of gleaning in the fields, so we should not be surprised to find the word used frequently *[Village Farming]*. Gleaning, as practiced in ancient Israel, was aimed to assist those without natural access to food, such as the widow, the alien, and the orphan. In less obvious ways, the word *glean* carries the movement of the narrative from famine toward fertility. Gleaning does not secure the future, but it does provide for the present. For the widow and the alien, the present is often so precarious that they have no time to worry about the future.

This episode is bracketed by dialogue between Ruth and Naomi. In the opening exchange, Ruth sets out her plan for obtaining food and gains Naomi's agreement (2:2). The episode closes with the two of them assessing the results of Ruth's effort (2:18-22). In between those two conversations, we find Ruth in the grainfield. Measured simply by the amount of grain, Ruth has an outstandingly successful day. Though sufficient grain answers the immediate need for food, the narrative focus is not really on barley, but on the chance encounter of Ruth and Boaz. The narrator thinks it most important that we listen in on the conversation between these two individuals *[Characteristics of Hebrew Narrative]*.

OUTLINE
Introductory Statement, 2:1

Dialogue Between Ruth and Naomi, 2:2

Scene in the Field, 2:3-17
    2:3   Introductory Statement
    2:4-16   Dialogues
       Boaz and the Workers, 2:4-7
       Boaz and Ruth, 2:8-14
       Boaz and the Workers, 2:15-16
    2:17   Concluding Statement

Dialogue Between Naomi and Ruth, 2:18-22

Concluding Statement, 2:23

This presents the episode in customary outline form. However, there is another way to display the movement of this episode, one that more clearly shows how the narrative flows. The dialogue between Boaz and Ruth forms the center of the episode (2:8-14). The narrative moves toward this conversation and then out from it. A narrative structure with such a formally balanced movement is called *chiasm [Narrative Structure]*. The use of a chiastic structure provides the narrator an additional way to point the reader to what is at the heart of the matter—in this episode, the exchange between Boaz and Ruth. The episode in chiastic outline:

Introductory Statement, 2:1
    Dialogue Between Ruth and Naomi, 2:2
        Scene in the Field: Introductory Statement, 2:3
            Dialogue: Boaz and the Workers, 2:4-7
                Dialogue: Boaz and Ruth, 2:8-14
            Dialogue: Boaz and the Workers, 2:15-16
        Scene in the Field: Concluding Statement, 2:17
    Dialogue Between Naomi and Ruth, 2:18-22
Concluding Statement 2:23.

EXPLANATORY NOTES

Introductory Statement 2:1

To open the second episode, the narrator introduces us to the other major character in this story, *Boaz*. Besides the name of this man, we learn something of his character and his relationship to Naomi. The statements made about Boaz, however, leave as many questions as they provide answers.

The narrator describes Boaz by using a Hebrew phrase that we might translate as *a man of substance* (Campbell, 1975:90). What does it mean to describe a person as a man of substance? It might point to his economic wealth or to his prestige in the community (NRSV: *a prominent, rich man;* NIV: *a man of standing*). It might refer to his physical stature or his reputation for valor. The phrase can even have military connotations (Gray: 390). Perhaps we are to identify him as a man of strong moral character and integrity (Cundall: 269). The latter interpretation, however, seems based more on an evaluation of Boaz's role in this story than on the words themselves. Whichever the better nuance, *man of substance (khayil)* points to Boaz's position in the village and contrasts him with Naomi (Trible, 1978:175). Boaz has wealth and prestige; Naomi lacks both resources and standing.

However sharp the contrast between Boaz and Ruth, the narrator twice informs us that they have a relationship, perhaps both informal and familial. Quite explicitly, the reader learns that Boaz belongs to the extended family of Elimelech and as such is a relative of Naomi by her marriage. With this bit of information, the narrator likely signals that Boaz has both a role and maybe even a responsibility for the family, including his relative-in-law Naomi.

Besides being related to Elimelech, Boaz also has another relationship to Naomi. Whether he is her *kinsman* (NIV: *relative*) is difficult to discern from the Hebrew word myd'. This adjective, related to the Hebrew verb, "to know" indicates some manner of relationship between Naomi and Boaz, a relative, a friend, or perhaps only an acquaintance. The ambiguity of the phrase counsels the reader not to be too quick to assume that the person will be of help to Naomi (Farmer, 1998:914).

Whatever the precise relationship between Boaz and Naomi, this man of substance has not heretofore responded to the needs of a friend and relative who has lost everything. Boaz waits until the women take the initiative before acting to assist them. Some wonder why it takes him so long.

Dialogue Between Ruth and Naomi 2:2

Ruth takes the initiative. This woman, whom the narrator reminds us was from Moab, decides to go after food. At first glance, the words used, both in Hebrew and in English, suggest that Ruth comes to Naomi with a request: *"Let me go . . ."* (2:2). But a closer reading reveals that Ruth has actually decided on a course of action. She comes as much to inform Naomi as to ask her permission.

Ruth decides to obtain food by using the customary practice of gleaning, picking up grain left in the field after harvesting (barley first, then wheat; 1:22; 2:23) *[Village Farming]*. Although custom permits her to glean in the field of her choice, Ruth is determined to glean only in the field of *"someone in whose sight I may find favor"* (2:2). We do not know exactly what Ruth intends by that phrase, which frequently indicates a difference in status: one of low estate is noticed and treated kindly by a person with power and status. If so, Ruth has indicated that she intends to glean in the field of a landowner who treats her kindly.

Ruth may be saying more. She has set out not only to gather grain but to be noticed. Nevertheless, we ought not read the end of the story into this comment. It is doubtful that Ruth sets out intent on finding a husband. Naomi responds to Ruth's request/decision by granting permission.

Scene in the Field 2:3-17

2:3 Introductory Statement

The narrator begins with a sentence that summarizes the action of the entire scene. Such an introductory summary sentence is not unusual in Hebrew narrative. It is commonly balanced with a similar summary at the end of the scene. That is the case here in 2:17. Not unexpectedly, we find the key verb *glean* in this introductory sentence. *Glean (laqat)* will reoccur twelve times throughout the entire episode and thus becomes the word that holds the unit together (Preview) *[Characteristics of Hebrew Narrative]*.

This opening sentence does more than summarize the action in the scene. It goes on to inform the reader that Ruth has *happened* to choose the field of Boaz in which to work. As we read the statement, we suspect that this selection of a field is more than chance. It may be that Ruth knows what she is doing and comes intentionally to this particular field. More likely, the narrator signals God's quiet presence in the course of events (Hals: 13). Only twice in the story does the narrator mention God's active presence, behind the fertility that returns to the fields (1:6) and Ruth's pregnancy (4:13).

In this narrative, the activity of God is experienced mostly in the quiet blessings that happen in the course of daily life: the fertility of the fields, the birth of a baby, and the surprising good fortune that comes by "chance." The narrative may also assume the presence of God in the misfortune with which the story begins, the famine and death. Naomi certainly does (1:21).

Once again, the narrator tosses in a phrase about Boaz that appears redundant: he is again identified as being *of the house of Elimelech* (2:3, EFR; cf. 2:1). This note reinforces our awareness that there is a connection between Boaz and Naomi through her deceased husband.

2:4-7 Dialogue: Boaz and the Workers

Boaz arrives at the field either at the same time as Ruth (*just then,* NRSV, NIV) or perhaps sometime later (Campbell, 1975:93). The Hebrew grammar permits either interpretation. With the arrival of Boaz, however, all attention turns to him. He addresses the workers with a traditional greeting, common at the time of harvest (Gray: 391). The reapers return his greeting (2:4).

Boaz immediately spots a woman: *"To whom does this young woman belong?"* (2:5). His choice of words echoes Genesis 32:18 and 1 Samuel 30:13. In all three cases, a person (or persons) with low standing is defined in relationship to someone who has standing (Nielsen, 1997:57). The foreman of the workers identifies Ruth as *"the Moabite who came back with Naomi"* (2:6). Ruth is an alien, and her primary relationship is to a woman, a childless widow.

The foreman goes on to describe Ruth in what interpreters take to be complimentary terms. Yet the meaning of 2:7 is uncertain, as a comparison of English translations and commentaries shows. The difficulties warn us not to rely too much on this verse as we try to understand the story and its characters (Beattie, 1987:423). Most interpreters suggest that the speech by the foreman indicates two things about Ruth: (1) She has sought permission to glean in the field, even though by custom the poor need no permission to glean. (2) Either Ruth has been standing and waiting for permission from the owner (NRSV), or Ruth has already been working hard for a long time before Boaz arrives (NIV). The ambiguity of the Hebrew text allows us to say little more.

2:8-14 Dialogue: Boaz and Ruth

The dialogue between Boaz and Ruth comes at the center of the episode (Preview). Boaz begins the dialogue with a directive speech to Ruth (2:8-9). His instructions, along with his address *("my daughter"),* indicate that Boaz has assumed responsibility that goes beyond giving her permission to glean. Boaz directs Ruth to glean only in his fields and to stay close to the young women who work for him. Boaz informs Ruth that he has ordered his young men not to harass her (2:9). In addition, Boaz invites Ruth to drink from the water that his young men have drawn.

What are we to conclude from this solicitous initial speech by Boaz? By instructing Ruth to stay next to his women workers as they tie up the sheaves, Boaz has given Ruth first chance at the dropped grain (Hubbard, 1988a: 158). Access to water and protection from harassment provide Ruth additional assistance not available to most gleaners. Perhaps Ruth's arrival in his field prompts Boaz to accept his responsibility as a member of Elimelech's family (2:1, 3). He certainly plays a role that fits a benevolent family elder.

Nevertheless, there are hints that Boaz may have interests that go beyond family responsibility. His speech is sprinkled with words that have sexual as well as nonsexual connotations, including his persistent concern that Ruth not be molested (cf. 2:9, 15-16, Fewell/Gunn, 1990:84-5, 101). Boaz's speech hints that this may be the beginning of a relationship between a man and a woman.

In response, Ruth answers with a deference at least equal to

Boaz's concern. Ruth falls on her face before Boaz. This sign of complete submission is usually offered to royal figures, victorious generals, or even God (Sasson, 1987:324). We do not know whether to take Ruth's response as irony or as genuine servility. Good irony keeps the reader guessing [Comedy, Irony, and Satire].

Ruth has intended to glean in the fields of one in whose eyes she might find favor (2:2). She finds the "right" person. So she asks Boaz to explain his special consideration for her—an explanation that the readers might wish to hear. Ruth makes sure he understands that she is a *foreigner* (2:10). Some feel that the pillars of Bethlehem's society might find this aspect of Ruth's identity most objectionable (LaCocque: 85-7).

Boaz does not directly answer Ruth's question about the reason for his special favor. Instead, he responds more directly to another aspect of her speech. Ruth has explicitly set herself outside the community as a foreigner. Boaz responds with language that equates Ruth with Israel's ancestral families (2:11). Israel traces its beginnings to Sarah and Abraham, who left their homeland to journey to a foreign land. Echoes of this memory sound in the words of Boaz: *"You left your father and mother and your native land and came to a people you did not know before"* (2:11).

Boaz then goes on to pronounce a blessing on Ruth, one that echoes Naomi's blessing on her as the women began their journey from Moab (2:12; 1:8). In that previous blessing, Naomi prayed that God would bless Ruth as she returned to her own people. Ruth refused to return that direction (1:10). Unlike Sarah and Abraham, Ruth has left home without divine blessing (Trible, 1978:177), though one suspects not without divine presence. Now through Boaz, Ruth has heard God's blessing.

As for Boaz, he may have said more than he realized: *"the God of Israel, under whose wings you have come for refuge!"* (2:12b). The word *wings (kanap),* under which Ruth has taken refuge, will in the next scene be translated with its other meaning, *cloak* (3:9). Boaz's blessing includes the anticipation of divine protection for Ruth. Ruth will ask Boaz to provide the needed "cover."

Ruth's second response seeks to reaffirm and even strengthen her relationship to Boaz (Nielsen, 1997:60). Addressing Boaz as *"my lord,"* Ruth now identifies herself not as a foreigner (as she has been introduced to Boaz, 2:6), but as one treated as a *servant,* even though "I am not one of your servants" (2:13). The word Ruth uses for *servant (šipkhah)* designates the lowest rung on the social ladder, lower than other words that might be used to identify a woman servant

(Sasson, 1989:53-4). Though not claiming to be even among the lowest servants, Ruth has used servant language, moving her into the network of social responsibility in a way different from what a foreigner, a Moabite, could normally expect.

There is more. Ruth seems to take a step closer to Boaz, observing that he has *touched my heart* (EFR; *comforted* and *spoken kindly*, NRSV). With sophisticated artistry, Ruth describes the actions of Boaz as the cause of their strengthened connection.

In their conversation, we see not simply mutual admiration. Both Ruth and Boaz try to define the relationship. In bowing down, Ruth symbolizes the relationship as one of enormous social distance: servant and master. In response, Boaz grandly equates Ruth with heroes of Israel's past, Sarah in particular (2:11). Ruth returns to their reality. However far apart they may be in community position, Ruth points to an element of intimacy, thereby making that intimacy part of their relationship (2:13).

The narrative pauses for a moment after the end of Ruth's speech. Perhaps Boaz, like the reader, needs time to ponder their conversation. Apparently Boaz has acted to raise Ruth's social place, bringing her more intentionally into his orbit (Sasson, 1989:54; Hubbard, 1988a: 173-4). At the noon meal, he invites Ruth to sit among his workers. In addition, he serves her, and even serves her more food than she can eat (2:14a).

A conversation that has begun with a lecture by Boaz (2:8-9), concludes with a foreign widow sitting among workers and being served food by the man of substance. Ruth has left home that morning, intending to obtain food and favor (2:2). She has managed both. Clearly, initiative in the story remains in Ruth's hands (Trible, 1978:178). She has drawn a family member and pillar of the Bethlehem society into her story.

2:15-16 Dialogue: Boaz and the Workers

After the meal, Boaz continues to make special provisions for Ruth. He instructs his workers to let Ruth gather grain among the piles of harvested stalks before they have even been bundled up [*Village Farming*]. Even more surprising, Boaz directs the workers intentionally to leave some extra grain for Ruth to pick up. We are left to wonder about the reaction of the young men upon receiving these unusual orders.

Twice in this speech, Boaz orders these young men not to harass Ruth (2:15-16). The words he uses are different from his previous directive (2:9), but the idea remains the same. Boaz's command forbids everything from abusive actions to verbal harassment (Fewell/Gunn, 1990:76). Perhaps such harassment is part of the usual hazards of gleaning. Or maybe Boaz anticipates that his commands will not be favorably received by the workers. They might decide to take out some resentment on the favored woman. Boaz wants this woman cared for and protected.

2:17 Concluding Statement

The scene in the fields concludes with Ruth working the rest of the day, gathering grain and threshing it by hand. An additional surprise comes with the concluding comment by the narrator. Ruth's work produces an ephah of barley. We do not know exactly the amount of an ephah. Information from other locations in the ancient Near East suggests that an ephah would have been approximately twenty-two liters, about two-thirds of a bushel, weighing perhaps twenty-nine U.S. pounds or thirteen kilograms (Hubbard, 1988a: 179). This would provide enough grain to last the two women several weeks (Sasson, 1989:57). Ruth has certainly accomplished what she set out to do.

Dialogue Between Naomi and Ruth 2:18-22

As is common in this story, the narrator moves on with a quick-paced summary of action (2:18). Ruth picks up her grain and returns to town. Immediately, her mother-in-law sees the grain. In addition, Ruth adds to it the remainder of the cooked grain left from the extra large serving she has been served at noon. Their food shortage, obviously, is over for the near term.

Apparently startled, Naomi opens the conversation with two questions (2:19): "Where did you glean today?" "Where have you worked?" Lest we miss the emotion expressed in these questions, Naomi adds: "Blessed be the man who took notice of you" (2:19). The repetitive nature of these questions followed by a blessing suggests that Naomi can barely contain her excitement. The narrator reports Ruth's response and then mirrors it with Ruth's direct speech: she has worked for Boaz (2:19).

This interplay between report and speech serves to emphasize the name *Boaz* (Alter, 1981:77) *[Characteristics of Hebrew Narrative]*. The word order of Ruth's speech increases the emotional impact of the man's name. She withholds the name until the last word, *Boaz*. Apparently Ruth anticipates the effect of that name on her mother-in-law.

Naomi's reaction is immediate and ecstatic. Her first words pronounce blessing on Boaz: "Blessed be he by the LORD" (2:20). The remainder of her blessing contains some ambiguity: *the one who has not stopped showing kindness to the living or the dead* (EFR; cf. Sakenfeld, 1985:92). *Who* has not stopped showing kindness, God or Boaz? Neither Jewish nor Christian interpreters are sure (e.g., Beattie, 1977:69). Perhaps the answer is both. The response of God to the need of these women has merged with the decision of Boaz to grant special favor toward Ruth.

The help by God and Boaz toward the living is obvious—food for the widows, from *kindness/steadfast love [khesed]*. But what about the dead? How have they been helped? Is Naomi perchance looking ahead to more that Boaz might have to offer, such as marriage to Ruth? *[Kinship Marriage]*. The phrase *kindness to the living or the dead* may simply be an inclusive expression, such as "heaven and earth." Hubbard (1988a: 187-8) suggests that the entire encounter between the Ruth and Boaz presages that the future will bring a closer relationship between the two, a marriage that may provide an heir for the dead.

Naomi has made explicit to Ruth information the readers already have. Boaz is a relative, *"one of our nearest kin,"* Naomi says (2:20, NRSV), or *"one of our kinsman-redeemers"* (NIV). This is the first mention of the word *redeemer (go'el)*, a word that will play a central role in the episode at the threshing floor (3:1-18), leading to the decision at the city gate (4:1-12). Though this family redeemer (Boaz) may not have a primary obligation regarding the marriage of Ruth, Naomi's remark calls to mind the specific duties of a redeemer, especially the responsibility to restore the economic health of family members who have fallen on bad times *[Redeemer/Go'el]*.

Ruth's response to her mother-in-law indicates that the good news is not over. Ruth goes on to say that Boaz has invited her to continue throughout the entire harvest (2:21). Even after Boaz has carefully instructed Ruth that she is to stay close to his *young* **women** *(na'arot,* 2:8), however, Ruth tells Naomi that Boaz told her to stay close to his *young* **men!** *(ne'arim,* 2:21, EFR; *servants,* NRSV). Naomi quickly advises Ruth that she had better stay with the young women, to avoid harassment (2:22). Though they have not discussed the matter, Naomi and Boaz agree on the company Ruth should keep.

Concluding Statement 2:23

The narrator concludes by telling the reader that Ruth does indeed follow the advice to work near the young women, not the young men. She continues to gather grain throughout both the barley and then the wheat harvest *[Village Farming]*. Notably absent is any further comment regarding Boaz and Ruth. Apparently the lack of any further development in that relationship requires a woman once again to take the initiative. This leads us to the next episode.

THE TEXT IN BIBLICAL CONTEXT

The Poor in the Biblical Tradition

The biblical narratives, laws, and poems all recognize the plight of the poor. In the Bible, the "poor" is a general term including individuals and groups who, for various reasons, lack the ability and/or opportunity to obtain a secure life. The biblical tradition does not assume an economic leveling, that every one should have the same amount of wealth. In a world of limited resources, however, it was the responsibility of the community in ancient Israel to ensure that the poor were not left without adequate provisions for life. Indeed, in some traditions, the primary task of the king involved protection and care for the poor (Ps. 72). Hence, we find numerous warnings against mistreatment of the poor in both the Psalms and the prophets (e.g., Pss. 10:17-18; 82:2-8; Amos 4:1; Isa. 1:23).

God has special concern for the poor. The psalmist contends that this regard for the poor separates Israel's God from all the other deities in the ancient Near East (Ps. 82). God will not forget them, but will respond to their cry of anguish, just as God responded to the cry of those oppressed in Egypt (Ps. 9:12; Exod. 2:23-24).

Several practices in ancient Israel were intended to assist the poor. Newly harvested fields were to be opened to the poor so they could glean grain that had fallen or been left standing around the edges (Lev. 19:9-10) *[Village Farming]*. Every seventh year landowners were to leave fields, vineyards, and orchards to produce on their own. The produce of this "sabbatical year" belonged to the poor (Exod. 23:11; cf. Lev. 25:2-7, NASB). Family leaders had special responsibility to assist members who had fallen into debt and lost their land (Lev. 25:25-34).

Israelites were supposed to regard lending money as assistance to the needy, rather than as a matter of investment for financial gain. Therefore, creditors were not to charge interest or accept pledges of collateral that would cause hardship to the debtor (Exod. 22:25-27).

The statutes in Deuteronomy insist that the debts of the poor be canceled every seven years. This freed those who had sold themselves into debtor's service. It also gave other poor a chance to start over rather than being driven ever deeper into debt (Deut. 15:1-18). In

Leviticus 25, ancient Israel was directed to make the fiftieth year a special time of economic assistance, a "jubilee." Those who lost land through whatever debt or misfortune were to be given back their land, so that the community could once again be whole.

We do not know how consistently these procedures were followed nor how effectively they functioned. But we do know that the affirmation remained firm, carrying over into first-century Judaism and Christianity: "If there is among you anyone in need, . . . you should . . . open your hand, willingly lending enough to meet the need, whatever it may be" (Deut. 15:7-8; cf. Rom. 15:26; Gal. 2:10).

All the admonitions to charity and all the provisions for assistance will not work if the people who have enough fail to respond to those who need assistance. In Ruth 2, the program succeeds. It works because a poor foreign widow takes the initiative to seek help. It works because the man of substance responds, whatever motivates his response. In this narrative, the cause of poverty and the program of assistance seem simple enough. We experience the causes of poverty as complicated and solutions as elusive. Perhaps that is because we live now and not then. Yet this narrative suggests that it is possible to overcome problems such as ethnic antagonism and harassment of women. In Ruth 2, we see a singularly successful outcome as these difficult problems are faced.

THE TEXT IN THE LIFE OF THE CHURCH

God, Who Blesses

In Ruth, the women and men experience God's presence in daily routine and the rhythm of life. The fertility of the fields and the birth of an infant become particular moments to notice the wonder of God's work. Yet divine blessing is not expressed only in special moments. It comes also as the quiet, continuous flow of fertility, vitality, and companionship. Through the blessing of God, we receive life as a whole, especially its daily course in which nothing in particular happens (Westermann, 1979:44). Often the blessing of God comes to us as a seeming happenstance, even as Ruth *happened* to come to the field of Boaz (2:3).

The several pronouncements of blessing (1:8-9; 2:12, 19-20; 3:10; 4:11-12, 14-15) carry the basic theology featured in the story of Ruth. Hence, we should expect to find God in the background, hidden from view, but nonetheless a critical factor in the resolution of the famine and loss that has afflicted the family of Naomi. According to Hals (19), so deeply has the author hidden the divine presence that the intention and action of God almost completely disappear into the tapestry of everyday events.

Indeed, so hidden is the blessing of God that we might attribute the provision of food for Ruth and Naomi only to the courageous initiative of Ruth and the extraordinary response of Boaz. If so, we will miss the Character hidden in the shadows—not in the ominous shadow of death, with which the story opens, but in the quiet shadows of blessing that cool the heat of the day, satisfy the thirst of the parched, and relieve the hunger of the poor. The God who blesses can still be seen by those willing to turn from the human drama of the center stage and seek the quiet shadows of life's background.

Ruth 3:1-18

Episode 3
Seeking Security

PREVIEW

With this episode, the setting of the story shifts from the grainfield to the threshing floor, and from the light of midday to the dark of midnight. As for the relationship between Ruth and Boaz, the narrator moves them from the spotlight of the harvest field to the privacy of the farthest corner of the threshing floor, in a night so dark that friends cannot even recognize one another (3:14). Much of what happens that night, we will never know, for the narrator stays too far away to get a good look *[Narrator]*. We will be able to hear them speak, but not much else. Perhaps it is just as well. Some things may be best handled in private. However, be advised that the temptation will prove great for us to speculate on matters the narrator has not allowed us to see.

In terms of basic narrative flow, this episode proves to be the companion of the previous one (2:1-23). Both episodes begin and end with a conversation between Ruth and Naomi (2:2, 19-22; 3:1-4, 16-18). In both, the center of the unit features an encounter and dialogue between Ruth and Boaz (2:8-14; 3:8-15). That parallelism directs our attention all the more to the contrasts between the two meetings. Not only will readers find a direct contrast in time and place; they will also recognize that the first meeting happens by chance, and this one by choice (2:3; 3:3). In the initial meeting, Ruth wants food; in this encounter, she wants marriage (2:2; 3:2-5). Previously, Ruth and Boaz were at work, but this time they are at play (Trible, 1978:183).

A rendezvous between a woman and a man in the middle of the night at a remote location is electric with possibilities and fraught with danger. It should not surprise us that the narrator uses sexually charged language throughout this episode. Frequent use of both noun and verb forms of the word "know" *(yada')* and eight occurrences of the verb "lie down" *(šakab),* convey sexual overtones.

Ruth's action, however, rather than her language, captures the attention of most readers. Naomi instructs Ruth to *uncover* either Boaz's *feet*/legs or uncover herself at Boaz's feet (3:4). The ambiguity of Naomi's instruction (Nielsen, 1997:67-71) tells us right away that we will not have access to all the events on the threshing floor. Nevertheless, the precise nature of the act of uncovering has kept readers busy either imagining the possibilities or hastening to protect the two from even the appearance of impropriety.

Thus the episode raises many more questions than can be answered. The narrator draws a curtain of darkness, a fairly opaque curtain, between readers and the threshing floor. What matters is not the details that transpire that dark harvest night. Naomi sends Ruth to Boaz in the hope that at least one widow might have a secure future. Ruth apparently secures the future in the agreements made on the threshing floor.

As mentioned above, the flow of this episode displays much the same balance we found in the previous unit (Outline, Episode 2). This episode begins and ends with Naomi's speech to Ruth (3:1-4; 18). Structurally, this episode is less complex than the previous one. Ruth and Boaz alone occupy the central scene. All the other harvest workers are far away.

OUTLINE
Dialogue: Naomi and Ruth, 3:1-5

Scene at the Threshing Floor, 3:6-15
    3:6-8   Introductory Narration
    3:9-13   Dialogue: Boaz and Ruth
    3:14-15   Concluding Narration

Dialogue: Naomi and Ruth, 3:16-18

As with the previous episode (2:1-23), this one too can be laid out in a form that illustrates its chiastic balance *[Narrative Structure].* This way of balancing the parts of the episode points the reader to the central dialogue as the most important element. In addition, this type of symmetry moves us easily into and out of a situation beset with ambiguity. The episode in chiastic outline:

Dialogue: Naomi and Ruth, 3:1-5
    At the Threshing Floor: Introductory Narration, 3:6-8
        Dialogue: Boaz and Ruth, 3:9-13
    At the Threshing Floor: Concluding Narration, 3:14-15
Dialogue: Naomi and Ruth, 3:16-18

EXPLANATORY NOTES

Dialogue: Naomi and Ruth, 3:1-5

No narrative introduction provides a prelude to this dialogue. Instead, the dialogue begins immediately with Naomi's speech to Ruth (3:1-4). In the second episode, Naomi reacts to Ruth's plan to go after food (2:2-3), but this time the mother-in-law takes the initiative.

Naomi assumes the role she has taken as they left Moab (1:8-13), instructing Ruth on what she is to do. At that time, Naomi directed Ruth to return to her own people so that she might find a husband (1:9). Now we hear not only the same tone from Naomi, but the same subject, marriage, and the same purpose, to *seek some security* or a *home* (NIV, 3:1). Some interpreters question Naomi's motives. Does she only have Ruth's interests at heart? Perhaps Naomi seeks to use Ruth to secure her own future as well as Ruth's (Fewell/Gunn, 1990:74, 77). The narrator does not tell us Naomi's motives. It would not be out of character for Naomi to act out of concern for both herself and others (2:20).

The narrator has chosen to reveal nothing more about the relationship between Ruth and Boaz throughout the remainder of the harvest work (2:23). In this episode, however, Naomi decides to rekindle that relationship. Thus Naomi directs Ruth to dress seductively (3:3; cf. Esther 2:12-13) and go to the threshing floor, where she will find Boaz. Naomi further instructs Ruth not to approach Boaz immediately. Instead, she is to wait until after the eating and drinking is over. Then Ruth is to observe where Boaz retires for rest. Finally, she is to approach Boaz, *uncover his feet* or *uncover at his feet*, and lie down (Nielsen, 1997:67-71). From that point on, it will be up to Boaz (3:3-4).

This plan is fraught with all manner of danger. Circumstances have forced Ruth the Moabite into the role of foreign woman, a fact the narrator continues to call to our attention (2:10, 21). Now her mother-in-law adds the corollary to that role: the temptress (Brenner, 1985:90). Israelite tradition has warned that the foreign temptress can compromise Hebrew men and their faith (Num. 25:1) *[Moab]*. Israel's sages issued frequent warnings about the words of the "strange" and dangerous woman (Prov. 5:3; 7:5; 22:14). How will Boaz respond to a midnight approach by a woman? Can anything good come out of such a plan?

There is yet another threat. Sending a woman out at night is in itself dangerous, especially for one dressed as Ruth will be. Another woman, unnamed, was assaulted by the village sentinels when she ventured out at night to find her lover (Song of Sol. 5:7).

Finally, Ruth is instructed not only to dress provocatively but to initiate some manner of contact with Boaz. Exactly what is Ruth to uncover? Naomi's words hide as much as they reveal. The Hebrew word, *margelot*, may refer to the feet, the genitals, or even the whole body from the waist down (Gray: 394; Phillips, 1980:38-42). The word may also refer to a location, *at the feet* (cf. 3:8, 14). If the word refers to location more than anatomy, then we are not told what was to be uncovered. Kristen Nielsen (1997:68-9) observes that nowhere else in the Bible does a woman explicitly uncover a man. Instead, she suggests that Ruth is instructed to uncover herself. Ruth follows those instructions, asking, in response, to be covered by Boaz (3:9).

Whichever may be the case, Naomi, who has previously directed her daughter-in-law to play it safe (1:8-9; 2:22), has now requested that Ruth take an enormous risk. Ruth herself, in setting out to glean, has operated within the customs of ancient Israel. She may have pushed the edges of propriety by intending not only to obtain food, but also favor (2:2). However, this nocturnal scheme clearly lies outside the realm of acceptable behavior within Israel. Since Ruth is a Moabite, a foreign woman, this makes the scheme all the more troubling. Yet Naomi, the childless widow, apparently decides she needs to take this road to provide a secure home.

Even though Ruth has previously refused to comply with the instruction of her mother-in-law (1:16-17), she agrees to this plan (3:5). She asks no questions and seeks no reasons.

Scene at the Threshing Floor 3:6-15

3:6-8 Introductory Narration

The scene at the threshing floor opens with a summary statement reporting that Ruth has done as instructed (3:6). The narrator, however, promptly changes the direction of the reader's attention

[Narrator]. Ruth drops out of sight, and we watch Boaz finish eating. As Naomi anticipates, Boaz leaves the meal to lie down *at the end of the heap of grain* (3:7). This puts Boaz far away from anyone, including the reader, who might see too much (Sasson, 1989:73). Probably we are to picture Boaz lying down near a large pile of threshed and winnowed grain ready to be bagged and sold.

We do not know why Boaz is sleeping on the threshing floor. Many interpreters assume that he is guarding the grain, but that would more likely be the task of the workers, not the *man of substance* (2:1). Furthermore, we do not know his physical state. Boaz has been eating and drinking, but whether he has taken enough wine to be vulnerable to seduction is left for the reader to decide.

Ruth, apparently watching from the shadows, moves silently to the place where Boaz is lying (3:7b). As she comes *stealthily* (NRSV), this silence *(ballat)* has an ominous ring. Sisera died in his sleep when Jael silently crept up on him (Judg. 4:21). David took a snip out of Saul's coat in another such silence (1 Sam. 24:4).

Just as we cannot be sure about Naomi's instructions, so we cannot know what Ruth uncovers and where she lies. Frequently readers have sought to clarify events on the threshing floor. Those who feel that the character of Ruth and Boaz would be unacceptably compromised by sexual contact, will most certainly conclude that there was no contact (McGee: 92-4). If, however, the readers' assessment of the situation assumes the probability that the relationship is sexually consummated, then their interpretation will allow for that (Green: 61). The encounter happens in the dark of night, far from the eyes of anyone. It seems best not to pry where the narrator will not take us.

Apparently Boaz shares the reader's confusion and uncertainty. Something startles him wide awake in the dark of the night. He may have been chilled from the lack of cover (Hubbard, 1988a:210-1). Or perhaps, shifting in sleep, he touches another person. Whatever may have awakened him, the narrator reports Boaz's shock at what he sees: "Oh, a woman!"

3:9-13 *Dialogue: Boaz and Ruth*

Surprised at discovering a woman beside him, Boaz exclaims, *"Who are you?"* (3:9a). This is a question different from what he asked when he first saw Ruth: *"To whom does this woman belong?"* (2:5). Some interpreters see the change as quite significant. Previously Boaz has inquired about Ruth's social place. The question *"Who are you?"* assumes that the woman belongs to no one (Laffey: 556-7). Nevertheless, we do well not to over-interpret Boaz's question

[Questions]. His may be the normal response of a man upon discovering a female visitor he did not expect or recognize.

Be that as it may, Ruth introduces herself by name: *"I am Ruth"* (3:9b). Only in Ruth's self-introduction do we hear the name of either of the two figures at the threshing floor. The narrator, after mentioning *Boaz* in 3:7, describes the whole night scene without naming either one, using instead pronouns or generic nouns: *the man, a near kinsman, a woman, my daughter.*

Ruth goes beyond her name to define her relationship to Boaz: *"I am . . . your servant,"* and the man's relationship to her, *"You are the redeemer"* (3:9, EFR; *next-of-kin,* NRSV; *kinsman-redeemer,* NIV). Her words mark a change in how Ruth defines their relationship. No longer does Ruth assume the role as foreigner, one who is below even a servant (2:13). Instead, Ruth declares herself to be his servant, using a word for servant *('amah)* that designates a woman who might be taken as wife or concubine (a marital associate secondary to the wife).

Naomi has instructed Ruth to approach Boaz and then let him take the lead (3:4). One senses that already in this self-introduction, Ruth is exceeding her mandate. But this woman does not just stop there. Ruth petitions Boaz for help by identifying him as one who has a special responsibility toward her, *next-of-kin, redeemer* (3:9b). The *redeemer* functions to assist a member of the family who needs financial assistance or legal advocacy *[Redeemer]*. In spite of all the sexual allusions surrounding this dialogue, Ruth's petition involves business, not romance (Bos, 1988:63).

Apparently Ruth has asked Boaz to marry her with a clever echo of Boaz's own words (Campbell, 1975:123). In the barley field, Boaz blessed Ruth for choosing to seek refuge *under the wings/cloak (kanap)* of God (2:12). Alluding to this previous blessing by Boaz, Ruth urges him, *"Spread your cloak/wing (kanap) over your servant"* (3:9). Ruth has turned the blessing back to him, challenging Boaz to make good on his own blessing.

This most likely constitutes a request for marriage, though we cannot be absolutely certain that Ruth has asked for more than protection (Berlin, 1988:266). The available biblical law does not clearly assign to the redeemer the responsibility to marry a widowed family member *[Redeemer]*. The responsibility to marry the childless widow, to protect the deceased family member's name and property, apparently belongs to the brother of the deceased man *[Kinship Marriage]*. However, we cannot be sure that everywhere in ancient Israel the customs were the same, or that the literature reflects practice as clear-cut as we understand the biblical legal stipulations.

Some interpreters feel that Ruth has asked for marriage for herself, expecting that the marriage would serve the purpose of providing offspring for Naomi and Elimelech. Clearly, that is what Boaz decides to do (4:5). Nevertheless, Ruth's words are suggestive rather than clear.

How will this man of substance respond to such an emotionally charged situation? Clearly, Boaz responds favorably to the daring venture of Ruth (3:10-13). Previously, Boaz has provided the widows with food assistance; in dark of the night, he again agrees to help Ruth.

Has Boaz agreed out of the strength of his character, or has he been compromised? Boaz finds himself in an extremely delicate situation: a woman at his feet, clothes askew. Has anything happened before he becomes fully alert? (Phillips, 1986:14). We are not told the motives of this man of substance, but we do know his response. Boaz pronounces a second blessing on Ruth (3:10). He declares that Ruth's marriage proposal represents a level of compassion and *loyalty (khesed)* exceeding even her first declaration of loyalty to Naomi *[Khesed]*. He declares himself flattered that Ruth has chosen him as her husband/protector rather than any of the many men her own age.

Boaz goes on, promising to do all that Ruth has asked, because everyone in town knows that she is *"a woman of substance"* (3:11, EFR; *worthy woman,* NRSV; *noble character,* NIV). With this phrase, *woman of substance (khayil),* Boaz describes Ruth just as the narrator has described *him* (2:1, *khayil).* At least in terms of character, even if not economics, Boaz acknowledges Ruth as his equal (Bos, 1988:62).

Ruth asks Boaz to assume his role as family redeemer. We do not know what all that means: marriage, protection, heir? However broad the request, Boaz agrees to do all that Ruth seeks. The dangerous and delicate plan of the two women (Naomi and Ruth) seems to have succeeded. When put to the test, Boaz, a man of substance, proves his character. As Nielsen (1997:76) notes, this is not a rendevous of self-absorbed lovers; instead, two people are assuming responsibility for "family."

In this narrative, regrettably, nothing works exactly as planned. At the very moment that the reader believes the problem is resolved, Boaz introduces a complication. He informs Ruth of a family member who is *more closely related* and whose right of redemption takes precedence over his own (3:12). Biblical law indicates that the responsibility of *redeemer* belongs to any family member in a position to help. We have no text that expressly assigns an order to that role (Lev.

25:48-49) [Redeemer]. Perhaps the practice of redeemer reflected in this narrative differs from what other biblical texts describe.

Is Boaz looking for a way to pass on to some other family member the responsibility to which Ruth has called him? At this point in the narrative, we do not know what is going on. Nevertheless, Boaz promises under oath ("as the LORD lives") that if the other next-of-kin does not act as redeemer, he will do it himself (3:13).

In spite of the complication of another redeemer, Boaz seems to accept the marriage proposal from Ruth. However, Boaz does so as indirectly as it has been given. Twice he directs Ruth to remain through the night: *"Lie down until the morning"* (3:13). This is the first occasion since her vow of loyalty that Ruth has lodged (1:16) other than with Naomi (Berlin, 1988:266). The narrator does not tell us anything else about their night together, except that Ruth complies with his request to stay the night, at least until very early morning (3:14).

3:14-15 Concluding Narration

Ruth's departure from the threshing floor is as mysterious as her arrival. She arises while it is still too dark for anyone to be recognized. Apparently Boaz does not want anyone to be aware that *"the woman came to the threshing floor"* (3:14). This seems to suggest that Boaz does not wish to arouse suspicion. Is he worried about her reputation or his? Perhaps both. As a man of substance, Boaz can ill afford to be compromised by a foreign woman. As a Moabite childless widow, Ruth has little to lose, but she also has little protection from charges of prostitution.

As she leaves, Boaz fills Ruth's *shawl* (NIV) with grain (3:15), but we do not know how much. Literally translated, the Hebrew text tells us that he gives Ruth *six of grain*. The versions generally say *six measures*. Some suggest six *seahs*, or about sixty pounds, nearly thirty kilograms (Hubbard, 1988a: 222). The other possibility would be six *omers*, over half a bushel or about fifteen kilograms, over thirty pounds (Gerleman: 33).

In part, the decision of interpreters about the amount of grain depends on their understanding of the purpose of the gift. Some see it as a generous betrothal gift. For that, six seahs would be assumed (Sasson, 1989:98). However, the grain may be a symbolic gift, symbolic of fertility. If so, the reader might assume a smaller, more manageable amount (cf. Rashi in Beattie, 1977:109). Then again, this might be a gift to provide Ruth a "suitable" explanation for her return trip from the threshing floor in the early morning hours (Hubbard, 1988a: 222).

The narrator does not explain this gift of grain, instead letting us watch, though from a distance that prevents us from seeing exactly how much Ruth has been given. After measuring out six portions of grain, we notice Boaz walk off toward town (3:15). We do not even see Ruth depart *[Narrator]*.

Dialogue: Naomi and Ruth 3:16-18

Ruth does depart, returning to her mother-in-law (3:16). Naomi's question to Ruth is the same as Boaz's question on the threshing floor (3:9): *"Who are you?"* (EFR). She adds her frequent term of address to Ruth: *"my daughter."* Obviously Naomi recognizes Ruth, so she does not want the same information Boaz needed. Apparently Naomi wants to know whether or not her plan has succeeded; hence the NRSV/NIV translation, *"How did it go?"* (3:16). If the marriage proposal has succeeded, then Ruth's world will change. She can define her identity in relationship to Boaz (Sasson, 1989:100-1).

Ruth tells Naomi only what the man has done for her, rather than what Ruth herself has done. Ruth amplifies Boaz's speech with an explanation for his gift of grain: *"For he [Boaz] said, 'Do not go back to your mother-in-law empty'"* (3:17, EFR). Either we missed that part of the threshing-floor conversation, or Ruth has created an explanation that she feels the situation demands (Berlin, 1983:98). Perhaps intentionally, Ruth's phrasing of the explanation echoes Naomi's complaint when she first returns from Moab: *"The LORD has brought me back empty"* (1:21). Emptiness is now past.

The episode concludes as it began, with Naomi instructing Ruth about what she should do (3:18; 3:1-4). In light of Ruth's risk and wit on the threshing floor, Naomi's act of resuming the role of parent or teacher may contain a tinge of irony (Fewell/Gunn, 1990:80) *[Comedy, Irony, and Satire]*. Nevertheless, Naomi expresses her trust that *the man* will carry through his promise. And he does, but in an unexpected way.

Dialogue between Ruth and Naomi has carried this narrative along, beginning on the road running between Moab and Bethlehem (1:6-18). That now comes to an end. We do not hear either woman speak again.

THE TEXT IN BIBLICAL CONTEXT

The Childless Widow

Ruth and Naomi lived as childless widows in a society organized around the family, not limited to parents and children, but the extended family. The family's present was controlled by men/husbands, and the future depended on women/wives with children. Hence, women with many children, especially sons, had a place of respect, even honor. The woman with no child lacked respect, and the women without either husband or children had no secure place and few possibilities for the future.

The Bible recounts several stories about the suffering of barren wives, such as Sarah, Rachel, Hannah, and Elizabeth. Even more anguish appears in those stories of women who lack both husband and children. These painful narratives have a common thread. Frequently a woman without mate or child chose to break the traditional norms of community and faith in order to have a chance for life, perhaps even respect. Compare, for example, the narratives of Lot's daughters (Gen. 19), Tamar (Gen. 38), and Ruth.

Genesis 19:30-38 narrates the story of the birth of Moab, the traditional ancestor of Ruth's homeland. According to Hebrew tradition, Lot and his unnamed daughters escaped the destruction of Sodom only to find themselves homeless, living in a cave (Gen. 19:30). Lot's eldest daughter reminded her sister that their father was aging and they had no prospects of ever having husbands or children. She proposed that they bring Lot sufficiently under the influence of alcohol that he would lie with each daughter, thus providing them with children (Gen. 19:31-32). The son born to Lot's eldest daughter from this planned incest was Moab. Lot's daughter successfully created a place for herself in the present and secured the family's future, but she had to go far outside the limits of acceptable sexual behavior to make it happen.

The narrative in Genesis 38 concerns Judah, an ancestor of Boaz (and Elimelech). Judah arranged for his eldest son, Er, to marry Tamar (Gen. 38:6). When Er died, leaving Tamar childless, Judah directed his second son, Onan, to fulfill his responsibility to his brother and make Tamar pregnant *[Kinship Marriage]*. Onan only pretended to provide sperm for Tamar. Subsequently, he too died, still leaving Tamar childless (Gen. 38:8-10). Judah promised Tamar that his youngest son, Shelah, would assume that responsibility when he was old enough.

Judah, however, fearing that his only remaining son would also die, never intended to keep his promise (Gen. 38:11). When Tamar realized this, she disguised herself as a prostitute and sold her services to her father-in-law, Judah (Gen. 38:13-18). When the truth came out, Judah declared Tamar innocent of the prostitution charge against her. She gave birth to twins (Gen. 38:24-30). Tradition identifies one of these twins, Perez, as the ancestor of Boaz (Ruth 4:18).

The connections between these two narratives and Ruth go beyond just genealogy. Each case portrays a woman without child or husband who struggles to secure not only a place for herself, but also a future for the family. In her desperation, she is forced to take measures that set her outside the traditional mores of society: incest, prostitution, seduction in the night. The biblical tradition condemns none of these women, even though the incest and prostitution, and probably seduction on the threshing floor, remain unacceptable behavior.

Most of us find these narratives as troubling as did the ancient readers. Our ethical commitments cause us to reject or ignore biblical narratives that seem to excuse behavior such as incest, prostitution, or secret seduction. Such shocking behavior compromises our appreciation of the stories. At the same time, we hear the cries of these women who had no place in the present or hope for the future.

We recognize that every society creates the equivalent of the "childless widow." Each generation has a list of circumstances that disqualify a person from truly belonging in the community. Often these marginal people choose "indecent" actions to provide for their present and to secure the future for themselves and others. Will they find a Boaz, who answers Ruth with blessing? (Ruth 3:10). Or a Judah, who responded to Tamar with confession of his own sin? (Gen. 38:26).

THE TEXT IN THE LIFE OF THE CHURCH

Beyond Assistance to Security

Ruth and Naomi find themselves involved in a high-risk venture. According to Naomi, they take the risk so that they might have security (3:1). Ancient Israel had developed several structures designed to provide the necessities of life for the poor. Gleaning in the fields helped to provide food, although the food available to the gleaners would have been minimal *[Village Farming]*. In the seventh year, landowners were to let their fields lie fallow; any grain that grew up as "volunteers" belonged to the poor (Exod. 23:10-11; cf. Lev. 25:2-7, 12).

By tradition (if not practice), every fifty years the debts of the poor were to be canceled, freeing them to begin anew (Lev. 25). Ancient Israel also adapted another institution common in the ancient Near East: the redeemer *(go'el)*. Members of the extended family of the poor were responsible to assume their debts, paying off creditors who took control of the family property or forced the poor into their service for debt repayment *[Redeemer]*. In Ruth, the responsibility of the redeemer seems to extend to marrying a woman widowed and without children.

In theory, the poor would be cared for. The story of Ruth shows that in practice, not all these expectations were realized. Gleaning seems to have its dangers, especially for women, who are subject to harassment if not assault. We do not know how conscientiously the provisions for the seventh year and fiftieth year were kept (cf. Jer. 34:8-17). Biblical laws suggest that creditors discovered ways to dodge the requirement that they periodically cancel the debts of the poor (Lev. 25). Although any family member could serve as redeemer for a poor person (Lev. 25:48-49), we do not know how successfully the redeemer system worked. Ruth's dangerous trip to the threshing floor for the purpose of prompting the redeemer into action, may indicate that wealthy family members did not always step forward to assist their poor "cousins."

Each society past and present develops ways to help the poor. Perhaps the most universal is to "allow" the needy to beg for money, thus depending on voluntary contributions. Contemporary societies seek to assist the poor with a variety of programs developed by governments and private organizations. Some denominations, such as those in the believers church tradition, have been leaders in this work, often developing programs that serve as models for governments and other agencies to adapt.

It is one thing to assist the poor with food, shelter, and clothing. Naomi wants security, not just assistance (3:1). Security for Naomi and Ruth involves a place in the social and economic structure where they are no longer dependent on provisions for the poor. Few societies are willing to provide a clear pathway out of poverty.

The drive for a secure place in Bethlehemite society requires that Ruth risk even the little she has. In our day, the poor often find the world of education and employment stacked against them as they struggle to escape poverty. Ruth's venture prompts Boaz to do his duty and can also prompt us to fulfill our responsibility, so that the poor may receive not only food but also the opportunity for a secure place in society.

Ruth 4:1-12

Episode 4
Agreement at the Gate

PREVIEW

A woman, either Naomi or Ruth, takes the initiative in each of the previous episodes (1:6; 2:2; 3:1). Boaz, however, asserts control over the action in this fourth episode, convening the legal assembly to decide the redemption of Naomi's land and the kinship marriage for Ruth. In the process, the parties always speak of the two women in the third person.

This fourth episode brings the characters back to the public world of Bethlehem. The first episode concludes with Naomi as the center of public attention in the town, the women's world of Bethlehem (1:19-21). The second episode follows Ruth outside the village to the barley fields of Boaz (2:4-16). In the third episode, the narrator takes us as far from the public spotlight as possible, midnight on the threshing floor (3:6-15). With this fourth episode, the narrative moves back into town, but to a different part of town, the men's gathering at the village gate, called by Boaz, an important man in that town (2:1).

We have found specific words featured as key in particular episodes of the narrative. The first episode (1:6-22) involved returning, the returning of fertility to the land and of Naomi to Bethlehem. Hence, we followed the frequent repetition of the Hebrew word *šub, return*. The second episode (2:1-23) was set in the midst of the barley harvest, with Ruth's decision to obtain food by gleaning. Thus repetition of the Hebrew verb *laqat, glean,* carried the narrative from beginning to end. This fourth episode involves redemption. Boaz redeems Naomi's land that she must sell to obtain money *[Redeemer].* The narrative reinforces the focus by reusing the Hebrew term *ga'al/go'el, redeem/redeemer,* fourteen times in these twelve verses.

We will not be able to untangle all the legal questions presented by this episode. Elsewhere in biblical law and narrative, we see the different legal matters of a family redeeming land scheduled to be sold for repayment of debt, and of the marriage of a childless widow to another member of the family *[Kinship Marriage; Redeemer].* One does not directly involve the other. In Ruth, the two customs are brought together. Nevertheless, Boaz first discusses with his relative the redemption of land (4:4), and then takes up the kinship marriage (4:5).

The extent to which this episode blurs an assumed distinction between land redemption and kinship marriage varies widely from one interpreter to another (e.g., Beattie, 1974:251-67; Hubbard, 1988a: 56-62). We do not have enough knowledge about the judicial institutions at specific times and communities in ancient Israel to clarify precisely the legal issues involved in this case.

Nevertheless, we must not allow the legal uncertainties to preoccupy us so that we miss the excitement of this scene in the village square, just inside the town gate. After the two family members work out their accord, with one voice the town joins in blessing Boaz for his action, especially his decision to marry Ruth. The foreign woman who arrived in town unacknowledged and perhaps unnoticed (1:19-22), is now accepted by the town as the intended bride of Boaz (4:11-12).

The narrative flow of this episode follows the legal process. First the necessary parties gather (4:1-2), then the two relatives work out the agreement (4:3-8). The elders and the onlookers have a passive role as the agreement is forged, and then they verbally endorse and bless the agreement.

OUTLINE
Calling of the Legal Session, 4:1-2

The Legal Proceeding, 4:3-12
    4:3-8   Agreement Between the Parties
    4:9-12   Formal Announcement and Witnessing

EXPLANATORY NOTES

Calling of the Legal Session 4:1-2

Boaz needs to call together all the concerned parties in order to consummate a legal agreement. Therefore, Boaz goes to the area near the town gate. Everyone who travels in or out of the village passes through this open area, probably just inside the entrance to the town.

Providence smiles on Boaz. No sooner has he arrived than his relative, the other involved party, comes along (4:1). The narrator does not give us the name of the relative whom Boaz summons. The customary translation of his greeting, *"Friend/my friend"* (NRSV/NIV), may indicate more warmth than the Hebrew words convey. The narrator explicitly does not give us the man's name, substituting instead a term of anonymity (Waard/Nida, 64-5). The substitution stands out so sharply that some suspect Boaz has used the man's name and the narrator has removed it (Berlin, 1983:101). We need not read that anonymity as negative, although frequently interpreters have done so (e.g., Craghan: 222-3). More important than the name, the narrator wants us to understand that this man is the redeemer of whom Boaz has spoken earlier (3:13).

The unnamed relative responds to the summons (4:1), so Boaz calls ten men from the elders in the town (4:2). We presume these men are among the respected heads of families in the village. Actually, however, we know little about the designation *elders* throughout much of the history of ancient Israel (Hubbard, 1988a: 235-6). They are to function in this legal proceeding primarily as witnesses. The elders are required to observe as the two formulate their agreement, thus insuring that the proceeding is done properly. In this case, they only became active when Boaz asks for their ratification (4:9).

The narrator's words convey that all this happens quickly and fortuitously (*No sooner had Boaz gone up to the gate . . .,* 4:1). We have become accustomed to such moments of Providence in this narrative (e.g., 2:2). Such gaps invite us to look for the hidden presence of God in the drama.

The Legal Proceeding 4:3-12

4:3-8 Agreement Between the Parties

Boaz opens the legal proceeding by identifying the matter that must be decided (4:3-4a). He addresses his remarks directly to his relative. Boaz has called the session not to try a case, but to witness and ratify an agreement regarding a family matter. According to Boaz,

Naomi is selling a parcel of land that has been part of Elimelech's estate (4:3). By inviting his relative to purchase the land, Boaz invokes the customary practice of land redemption. Any sufficiently wealthy family member is responsible to redeem/buy any family land that has to be put up for sale *[Redeemer]*.

Next Boaz indicates a specific order for any to function as redeemer within the family. In this case, his unnamed relative has the first option, and Boaz the second (4:4). We do not know if anyone else in the family has the means to redeem the land. Boaz is not about to let the land pass out of the family (4:4).

Boaz's legal action raises questions for which we have no answers. Previously, we have heard no mention of any land owned by Naomi. If she owns land from Elimelech's estate, perhaps the widow is not as destitute as we have thought. How did Boaz learn about Naomi's intention to sell? In the story, Naomi and Boaz never meet, let alone discuss property matters. If her land needs to be redeemed, why does not the closer relative or Boaz step forward early on to care for this responsibility?

In response to most of these questions, interpreters have only suggestions, no clear answers. Second Kings 8:1-6 tells the story of a woman urged by Elisha to flee her home to escape a coming famine (Campbell, 1975:157-8). She did so and lived elsewhere for seven years. Eventually she returned only to find her land occupied by someone else. An appeal to the king resulted in the restoration of that land to her. We might imagine that Naomi's land was being cultivated by others. Prompted by his encounter with Ruth, Boaz perhaps takes it upon himself to turn this inheritance into money for Naomi. Throughout the narrative, Boaz has acted to assist Naomi and Ruth, but only after being nudged by one or both of the women. Thus it may not be surprising that the land has gone unredeemed until the end.

Boaz's unnamed relative agrees to redeem the land (4:4). In so doing, he agrees to pay Naomi for the field. In return, the land will be his to till as he chooses. For Naomi, the land's sale will provide her some measure of financial security, at least for a while. However, if Elimelech would have a son still living, the land would be deeded over at no cost to the son when that lad comes of age or in the year of Jubilee (Lev. 25:8-10). The redeemer would have use of the land until that time, but then he would lose it. But since Elimelech's sons have died (1:5) and the surviving widow is past childbearing age (1:11), there appears to be little danger that the relative will lose his investment.

Yet Boaz has more to say about the terms of the agreement (4:5).

It concerns kinship marriage for Ruth. Boaz's proposal concerning Ruth depends on how we read the Hebrew text. Boaz states that on the day when his relative acts to redeem the land, Ruth will be married to a family member for the purpose of conceiving a son. That child will inherit the family property *[Kinship Marriage]*. Who does Boaz propose should marry Ruth?

If we read the text the way the ancient rabbis pronounced it (*qere'*, "speak"), Boaz informs his relative that the relative himself is obligated to marry Ruth. Both the NRSV and NIV take it this way: *"The day you acquire the field from the hand of Naomi,* **you** [emphasis added] *are also acquiring Ruth, . . . to maintain the dead man's name on his inheritance"* (4:5). However, if we read the verse the way the ancient rabbis wrote it (*kethib*, "write"), Boaz informs his relative, that he, Boaz, will marry Ruth: *"The day you acquire the field from the hand of Naomi, I will acquire Ruth . . .* (4:5, EFR). Either reading is possible, and scholars divide on the matter (cf. Sasson, 1987:326-7; Berlin, 1988:266).

Nielsen (1997:86) observes that since the relative does not anticipate the necessity or even possibility of kinship marriage, it is not necessarily an obligation of a distant relative. Therefore, the most likely reading is that Boaz, himself, will marry Ruth. Boaz intends that he and Ruth will have an heir who will inherit the land. Suddenly, this closer relative faces the likelihood that one day a rightful heir to the property of Elimelech may claim this property. Hence, the land would need to be given to the heir without charge. If that were to happen, the relative who has redeemed Naomi's land would loose his money invested. It would become a gift to Elimelech's heir.

For the unnamed relative, this stipulation to the agreement changes everything. He declares to Boaz that he cannot afford such a purchase/gift: *"I cannot redeem it for myself without damaging my own estate"* (4:6, EFR). Apparently the purchase would take a large bite out of his capital; he cannot afford to pay the needed price and then lose ownership of it in a decade or so. In addition, custom seems to require the one who marries Ruth to assume long-term responsibility for her and any subsequent children. If the unnamed relative were to marry Ruth, this would further divide his income and estate (LaCocque: 97-9). Hence, he hands the right of redemption and kinship marriage over to Boaz (4:6).

The two relatives then engage in a ritual to seal the agreement. Apparently this ritual was not well-known even to an early audience. Therefore, the narrator takes a moment to explain the procedure (4:7). A sandal is handed from the one relinquishing the right of redemption to the one assuming that responsibility. Evidence from legal rituals in the ancient Near East suggests that this symbolized one person's act of removing his foot (his claim) from the property, and the other person's act of receiving that right to step on the land (Thompson/Thompson: 92).

4:9-12 Formal Announcement and Witnessing

Upon reaching the agreement with his unnamed relative, Boaz turns to the elders and onlookers, those who have gathered to watch the proceeding. He details the agreement by which he will purchase from Naomi all the property belonging to Elimelech and his sons, Chilion and Mahlon (4:9). What has sounded like the purchase of a single field that Naomi needs to sell, Boaz describes to the witnesses as Elimelech's entire family estate. Perhaps in his summary of the agreement, Boaz uses language that is more precise for legal purposes. Some suggest, however, that this may have been a second surprise sprung by Boaz. Not only will there be a kinship marriage to produce an heir, but the unnamed relative has also given up his option on far more property than we, the readers, know about (Hubbard, 1988a: 255).

A second agreement involves Ruth. Boaz will take Ruth within the custom of kinship marriage *[Kinship Marriage]*. According to this custom, the firstborn son of this union will be not only the son of Boaz, but also the heir of Elimelech. This son will perpetuate the family line of his deceased grandfather/father. Elimelech's property will belong to his legal descendants through this surrogate son, and his name and memory will be a part of the ongoing life of the village of Bethlehem.

Boaz brackets his speech by calling the elders and onlookers to their role as *witnesses* (4:9a, 10b). The narrator creates an anxious pause with an unusually long introductory narration (4:11a). Through that narration, we slowly look over the crowd who has gathered, and then specifically at the elders. Finally we hear their affirmation as one voice: *"We are witnesses!"* (4:11b).

The witnesses continue, still as one voice, with a blessing in poetic form (4:11b-12) *[Poetry]*. The blessing appears as a three-part pronouncement: a blessing on Ruth *(the woman),* a blessing on Boaz *(you),* and a blessing on the household *(family,* NIV; *house,* NRSV).

In their blessing on Ruth, the witnesses bring her solidly within the family of Israel. Their hope is that Ruth might be known as one of the founding mothers, joining Rachel and Leah (4:11a). Nevertheless, it is hard to know how to interpret the fact that Ruth's name is not used when she is blessed. Boaz has explicitly called her by name both in discussion with his relative (4:5) and in the formal stipulations of the agreement to the witnesses (4:10). In fact, Boaz has named Ruth and also twice identified her as *the Moabite.*

In spite of the elders' acceptance of her, they may still be distancing themselves from Ruth. We have seen such distancing elsewhere in the story. Both the narrator and Boaz have avoided using names on the threshing floor. We, the readers, are not able to get close enough to see what really happens there (3:8-15). In this episode, the narrator also avoids naming Boaz's relative in the legal proceedings, thus keeping that person at a distance (4:1-8). Why keep Ruth away? Perhaps because the village scene is a man's world, this episode is designed to feature Boaz and him alone (Trible, 1978:188).

The blessing on Boaz wishes that this *man of substance* might become even more famous: *"May you have standing in Ephrathah and be famous in Bethlehem"* (4:11b, NIV). Ephrathah is used here poetically as another name for Bethlehem (cf. 1:2, notes).

The focus on Boaz continues in the third blessing, even though the blessing is pronounced on the *house* or *family* of Boaz: *"May your house be like the house of Perez, whom Tamar bore to Judah"* (4:12). According to the traditional genealogy, Perez, one of Tamar's twin sons, is the ancestor of Boaz (Gen. 38:27-30; Ruth 4:18-21; 1 Chron. 2:4-15). Suddenly the house of Elimelech has disappeared into the background. Not only does the scene belong to Boaz, but the witnesses expect the same to be true of the genealogy.

Does the episode revere Boaz for his actions, or has Boaz acted to save his own honor compromised on the threshing floor? (cf. Nielson, 1997:86; Fewell/Gunn, 1990:90-2). In favor of Boaz, he has exceeded the requirements of custom and law in his response to the plight of Naomi and Ruth. In contrast to the sons of Judah and even Judah himself, who tried to avoid providing an heir for the widow Tamar (Gen. 38), Boaz appears as a model redeemer.

The story, however, has arrived at this point through the determination and schemes of Ruth and Naomi. Suddenly, the women are missing, mentioned only formally in the legal negotiations. The public world at the village gate belongs only to Boaz. Perhaps he must get ahead of any questions asked about his relationship to Ruth, whom Boaz has sent away before anyone could recognize *that the woman came to the threshing floor* (3:14).

THE TEXT IN BIBLICAL CONTEXT
The Unrecorded World of Women

The public world in ancient Israel and the Near East belonged to men. The realm of the woman tended to be the home and everyday life, a world less visible to us as we look back on those times. Most of the literature preserved from ancient times told about public events, usually the life and actions of important men. By sacral tradition, only men served as priests. Political tradition throughout the ancient Near East reserved most national leadership for men. The military was a male world as well.

Apparently the public realm of village life tended also to be male-dominated. Hence, we note the difference when women make their way into the public roles. They are unusual: Deborah (Judg. 4–5), Jezebel (1 Kings 18–19, 21), and Athaliah (2 Kings 11). No doubt we notice the women in the biblical narrative less than we ought because narrative attention focuses mostly on the men. We do not remember that Miriam was known as a prophetess (Exod. 15:20, Heb.), or that a reform movement credited to King Josiah was begun by Huldah, also a prophetess (2 Kings 22:14-29).

In the legal literature of the Bible, the woman appears as dependent on the man, having a status often on a par with a child. However, the wisdom literature (Prov.; Song of Sol.) portrays a much more active role for women, certainly in the home, but also in the community (Bird: 48-60). Even so, a woman's influence upon the public world of men frequently came more often by quiet planning or advice to a husband than by actual participation.

The story of Ruth fits into that ancient world as far as we know it. Either by direct appeal or secret plot, Ruth and Naomi try to activate the structures of assistance in their behalf. But when matters move into the public realm, it is a man's world (Trible, 1978:192). The women appear mostly as a part of agreements the men make. Most of the revered women are the famous mothers.

Yet the story of Ruth signals that what we usually see in the ancient Hebrew world may not have been all that was there. The world of women went largely unrecorded and unremembered. Faith, care, courage, risk, and tears seem to have carried these women along. This faith, apparently practiced in the home and at the village sanctuary, enabled them to form a society largely invisible in the preserved literature, held together by commitment, and surviving on work, wit, and wisdom.

These women of faith carried on, valued by the public record as the mothers of the next generation. Perhaps these women knew what the men did not. Each new generation brings with it God's promise of a new world. From the house that Ruth "built" would come One, through whom everything old would pass away and all things would become new (2 Cor. 5:17).

THE TEXT IN THE LIFE OF THE CHURCH

The Person of Substance

This episode belongs to Boaz. Tradition has celebrated this man as one who is at the same time successful in public affairs and concerned for those in need. He provides food for the widow and alien. He promises an heir so that *"the name of dead may not be cut off from his kindred and from the gate of his native place"* (4:10). Because of Boaz's skill in handling the agreement at the village gate, Ruth becomes a blessed member of her adopted people.

Close reading of the narrative reveals Boaz as a complex character. We should not reduce him to a literary type instead of a fullfledged character (Berlin, 1983:23-4). Our temptation is to read Boaz as the type of the ideal Israelite man. Such a reading not only compromises the complexity of the narrative; it also limits the value of Boaz for the church. A type may help to provide an idealized model, but it does not enable us to live with the person. A full-fledged character can help us understand our own impulses and the actions of others.

Boaz does assist Ruth and Naomi, providing food, home, and security. His benevolence far exceeds what custom expects and law dictates. Boaz acts because God (sometimes hidden in happenstance) provides the opportunity. Ruth happens to come to his field (2:3). The very relative Boaz needs to see happens to arrive at the city gate so that Boaz can conclude his agreement to redeem the family land and marry Ruth (4:1).

Nevertheless, Boaz also acts because Ruth and Naomi prompt and even trap him. Ruth is determined to obtain grain and to develop a special relationship with someone (2:2). Naomi conspires with Ruth to place Boaz in a compromising position (3:1-4). Boaz acts in his own self interest. He is attracted to this young woman who happens into his field to glean and who lies beside him at night on the threshing floor (2:8-16; 3:10).

Boaz acts, not out of pure virtue, but out of real life. In the midst of this normal mixture of virtue, providence, circumstances, and self-interest, Boaz makes decisions that enhance life, not only for the widow and the alien, but for himself. The widow receives food, the alien a home, and the man a renowned name.

We often look with a cynical eye at the person of substance, the one who functions influentially in the public arena. We view them as operating out of self-interest, with little concern for others. On the other hand, a Christian is expected to be self-sacrificing, living for others. This cynicism has frequently led church people to address public figures in business, industry, and government with automatic suspicion and criticism. Many Christians conclude that the very position compromises persons of substance, requiring them to be accountable to financial balance sheets and political interest rather than Christ. Even if that were the case, the apostle Paul recognized that public figures are not the only ones who "fall short of the glory of God" (Rom. 3:23). From Paul, we can conclude that people of substance may not "fall short" in any greater numbers than people in other sectors of society.

This narrative reminds us that we are all complex characters, not literary types, whether as people of substance or widows and aliens. Rather than condemning public actions that do not square with pure virtue, we more faithfully serve Christ as we search for ways to bring the interests of the publicly powerful together with the needs of the widow, the orphan, and the alien. When that happens, as it did in Bethlehem *in the days when judges ruled* (1:1), the community can join together in pronouncing God's blessing on each one.

Part 3

Conclusion and Coda

Ruth 4:13-22

Ruth 4:13-22

PREVIEW

What began in complaint ends in praise. In the first episode (1:6-22), Naomi returns to Bethlehem from Moab, declaring to those who met her that she is empty. A woman, whose life has been full, through a series of tragedies has lost food, home, and family (1:1-5). Devastated and angry, Naomi brings her case against God to the women of Bethlehem:

> The LORD has dealt harshly with me,
> and the Almighty has brought calamity upon me. (1:21)

This concluding unit (4:13-22) finds Naomi again in the company of the women of Bethlehem. This time, however, everything is different. God's action has brought fertility to Naomi's daughter-in-law (4:13). This son will restore life to Naomi (4:15).

Campbell notes that, even to the end, the disaster in Moab remains unexplained (Campbell, 1975:168). Naomi has a legitimate complaint. God responds to Naomi's lament, by restoring fertility first to the fields (1:6, 22) and then to family (4:13). The women of Bethlehem recognize that with the birth of this boy, Naomi has the prospect of living out her years in peace (4:15).

The narrator carefully crafts this concluding paragraph (4:13-17) to bring the story to a close. The section (4:13-22) is a combination of two distinct units: a concluding narrative of the birth and naming of Obed (4:13-17), and a coda, a note of what happens afterward, in the form of a genealogical table (4:18-22).

We find the resolution of the primary tension: the disasters in Moab have been replaced by food and family. The narrative also picks up words from previous units to signal closure. For example, the first episode features the word *return* (šub, 1:6-22). In this final unit, the women's chorus celebrates the birth of a one who will *return* life to Naomi (4:15, EFR; *renew,* NIV; participle from *šub,* as a *restorer,* NRSV). In episode 4, the men met at the city gate to decide on a *redeemer* (*go'el*) for Naomi (4:3-6). Boaz is selected to redeem Naomi's property on that occasion. Now, however, the women rejoice that with the child, Naomi has a *redeemer* from this day forth (*next-of-kin,* 4:14; *kinsman-redeemer,* NIV).

The mention of David in the genealogical conclusion has prompted energetic debate among interpreters of the story. Some have suggested that the connection between Ruth and David is a matter of later tradition rather than the work of the original narrator. Others have contended that this genealogical connection between Ruth and David constitutes the point of the whole story. A Moabite as the ancestor of David stands as an indictment of groups in Israel who were seeking to exclude the foreigner and discriminate against the poor (LaCocque: 84-116). Be that as it may, the name of *David* (future ruler and king) as the last word serves as an *inclusion* (or *inclusio*), the other bookend, bringing to an end a story that begins in the days *when the judges ruled* (1:1).

OUTLINE

A chiastic outline of the unit illustrates that the central focus rests on Naomi's action (4:16) *[Narrative Structure]*. Notice the careful balance. Not only do the women's speeches balance (4:14-15; 4:17a); the opening and closing statements also tell of the infant's birth and naming (4:13; 4:17b). Normally the report of naming would come immediately after the birth (cf. 1 Sam. 1:20). But here the two are split apart, to celebrate Naomi's restoration to a full life. The unit in chiastic outline:

Statement of Child's Birth, 4:13
   Speech of the Women, 4:14-15
      Action of Naomi, 4:16
   Speech of the Women, 4:17a
Statement of Child's Name, 4:17b

Recognition of the chiastic movement within 4:13-17 helps the reader acknowledge Naomi's new life. Yet the outline form employed throughout the commentary properly places this unit as Conclusion (4:13-17) and Coda (4:18-22) to the whole story ("Outline of the Book," in Overview). This produces the following outline:

Conclusion: Birth and Naming of a Son, 4:13-17
    4:13   Report of the Birth
    4:14-17   Response of the Women and Naomi

Coda: Genealogy of Perez, 4:18-22

EXPLANATORY NOTES

Conclusion: Birth and Naming of a Son 4:13-17

4:13 Report of the Birth

The crisis of childlessness with which the narrative begins (1:5) is resolved with the birth of a son to Ruth and Boaz. In spite of the importance of the birth in the flow of the story, the birth report is quite brief. Although this seems to us like hurrying over the crucial event, such brevity is customary in biblical narrative. Sarah waited past menopause for a child. When that child was finally born, the birth report is as brief as this one (Gen. 21:2). Hannah complained about her barrenness so vehemently that Eli thought her drunk or deranged. When she finally conceived and gave birth, the event is told quickly (1 Sam. 1:14, 20).

To be sure, the rapid sequence of verbs moves the reader swiftly through the marriage of Ruth and Boaz to the birth of the son: *took, became, came together, bore* (NRSV). Nevertheless, we notice that the sequence of action by Boaz and/or Ruth is interrupted at one point. The LORD causes the conception: *made her conceive* (4:13; cf. 4:11). The infant is God's child.

This marks the second moment in the story when the narrator tells of God's direct participation in the drama. The first occasion happens in 1:6. God restores fertility to the land. Hence, with Ruth's pregnancy, God has restored fertility to the barren land and to the barren woman. The blessing of God that brings fertility, prosperity, and community is central to the theology of the book of Ruth ("God, Who Blesses," TLC for 2:1-23). This is not a story in which God is said to act in dramatic and interruptive ways. Instead, aside from bringing fertility, God's action is present through what we frequently call happenstance, and through the loyal and loving actions of the people.

4:14-17 Response of the Women and Naomi

The fourth episode features the men of the village (4:1-12). They pronounce a threefold blessing—on the woman whom Boaz is taking in kinship marriage, on Boaz himself, and on the family the two will create (4:11-12). However, the conclusion of the story belongs to the women of Bethlehem. It is these women who respond to the birth of the child and receive him into the community.

The women give thanks to God on behalf of Naomi and the child (4:14-15). They declare that with this infant, Naomi has her own *redeemer*. It is difficult to know how to interpret this use of the term *redeemer*. This is the only place in the biblical traditions where *redeemer (go'el)* is used to refer to a child's future (Hubbard, 1988a: 271) [Redeemer]. Quite likely, this should be understood in poetic relationship to the rest of the women's blessing:

> Blessed be the LORD,
> Who has not left you without a redeemer—today;
> May his name be renowned in Israel.
> He will restore your life;
> And sustain your old age;
> For your daughter-in-law,
> Who loves you,
> Has given birth to him,
> she, who is better than seven sons. (4:14-15, EFR)

This child, as redeemer, will restore Naomi's life. The Hebrew uses the participle based on the verb *return (šub)*, a key word for Naomi's journey in the first episode (1:6-23). Through this child, Naomi's life-center, her soul *(nepeš)* has returned. This very day Naomi's life has been renewed. But this is not a momentary renewal. The infant will provide the prospect for Naomi to finish her life peacefully, as one would wish for all as they age: *"[The child shall] sustain you in your old age"* (4:15, NIV). The word translated *sustain (kul; nourisher,* NRSV) is frequently used in connection with food and water (Gen. 45:11; Hubbard, 1988a: 272). This word serves as another reminder that the famine beginning the tragedy will not again threaten Naomi.

As the women address Naomi, they remember the woman (Ruth) who made this possible. Like the blessing from the men (4:11-12), they do not use Ruth's name. Ruth is identified in relationship to Naomi as she is when the narrative opens (1:6). Ruth is the *daughter-in-law*. However, the value of Naomi's daughter-in-law exceeds that of a perfect family. Folklore regarded seven sons as the perfect number. Ruth is not even noticed when Naomi returns from Moab (1:19-21). Throughout the story, she is known variously as the Moabite woman (2:6) and Naomi's daughter-in-law. Eventually, because of her compassion and steadfastness, Boaz acknowledges her worth (3:11). Now the women recognize Ruth as the greatest asset Naomi can ever have.

The central moment in the unit comes in 4:16 (chiastic outline, above). Naomi takes guardianship of the child: *Naomi took the child, laid him in her bosom, and became his nurse* (4:16). Interpreters have debated the significance of Naomi's action. Some continue to take this as legal adoption (Gerleman: 37). Others insist that this represents little more than an expression of affection (Gray: 402). Though Naomi's actions may not correspond exactly to the common adoption process in the ancient Near East, the ritual amounts to more than an affectionate gesture. The response of the women after Naomi's actions suggests that in a special way, the child is Naomi's. Ruth has faded into the background. Naomi and the women have assumed the responsibility to mother and to name child.

Although some suggest that this amounts to foster care or daycare (Hubbard, 1988a: 265-6), such analogies depend too much on contemporary family patterns. Rather than explaining Naomi's action in sociological terms, it seems better to recognize this as another moment of closure in the narration. With the tragedy of the death of her two sons, Naomi recognizes that she will never again have a child (1:11-13). But with this action and the women's subsequent word (4:17a), what can never happen has come to be.

We can recognize why the narrative artist has shaped the conclusion with verse 16 at the center. Ruth is the story about the coming to be of what can never happen. Naomi, past childbearing age, takes a child to her breast. This miracle happens, not through the surprise of direct divine intervention, as some narratives portray, but through the blessing of God and the determination, wit, and risk of a Moabite woman.

The women of the neighborhood give voice to this miracle: *"A son has been born to Naomi"* (4:17a). The one who has come back empty *has a son* (NIV). Readers who have lived with Naomi from tragedy to triumph understand this joy. A son has been born to Naomi in a way that defies any simple description of the conception, pregnancy, and the birth of this infant.

The unit concludes with a statement of naming the child (4:17b). As mentioned earlier (Outline), in biblical narratives the report of naming the infant normally comes immediately after the birth (as in Gen. 21:2-3; 29:32; 30:24; Matt. 1:25). However, the narrator has split apart this literary connection between birth and naming, thus allowing us to celebrate an event that can never happen.

Additional surprises come with the naming of the child. In the first place, it is the *women of the neighborhood* who name the child, not the father or even the mother. The only other biblical narrative where community members try to name an infant happens in Luke's story of

Elizabeth. There the neighbors and friends decide to name Elizabeth's son after his father, Zechariah. But Elizabeth stops them. Instead, she names her child John, a decision with which the boy's father agrees (Luke 1:57-63). With Naomi's son, no one interferes with the women's decision to name the child Obed.

The name itself is a surprise. Traditionally, the words spoken just before the infant's naming become in fact the child's name (Gen. 29:32—30:24). Therefore, literary convention suggests that the women are about to name the child *Ben Naomi (son of Naomi)*. That does not happen. Instead, the narrator reports that the women name the child after neither his mother or father. They name him *Obed*, a Hebrew word that means "the one who serves" or "servant."

Some interpreters suggest that the name *Obed* was not present in the original story. They propose that the various stories of David's family came together as these narratives were retold through many generations. As this happened, David's ancestral names merged into a single genealogy. In this standard genealogy, Obed was the son of Boaz. Therefore, as a part of the process of bringing these stories together, Obed was inserted into the narrative of Ruth, displacing another name (Gerleman: 38). We cannot know that for sure. However, we can recognize the significance of the name *Obed* in the narrative as we read it. The child's name reflects the role his birth mother has assumed in the story. The woman from Moab has brought the fertility of the fields to Naomi's table and carried the renewal of Naomi's life in her womb.

The narrator announces that the significance of the *servant* will reach far beyond the people in this narrative. Obed will be the grandfather of David. The narrative of two struggling widows has become part of the fabric of Israel's national epic and faith's Messianic story.

Coda: Genealogy of Perez 4:18-22

The narrative concludes with a genealogy that reflects the style of Israel's priestly tradition (Campbell, 1975:170-2). The genealogy identifies ten generations from Perez (one of Judah's twin sons by Tamar; Gen. 38) to David. Comparison with other genealogical lists suggests that some generations may have been left out to make this reflect the ideal ten-member royal genealogy. Recognizing that Nashon (4:20) was a contemporary of Moses, the genealogy's five members from the time of Moses to David do not account for even the briefest possible time span from the Exodus to the monarchy (Hubbard, 1988a: 284; only five generations in 250 years, 1250-1000 B.C.).

Hence, the genealogical table likely has other purposes than to provide complete data on David's ancestors. Certainly the ten-member table affirms the royal stature of David. In addition, the genealogy ties David directly to the ancestral stories of Israel: Jacob and Judah. David, the royal son, is born of roots deep in the story of Israel's formation.

But there is more to the story of David's ancestors than a list of fathers. Joining the genealogy to the narrative makes this women's story stand out among all the threads that weave the fabric of the Davidic cloth. Indeed, the story of David begins with a determined Moabite woman, her destitute mother-in-law, and the God who has blessed them.

THE TEXT IN BIBLICAL CONTEXT

The Women in the Genealogy

Matthew begins his Gospel with a genealogy (1:1-17). Most readers skip past this genealogy because of their interest in the Christmas story (1:18ff.). With this genealogy, however, Matthew insists that Jesus was born into a great story. We cannot understand the mission and message of Jesus, except as we listen to the stories of his ancestors. Many of the names that appear early in the genealogy, we easily recall from the biblical narratives: Abraham, Isaac, Jacob, Judah. The names in the middle of the list are kings: David, Solomon, Rehoboam, and others. For several of the later members of Matthew's genealogical table, little has been preserved other than their name: Abiud, Achim, Eliud.

Occasionally Matthew breaks his pattern of straight genealogical listing of father and son. One such moment comes in Matthew 1:5b: "and Boaz the father of Obed by Ruth." Matthew recalls Ruth as one of four women (including Tamar, Rahab, and the wife of Uriah, Bathsheba) who have a special place in the account of the "Jesus the Messiah" (1:1). The diverse women of Matthew's genealogy have several common elements. They do not fit what most of us imagine as the ideal woman in ancient Israel.

Tamar tricked her father-in-law into making her pregnant, when Judah did not carry through on the promise to provide her husband a child (Gen. 38). Rahab, a prostitute in Jericho, hid the spies sent by Joshua and lied about the matter to the city authorities (Josh. 2). Ruth, the Moabite widow, followed a man of renown from grainfield to threshing floor, where no woman ought to be (Ruth 3:14). David had Uriah the Hittite killed so that he, David, could marry Uriah's beautiful wife, Bathsheba (2 Sam. 11). Subsequently, Bathsheba conspired to gain the dying David's promise that her son, Solomon, would succeed David as monarch of Judah and Israel (1 Kings 1).

Another common thread connecting these women concerns their character. The determination and courage of each changed the direction of the story of faith. Each woman pushed beyond the boundaries of proper behavior. They entered the treacherous world of deceit and conspiracy, a world that the Bible recognizes as dangerous and potentially destructive. These women avoid biblical condemnation because they put themselves at risk in behalf of others. They are precisely the mothers of the One whom respectable society condemned as a companion of sinners and tax collectors (Matt. 11:19). These women mothered the Man from Bethlehem who not only risked himself, but also gave up his life for others (Mark 10:43-45).

THE TEXT IN THE LIFE OF THE CHURCH

Good and Faithful Servant

Ruth appears by name in this final unit only in the narrator's summary of her marriage and pregnancy (4:13). The women of the village celebrate Ruth's inestimable value, but only in relationship to Naomi, her mother-in-law (4:15). This woman of Moab has remained with her mother-in-law when Naomi was a destitute widow; now she fades into the background as Naomi's present and future becomes secure. It is so natural to celebrate with Naomi that many readers do not notice Ruth's absence. The woman who has made such a surprisingly loud entrance into the story makes a surprisingly quiet exit. What has happened to Ruth?

Some interpreters speculate that Ruth has a good life in the house of Boaz, but of course, we do not know that. As an active character in the drama, Ruth has left. She has actually left after the night on the threshing floor, when Naomi assures her that Boaz will take care of everything (3:18).

More than any person in the story, Ruth has made things happen that turn emptiness into fulfillment. She refuses to use common sense and abandon her destitute mother-in-law. She determines to get food and win someone's favor. She risks her life to prod a relative into kinship marriage, to provide a future for her mother-in-law. She gives birth to a son whom the women of the village receive with the words *"A son is born to Naomi"* (4:17).

But when it comes time to celebrate the tragedy turned to triumph, Ruth is gone. In her stead is an infant son surprisingly named *Obed*, "the one who serves." Yet considering the child's mother, the baby cannot be more aptly named.

Campbell, followed by most later interpreters, observed that this story is a narrative about the Hebrew word *khesed,* voluntary service given to someone in desperate circumstances (Campbell, 1975:28-30; Sakenfeld, 1985). That is why the name of the book is Ruth. The story begins and ends as Naomi's story. She even assumes motherhood in relationship to the newborn baby. But tradition recognizes that this is the story of Ruth. She is the mother of Obed, and the ancestor of Christ the Servant (Matt. 12:18; Phil. 2:7, NIV).

Servanthood remains one of the most celebrated virtues in the believers church tradition. The importance of this virtue is rooted in the thought of the church's ancestors such as Gottfried Arnold and Menno Simons (Stoffer: 29-31, 54-55). Throughout our history, our most valued leaders have been those for whom the church could use the word *servant.* However, the importance of service has often turned the servant's role into a position of glamour. The strong among us are exhorted to help the weak and faithfully finish the work, receiving the accolade "Well done, good and faithful servant" (Matt. 25:23, KJV).

In addition Katharine Sakenfeld reminds us of the danger when servanthood is defined as self-sacrificing fulfillment of cultural expectations (1999:13, 34). She notes that in some Asian churches Ruth is used as a model to insist that young Christian women serve the needs of their mothers-in-law rather than their own family or pursuing a professional vocation. Ruth's acts of loyal living (Sakenfeld's word) did not simply reinforce the social traditions and expectations. In fact Ruth chose to stay with her mother-in-law against the expectations of the culture. Throughout the story she took significant risks, stepping beyond the social boundaries in order that the shalom of the community might be more fully realized.

The story of Ruth may be central in the believers church and other traditions because it features service, a most valued Christian virtue. However, it may be crucial for Christians to reread Ruth, remembering that the key figure is a foreign widow not wanted in the beginning and gone in the end. Naomi and Boaz may fit the role of "servant" in the contemporary church: the one of substance who comes to the aid of the disadvantaged, and the one who carries on the work of the church in spite of personal pain and suffering.

Yet no matter how good and helpful Naomi and Boaz may be in the readers' view, they are not God's most trusted servants in this story. That person is *Ruth,* a woman, a Moabite woman, a woman whom the men and women of Bethlehem neglect to mention by name (4:11-12, 15). She is the mother of Obed, the one who serves.

Outline of Ruth

Introduction: Famine, Displacement, and Death	**1:1-5**
Opening Statement: The Family	1:1
A Report of Death in the Family	1:2-5a
Concluding Statement: The Woman	1:5b
The Story of Two Widows	**1:6—4:12**
Episode 1: Return to Bethlehem	1:6-22
The Journey to Judah	1:6-18
Preparations and Departure	1:6-7
Farewell Dialogue	1:8-18
The Arrival in Bethlehem	1:19-21
Reception in Bethlehem	1:19
Response by Naomi	1:20-21
Concluding Summary	1:22
Episode 2: Going for Grain	2:1-23
Introductory Statement	2:1
Dialogue Between Ruth and Naomi	2:2
Scene in the Field	2:3-17
Introductory Statement	2:3
Dialogues	2:4-16
Boaz and the Workers	2:4-7
Boaz and Ruth	2:8-14
Boaz and the Workers	2:15-16
Concluding Statement	2:17
Dialogue Between Naomi and Ruth	2:18-22

Outline of Ruth

Concluding Statement	2:23
Episode 3: Seeking Security	3:1-18
Dialogue: Naomi and Ruth	3:1-5
Scene at the Threshing Floor	3:6-15
Introductory Narration	3:6-8
Dialogue: Boaz and Ruth	3:9-13
Concluding Narration	3:14-15
Dialogue: Naomi and Ruth	3:16-18
Episode 4: Agreement at the Gate	4:1-12
Calling of the Legal Session	4:1-2
The Legal Proceeding	4:3-12
Agreement Between the Parties	4:3-8
Formal Announcement and Witnessing	4:9-12

Conclusion and Coda   **4:13-22**

Conclusion: Birth and Naming of a Son	4:13-17
Report of the Birth	4:13
Response of the Women and Naomi	4:14-17
Coda: Genealogy of Perez	4:18-22

Jonah

Jonah: A Story for All Times

OVERVIEW

Jonah as Understood in the Past

Ishmael, in Herman Melville's 1851 classic novel *Moby Dick*, tells of his visit to Whaleman's Chapel in New Bedford (Mass.) in the company of other fisherman about to set off to sea. Ishmael watched as a robust chaplain, Father Mapple, mounted the lofty pulpit and began preaching. The prophet Jonah served as the biblical text for the sermon. Father Mapple proceeded to tell the story of Jonah's departure for sea and subsequent misfortune in far more detail than one finds in the biblical narrative itself. Finally the preacher reached the main point of the sermon, which for him was the lesson from Jonah:

> Shipmates, I do not place Jonah before you to be copied for his sin, but I do place him before you as a model for repentance. Sin not, but if you do, take heed to repent of it like Jonah. (Melville: 46)

The story of Jonah fits well Melville's novel of a whaling ship with a captain obsessed by the desire to kill the huge sperm whale, Moby Dick. In fact, the story of Jonah has captured the imagination of the earliest church, even of believers who have never stepped aboard a ship. In spite of its popularity, Christians through the centuries have never agreed on a single interpretation of this four-chapter narrative placed in the middle of the Bible's twelve minor prophets. As a char-

Jonah Overview

acter, Jonah seems to model disobedience and stubbornness rather than the traditional prophetic virtues of obedience and responsiveness. Indeed, Jonah seems to be the only biblical book named for a rogue. Hence, like Father Mapple in Whaleman's Chapel, preachers to this day have struggled to agree on the teachings the church should take from the story of Jonah.

The Christian church did not originally look on Jonah as a negative figure. Stimulated by Matthew 12:40-41, many of the early church writers saw Jonah as a "type" of Christ (Bowers: 21). These early Christian interpreters found in many OT events and persons models that they construed as foreshadowing particular events or attributes of Christ. The story of Jonah, as swallowed by a great fish and then "resurrected" after three days and nights, functioned frequently as a type of Jesus' death and resurrection.

Current Christian interpreters connect Jonah with the NT in a variety of ways, but few follow the christological path of the early church scholars. Jacque Ellul is one whose approach does have clear continuity with this past. He sees the whole drama as a parallel of Christ and the world, with Jonah playing a type of Christ (26-37, 100-103).

Early writers were not alone in turning to Jonah as a positive model. Prior to Emperor Constantine's acceptance of Christianity as one of the permitted religions in the Roman Empire, Jonah appeared frequently in Christian art (Snyder: 45-9). However, the emphasis of this art falls not on prefiguring the resurrection, but on God's action to deliver Jonah from danger and provide him peaceful rest under a vine. Many ancient Christian pictures show a sequence of three scenes: Jonah "handed" into the jaws of a sea monster, Jonah vomited out on shore, and Jonah reclining peacefully under a tree or vine.

Of course, Jonah's unsavory reputation did not entirely escape early interpreters in the church. Origen (ca. 182-251) noted that Jonah was swallowed for his disobedience, whereas Jesus was "swallowed" for obedience. Jerome (340-420), the ablest biblical scholar in the ancient church, scolded Jonah for some of his behavior; yet he sought to preserve a positive image for the prophet by insisting that Jonah's actions reflected his love of his people, whom Assyria threatened to destroy (Bowers: 24-7).

Apparently Jonah's reputation steadily deteriorated as later generations reread the story. Luther reflected the opinion of Jonah as it had developed through the Middle Ages to his day, an interpretation influential even in our day. For Luther, this is the story of the patience of God and the disobedience and obstinacy of Jonah. This story reminds us, Luther insisted, that "God permits His children to blunder and err greatly and grossly" (92). About the only thing Luther could say in the prophet's behalf is that Jonah is "God's dear child," and he "chats so uninhibitedly with God."

Visual artists, however, did not follow the lead of their literary counterparts. The focus of the artists throughout the centuries continued to pick up the perspective of the early Christian writers and the pre-Constantinian artists. Some of these early artists preserved the tradition of Jonah as a type of Christ, one who was resurrected after three days. This artistic interpretation has continued even to the contemporary portrayal of Jonah in the Cologne Cathedral (Limburg, 1990:22-3). Other artists revisited Jonah as one delivered from the dangerous seas of life.

Some later artists turned away from Jonah as the center of attention. In a seventeenth-century window at Christ Church Cathedral in Oxford, England, the Van Linge brothers focused instead on Nineveh as the city that repented (Limburg, 1990:25). They reflected the concern of preachers and writers who compared Nineveh's repentance with the persistence of evil in the cities of their day. In general, the paintings, etchings, and stained glass preserved from the past several centuries seem to indicate that visual artists have consistently evaluated Jonah more favorably than did their contemporary literary interpreters.

Current interpreters continue to use Jonah as an example of what we ought not do. Educational material for children insists that Jonah did what a Christian ought never to do: he ran away from God. Along with that emphasis, educational material for adults focuses on the "unchristian" attitude to the foreigner, Jonah's desire that Nineveh be destroyed. Scholars, frequently following the same interpretive line, identify Jonah as an antiprophet, an example of everything a prophet is not supposed to do and be (Payne: 131-4). Calvin (144) articulated a position similar to many current interpreters: while we may understand Jonah, perhaps even appreciate the prophet's zeal, we dare not emulate him.

We may arrive at a similar negative view of Jonah as we reread the narrative. Nevertheless, we need to recall that the Christian church has not always held the prophet in low regard. It may serve us well as we restudy this familiar story to remember the early church's positive regard for Jonah, as well as the contemporary portrayal of him as an anti-hero. Such memory may enable us to experience more depth in the story's main human character. Indeed, this commentary will expect us to look at Jonah as one whom God takes seriously, not as a clown and an object of ridicule.

What Manner of Narrative?

It may seem obvious and unnecessary to identify Jonah as a short story. Yet the definition of its genre has been much discussed, for good reason. Proposals of genre ranging all the way from *historical account* to *allegory* have created so much debate that the narrative itself has sometimes been lost in the process. To call this a "historical account" turns attention away from the narrative itself, in an effort to locate the names and places in history (Simon, 1999:xv).

Chapter 2 in particular has become a battleground for argument about the *large fish* (1:17). Can a fish swallow and then vomit a person without physical harm to the individual? The debate usually stalls, with one side insisting that the digestive processes of the sea animal make such an adventure impossible, and the other side countering that with God nothing is impossible (cf. Mark 10:27).

The genre designation of *allegory* marks the other extreme. In an allegory, the characters and events of the narrative do not have importance in themselves but only for what they symbolize in hidden or figurative meanings. In such an approach, the great fish may represent Satan swallowing the sinner, Jonah. The Ninevites stand for a group of sinful pagans, usually a group who "should" repent in the interpreter's own world.

The literary characteristics point to *short story* as the genre of this narrative [Short Story]. Even that designation does not settle the matter. Scholars continue to discuss the kind of short story we find in Jonah: perhaps a parable, a fable, or maybe satire.

The term *parable* suggests to most readers that we should look for a single teaching in Jonah. The history of the church's interpretation warns us against trying to reduce the story to a single moral. The term *fable* points to certain elements in the story, such as the great fish and the vine. Yet the story itself centers on the interaction between God and Jonah; the fish and the vine are simply agents of divine action. Throughout the narrative, we find *irony*, perhaps even satire. But to call the story irony or satire predisposes the reader to view the main character in a one-sidedly negative way.

The genre *short story* asks that each reader be open to enjoy, experience, and learn from the narrative. That learning is not prescribed ahead of time. Its discernment and application is entrusted to the community of faith. Indeed, candid and careful listening to Jonah's story may open our ears, perhaps enabling us to hear voices in our midst that have been quiet or overlooked.

Message and Meaning

Readers have discovered a wide variety of messages from their study of Jonah. In part, these different messages arise from different interpretative approaches. Scholars who decide on a specific date for the origin of the narrative, usually relate the message of Jonah to events in that particular era. Other scholars read the book from a particular doctrinal or theological perspective. They frequently experience the story as illustrating or reinforcing a doctrine of the church, such as repentance/forgiveness. The more recent literary approach to the narrative has yielded still other interpretations.

An interpretation of Jonah as protest literature has a long history, especially with scholars who have connected the narrative to the religious reforms of Ezra and Nehemiah (fifth-fourth centuries B.C.). With that backdrop, they interpret the narrative as a protest against religious and ethnic exclusivity frequently ascribed to that reform. That interpretation, however, has become problematic in several respects. Not only is the dating difficult [*Jonah and Historical Analysis*], but the narrative itself does not portray Jonah as a ethnic zealot or a religious bigot. The story certainly does portray God as anxious to extend mercy beyond boundaries frequently enforced by religious communities. Yet the focus of Jonah is not on combating religious bigotry (Simon 1999:viii-x).

Other interpreters place the story in an earlier era, connecting Jonah with the prophetic theme of repentance and forgiveness (Dyck, 1986:249). The narrative pictures God as merciful, anxiously awaiting repentance so as to forgive and turn away judgment. Without doubt, Jonah 3 features the theme of repentance. In response to Jonah's announcement of judgment, the citizens of Nineveh repent, and God turns away from the declared destruction.

The language of repentance, however, only appears in chapter 3 and in 4:2 (Trible, 1996:490). God's final speech (4:10-11) insists that Nineveh's continued existence is grounded squarely in divine compassion. As Uriel Simon notes, there is no mention in 4:11 of the repentance of the citizens of Nineveh as the reason for the divine action, simply that they do not *know their right hand from the left* (Simon, 1999: vii-viii). Repentance constitutes a thread in the narrative, but it does not define the message of Jonah.

Other readers interpret Jonah as concerned about his own vocation as a prophet. Deuteronomy 18:22 defines a false prophet: "If a prophet speaks in the name of the LORD but the thing does not take place or prove true, it is a word that the LORD has not spoken." Perhaps Nineveh's continued existence taints Jonah's prophetic credentials (Bickerman: 38-45). But Jonah does not complain to God about his image as a prophet. Jonah connects his anger to God's character: *"You are a gracious God and merciful, slow to anger, and abounding in steadfast love, and ready to relent from punishing"* (4:2).

Increasingly, scholars advise against quickly assigning Jonah a single message or meaning. Our inability to define the exact era in which the narrative was first told, makes us reluctant to interpret the book in light of particular historical events or a single cultural milieu. The character of biblical narrative alerts us to expect a variety of interpretive possibilities *[Short Story]*. We have been entrusted with the responsibility of listening carefully to the story, anticipating that various threads and themes will speak to different readers and to us at different times.

Among those threads of meaning and message in Jonah, many readers discover the compassion of God reconciling and restoring life—reaching out not only to the sailors, the citizens of Nineveh, and Jonah, but also in behalf of all for whom Christ died. Sometimes this divine compassion blesses us, releasing us from the tyranny of evil that controls our direction and destiny. Other times God's compassion irritates us, extending mercy to those whose sin has damaged or destroyed us or those we love. Jonah expresses his rage at God's apparently indiscriminate compassion. The concluding question suggests that only through compassion can we understand God's undying devotion to the world and all who dwell therein.

A Glance at the Whole

Even a quick glance at the narrative reveals several strands that connect the various parts to the whole. Let us look at some of those strands. Perhaps most noticeable is the nearly identical wording found in Jonah 1:1-3 and 3:1-3a. In both of those units, *the word of the* LORD comes to Jonah, instructing him to go to Nineveh (1:2; 3:2). These two speeches of God divide the narrative into two parts. For both part 1 (1:1—2:10) and part 2 (3:1—4:11), Jonah's response to the divine instruction determines the following action. After the first divine speech, Jonah heads to Tarshish rather than Nineveh. After the second, he goes to Nineveh.

We can discern other threads weaving the narrative fabric together. The location of action in various parts of the story reveals additional symmetry. Jonah's decision to go to Tarshish by ship places the following action on the sea (1:4ff.). The scene changes to "under the sea" when Jonah "leaves" the ship (2:17ff.). Correspondingly, Jonah goes to Nineveh the second time around (3:3a). Hence, the action in this section takes place in the city (3:3bff.). Then the scene switches to "outside" the city (4:1ff.).

Plot involves the establishment of a tension in the narrative and its later resolution *[Short Story]*. Jonah 1:1-3, with its parallel in 3:1-3a, establishes the tension in the story. God directs Jonah to go to Nineveh with a message. That tension is resolved at the end of chapter 3. Jonah has gone to Nineveh and delivered a message. The Ninevites have repented, and God has decided not to carry out the planned destruction. In terms of plot, the story is over.

Nevertheless, the book has yet another scene, outside the city and beyond the main plot. While the story is over for God and the Ninevites, it is not over for Jonah. The affect of this narrative movement startles the reader, who has already relaxed with a happy ending. The flow of the narrative isolates chapter 4, emphasizing the isolation expressed by Jonah's wish for death (4:3, 9). Readers who have been similarly victimized by such isolation, will doubtless feel with Jonah. With the drama over, the concerns of one person remain unanswered. Jonah sits alone.

An Outline of the Major Units

Any outline of Jonah forfeits some of the complexity and depth in the story. No matter how carefully chosen to fit the narrative, an outline selectively emphasizes some elements and relegates others to the background. Be that as it may, such organization assists us as we move through the story, enabling us to interpret the individual parts in relation to the whole:

The Unfulfilled Prophetic Mission, 1:1—2:11
    1:1-3   The Commissioning of Jonah
    1:4—2:10 The Drama at Sea
        On the Sea, 1:4-16
        Under the Sea, 1:17—2:10

The Unfulfilled Prophet, 3:1—4:11
    3:1-3a   The Recommissioning of Jonah
    3:3b—4:11 The Drama on Land
        In the City, 3:3b-10
        Outside the City, 4:1-11

The short story of Jonah asks to be read in one sitting. Before we look in detail at each piece in turn, take time to read the whole narrative, preferably more than once. With each reading, experience the adventure from the perspective of different characters in the drama: God, Jonah, the sailors, the Ninevites, and even the king of Nineveh. Try to sense what is going on in each character. You will find it easy to identify with some. Many listeners struggle to sympathetically experience the drama from Jonah's perspective, except as he acts out our dark side. While the character of Jonah may provide the most challenge, such sympathetic identification may be the most important and finally the most rewarding.

Part 1

The Unfulfilled Prophetic Mission

Jonah 1-2

Jonah 1:1-3

The Commissioning of Jonah

PREVIEW

The reader has scarcely drawn a breath before being caught in the middle of a dispute between God and Jonah. The compact narration introduces the main characters, establishes the tension of the story, and sends the plot on its way. This fulfills the responsibility of the exposition in a short story *[Short Story]*. However, it all happens so quickly that the verses almost require rereading for the listener to get on board.

Even after rereading, the paragraph may raise more questions than provide information. Who is Jonah? How does the prophet receive this word from the LORD? Where is he at the time? How will God respond to Jonah's flight? Some of our questions will eventually be answered; others will not. Such a lack of descriptive detail is characteristic of much Hebrew narrative *[Characteristics]*. We will fill in many missing details ourselves. In so doing, the reader becomes a fellow traveler with the story's narrator. Other informational gaps are left open as the story bids us to hurry on.

This exposition introduces the two main characters, God and Jonah. But that happens almost as a matter secondary to God's speech and Jonah's action. The speech-action sequence divides the unit in two parts, 1:1-2 and 1:3. Given the content of God's instruction and the nature of Jonah's response, that split seems to mark more than a division in the unit.

Jonah 1:1-3

OUTLINE

The Word from the LORD, 1:1-2
    1:1   Introduction of the Characters
    1:2   Divine Word

The Response of Jonah, 1:3
    1:3a   Statement of Flight
    1:3b   Detail of His Action

EXPLANATORY NOTES

The Word from the LORD 1:1-2

The narrative opens with phrases typical of introductions found in the book of the Twelve *[Twelve Prophets]*. In terms of length and information, the closest parallel to Jonah 1:1 appears in Joel 1:1, "The word of the LORD that came to Joel, son of Pethuel." Most of the other prophetic books have much more extensive introductory words. Yet, reading the introduction to Jonah and Joel shows an important difference:

    The word of the LORD came to Jonah.
    The word of the LORD *that* came to Joel.

The word *that* signals the introduction of a list of oracles or prophetic sayings. That is just what the reader finds in Joel. On the other hand, the opening of Jonah introduces a narrative. Of all the prophetic books, only Jonah is essentially a narrative. While some of the other prophetic books have narrative sections, such as Isaiah and Jeremiah, they are mostly oracles. The story character of Jonah has led to a discussion about whether Jonah should even be included with the other prophets (Dyck, 1986:210).

This narrative opening, though unique in the prophetic books, is found in other narratives about prophets. A glance at Elijah provides not only a parallel with the opening words in Jonah, but a striking contrast in the prophetic response:

    The word of the LORD came to him [Elijah], saying, "Go now to Zarephath, which belong to Sidon, and live there. . . ." So he set out and went to Zarephath. (1 Kings 17:8-10)

Hence, the opening words of Jonah have a familiar ring to those acquainted with both the prophetic books and with other stories about prophets. Here we have a narrative about a prophet, even though Jonah—like Joel, Obadiah, and Nahum—is not explicitly called a prophet in the account (cf. Matt. 12:39).

The name *Jonah son of Amittai* directs us to 2 Kings 14:25. We know little about this prophet active in Israel during the time of Jeroboam II (787-747 B.C.). Jonah, as pictured in 2 Kings, announced to Jeroboam that God would expand Israel's borders, because "the LORD saw that the distress of Israel was very bitter" (2 Kings 14:26). It is difficult to say how much we are to take from this brief note in 2 Kings for use in interpreting the narrative of Jonah. Daniel and Job provide other examples of narrative figures briefly mentioned elsewhere in the OT (Ezek. 14:14, 20; 28:3). The proverbial wisdom and righteousness of Daniel and Job figure in the narratives about them. The association of Jonah with anger over oppression by Assyria (733ff. B.C.) may lead us to understand that the prophet deeply identifies with the bitter distress of his people.

In translation, the name *Jonah son of Amittai* means "Dove, the son of truth (or trust)." Those who interpret the narrative as a parody, interpret Jonah's name as satire (Holbert: 64). As a "dove," Jonah neither carries out his responsibility, as did the dove of the flood (Gen. 8:6-12), nor does Jonah come bearing peace, as when the dove brought back the olive leaf. Furthermore, Jonah can scarcely be labeled a man of either truth or trust. He hides the truth from the sailors and ignores his trust from God.

However, we must not too quickly label Jonah a villain who betrays his own good name. The narrator gives us no cause to use such an interpretation of Jonah's name as a key to understanding the story. If the dove signifies anything, it may be Jonah's decision for flight and his subsequent passivity (Hauser: 22-3). As for Jonah, the son of truth or trust, not even God impugns Jonah's integrity—his inadequate understanding of *compassion,* perhaps (4:10-11), but not Jonah's integrity. In fact, ancient rabbinical commentary celebrated Jonah as a person of integrity and righteousness (Zucker: 366). The rabbis pointed out that no other biblical character sank into the depths of the sea and lived.

God's instructions to Jonah (1:2) feature the same language we find in the commissioning of Elijah: *"Go now/at once to Zarephath/Nineveh"* (1 Kings 17:9; Jon. 1:2). The narrator wants us to know that, at least formally, Jonah's commission is quite traditional. Furthermore, Jonah like Elijah is instructed to go to a foreign land. But the two prophets are not sent to the same land and not for the same purpose. Elijah goes to a Phoenician town to be cared for, perhaps even to be protected from Ahab (Gray: 380). Jonah is directed to go to Nineveh *to cry out against it.*

The text tells us only two things about Nineveh *[Nineveh]*. Nineveh is a great city, and the people are known by God for their wickedness. These two phrases tell us all we need to know about Nineveh for the purposes of this narrative. But the phrases carry even more significance than that. The terms *evil/wicked (ra'ah)* and *great (gadol)* reappear frequently in various forms throughout the narrative *[Characteristics of Hebrew Narrative]*. Along with Nineveh, storm, fish, and anger are described as *great*. Hence, the story points to some element in every episode of the story as unusually large or intense. The repetition of the word *great* contributes to the humor, danger, and pathos of the narrative. Elements in this story grow to be as large and intense as the readers imagination will allow.

The word *evil* is a second key term in Jonah. It appears in every scene but chapter 2. The story of Jonah uses the word *evil* in a variety of ways. Sometimes *evil* is employed in a way we find quite unexpected. Therefore, when God intends *evil* (3:10), translations usually select a word quite different from *evil* (*calamity*, NRSV; *destruction*, NIV; cf. 1:7; 4:2). Jonah as well as God is associated with the word *evil* (4:1-2, 6). *Evil* is used to describe the circumstances that have enraged Jonah (4:1). He does not do evil, but *great evil* inundates Jonah (*this was very displeasing*, NRSV; *greatly displeased*, NIV). In summary, even as Nineveh, God, and Jonah are connected by the word *great*, so they are also bound together in a web of *evil*.

This story is not about evil versus good or great versus small. *Evil* touches the actions of all the characters in the drama: Nineveh, God, and Jonah. This is a "great" story, featuring a *great* city, a great storm, a great fish, and great evil. We do the narrative a disservice if we assign all the positive adjectives to one character and the negative ones to the another. God does not do that, and neither does the literary device of word repetition.

God instructs Jonah to cry out against Nineveh (1:2). Jonah receives no instructions as to the exact words he must announce. The text leaves little doubt, however, that God calls for the announcement of disaster or judgment. We will see that in the second commissioning speech to Jonah, God's instructions are somewhat more specific (3:2, 4). In this case, however, God commissions Jonah to go the great city of Israel's hated enemy and to denounce the evil of its people *[Nineveh]*.

The Response of Jonah 1:3

To sense the shock inherent in Jonah's response, we need only to remember the parallel commissioning of Elijah.

> The word of the LORD came to him [Elijah], saying, "Go now to Zarephath, which belongs to Sidon, and live there." . . . So he set out and went to Zarephath. (1 Kings 17:9-10)

In the Bible, reluctance on the part of an individual receiving a divine commission is not uncommon. Moses, Gideon, and Jeremiah all responded to God's commissioning by raising some objection, usually based on their personal inadequacy (Exod. 3:11; Judg. 6:15; Jer. 1:6). They were all eventually persuaded to accept their responsibility. Jonah does not say a word in response to the divine commissioning. Neither did Elijah. Elijah's silence issued in compliance; he did as instructed. Jonah's silence issued in a different action; Jonah fled. He did exactly the opposite of his instructions. God told him to rise up and *"go at once."* Jonah *rose up and fled* (EFR; *set out to flee*, NRSV).

The direction of Jonah's flight is *down*. Indeed, this will be the direction of Jonah's movement until he ends up in the belly of a fish. The word *down* is reinforced by other directional words. Jonah not only goes down, but *from: from the presence of the* LORD (1:3). Further, he goes toward Tarshish. All the words in this tightly packed narration work together to put distance between Jonah and God.

We do not know the exact location of *Tarshish*. Much interpretive tradition locates Tarshish on the west coast of Spain. However, the various places for which the Bible uses the name point in different directions (Gordon: 517-8). All the references to Tarshish have two elements in common. Getting to Tarshish always requires a sea voyage. All references agree that Tarshish is a long way from Israel. In terms of this narrative, Tarshish is the geographical opposite of Nineveh, regardless of the precise location or direction (Ackerman, 1987:235). Hence, all the directional words and locational words reinforce the initial verbs: *Jonah rose and fled*.

The narration of Jonah's response concludes by repeating the purpose of his flight. Jonah intends to get *away from the presence of the* LORD (1:3). Frequently in the biblical stories, one flees to escape an intolerable relationship (Limburg, 1988:140). Hagar fled Sarah (Gen. 16:6), Jacob fled Laban (Gen. 31:20), and Moses fled Pharaoh (Exod. 2:15)—all hoping to reach a place outside the threatening power of the other party.

Israel constantly wrestled with the question of whether one could go to a place beyond God's reach and power. Those relocated from Jerusalem to Babylon by Nebuchadnezzar's army were not sure they could sing and worship God in a foreign land (Ps. 137:4; 2 Kings

24–25). God's power and presence might not reach that far. Several times the psalmist suggests that death lies beyond the realm of God's relationship if not reach (Ps. 6:5; 30:9; 88:10).

We do not know what Jonah is thinking. The narrator leaves Jonah's inner thoughts to readers' imagination. Conceivably, Jonah believes he can escape God's domain. But that seems unlikely. Amos declared that even Sheol does not exceed God's reach (9:2; cf. Ps. 139:8). Jonah's own confession of faith denies the possibility that Jonah could escape God's presence: *"I worship the LORD, the God of heaven, who made the sea and the land"* (1:9). The reader knows this, and one can suspect that Jonah does also. However, Jonah does not explain his action—not yet. We have only the narrator's description of what Jonah does, nothing about why he does it.

THE TEXT IN BIBLICAL CONTEXT

Commissioning of the Prophet

We have many biblical narratives that describe the commissioning of a prophet. These commissioning moments each have their own distinctive elements, but they also have much in common. In one set of narratives, the prophet responds to God's address with an objection. God responds to the prophet's objection with a promise of presence and assistance and usually confirms this promise with a sign. For example, Jeremiah objects because of his youth (1:6). God promises to be with him (1:8) and reaches out to the prophet's mouth with a divine touch (1:9).

A visit to the divine council constitutes the prime feature in other reports of the commissioning of a prophet. For example, in a terrifying experience in the temple, Isaiah tells of being carried to a divine council meeting (6:1). After his confession and pardon, this prophet volunteers to be the council's messenger (6:5-8). Surprisingly, Isaiah is commissioned to assist God in bringing disaster on the prophet's own people (6:9-10).

There is at least one other type of commissioning of a prophet, as represented by Elijah (1 Kings 17–19). After receiving a divine commission, Elijah offers no verbal response at all; he simply acts to carry out God's instructions. This pattern we also find in the NT narratives reporting the call of the disciples. Jesus tells the disciples, "Follow me." Without saying a word, the disciples drop what they are doing and follow (Matt. 4:18-22; Mark. 1:16-20).

The commissioning of Jonah follows this latter pattern. The surprise to the earliest listeners was not that the prophet might receive instructions from God, even though that might be unusual in our experience. For the biblical narrative, the surprise is Jonah's response. He goes the other way. Reluctance would be considered normal. Jonah's flight makes him one of a kind. The reader has no biblical precedent for anticipating what will follow.

THE TEXT IN LIFE OF THE CHURCH
Reluctant Response

When confronted with a commission from God, an individual's life changes. From the moment of his call, everything depends on how Jonah will respond (LaCocque, 1981:33). Jonah decides to flee.

Interpreters often speculate about the reason for Jonah's refusal. In general, Christian interpreters have been critical of Jonah's decision, represented in Luther's declaration that Jonah "has sinned as gravely as Adam" (46). Calvin's (28) summary of the reasons for Jonah's flight echo the conclusion of many preachers and teachers. Calvin insisted that the problem was Jonah's weak character. In part, Jonah feared the outcome; but more than that, Jonah could not handle the novelty of the message, *Cry out against [Nineveh]* (1:2).

Jonah has frequently been accused of being narrow-minded, perhaps even bigoted against Gentiles. The text gives us no reason to ascribe bigotry to Jonah's motive for refusing to comply with God's instructions. Nor dare we conclude, as some have, that Jonah, the Jew, objected to the conversion of Gentiles (Luther: 50). Jonah shows no antagonism to the non-Israelite sailors (1:4-16). He volunteers to be thrown into the sea to save them. Later, Jonah tells God that the outcome is the primary issue. He objects to God's decision to spare Nineveh, whose evil offends Jonah and God. It is more likely that the evil and violent history of Nineveh and the Assyrians upsets Jonah rather than the fact that the city is Gentile.

Be that as it may, the narrator stirs the reader's imagination by not stating the reason for Jonah's flight. The movement of 1:1 (God's commission) and verse 2 (Jonah's response) can never be avoided. Whether one makes an oral response or lets one's actions speak, the one called must respond. A commission from God changes one's life regardless of the individual's response. Divine call and human response continues to trouble us, although our concerns are usually somewhat different from those that apparently upset Jonah.

In North America, Anabaptists expect to experience the call of God in interaction between an inner word (voice/conviction) and a community decision. Frequently, individuals find themselves skeptical of a community decision, unclear whether the announced call really originates from God. Others sense God's call but receive no confirmation from the community. This confuses and disturbs especially women and non-Anglo Christians. Nevertheless, occasions do arise when the divine commission seems clear, but the call is met with objection or even refusal. That objection may not be the result of a character flaw or weak faith. The one commissioned by God may correctly discern the enormous cost of compliance.

In spite of the tradition that treats Jonah's decision as foolish or sin, we are well advised to withhold judgment, even to show a bit more compassion. God does not condemn Jonah. Some rabbis suggest that the waiting ship at Joppa constitutes a sign of divine approval for Jonah's decision to flee. In any case, Jonah has many companions both ancient and modern, foreign and domestic. His may be a far more normal response to such a commission than we care to admit.

Jonah 1:4—2:10

The Drama at Sea

PREVIEW

Quickly the narrative action changes from land to sea. We have only been told that Jonah has gone on board *to go with them to Tarshish* (1:3). The sea will continue to be the location of the story until 2:10, when Jonah is delivered back onto land. Jonah 1:4 signals to us that God will control the action of this episode: *The LORD hurled a great wind upon the sea.*

Even a quick reading spots the literary division within this unit. The initial action takes place on top of the water (1:4-16). Later the adventure moves underwater (1:17—2:10). Still other literary elements signal this split in the unit. While on the water, the cast of characters includes Jonah and the sailors. Underwater, we find Jonah alone in the belly of a fish.

Two distinctive words are repeated throughout this first scene (1:4-16). These words hold the scene together and also carry the action forward. Several items are *hurled (tul)*: God *hurls* a wind (1:4). The sailors *hurl* their cargo into the sea (1:5, EFR). Then the scene closes with the sailors *hurling* Jonah into the sea (1:15, EFR), following his instruction that they do so (1:12). The word *fear (yara')* also plays a key role in this episode. When we first meet the sailors, they *fear* the storm (1:5, EFR). At the end of the scene, we find the same Hebrew word used, this time in a quite different sense. The sailors *feared/revered (yara')* the LORD (1:16). Much has happened to the sailors between those two meanings of the word *fear.*

Like 1:4-16, the second scene in this unit opens with God's

112

action. This time God *appointed* (NASB; *provided,* NRSV, NIV) a great fish as a divine instrument (1:17). The centerpiece of this episode is a prayer/psalm by Jonah (2:2-9). As we will see, this poem follows the typical pattern found in a biblical psalm of thanksgiving. The episode ends with God once again instructing the fish (2:10). With God's second directive to the fish, the action shifts back to the land. The drama on and under the sea is over.

OUTLINE
In these two units, the outline can be presented in chiastic format:

On the Sea, 1:4-16
    Introduction, 1:4
        Battling the Storm, 1:5-6
            Divining the Cause, 1:7-10
        Quieting the Storm, 1:11-15
    Conclusion, 1:16

Under the Sea, 1:17—2:10
    Action of God, 1:17
        Prayer of Jonah, 2:1-10
    Action of God, 2:10

On the Sea
Jonah 1:4-16

PREVIEW
This episode is powered by a *mighty* wind, a *violent* storm that God hurls on the sea (1:4). Then action happens on the ship, and the reader almost forgets the storm. But just as the sailors act, the narrator again reminds us of the storm, which has not abated. Instead, the danger is increasing (1:11, 13). Clearly, control of this episode belongs to the intense power of God. The human characters are required to react to this display of divine power.

The scene features two (or three) other characters. First and last on the stage are *the sailors* (NIV; *mariners,* NRSV). We are told little about them, except for their fear of the dangerous storm. Indeed, the sailors' *fear* intensifies as they sense that their plight grows ever more desperate (1:5, 10). The sailors' fear is transformed to reverence or awe as the storm is quieted (1:15). Meanwhile, the captain of the sailors acts to engage the one passenger not helping to save the ship from the storm—Jonah.

The passive Jonah seems out of touch with everything that is going on. He has slept through the storm until aroused. He answers the sailors' barrage of questions with a confession of faith inconsistent with his own actions (1:9). Then he volunteers to help still the storm by having the sailors throw him overboard. The sailors fear such "help" will put them in still deeper water. They might be responsible for the death of an innocent person (1:14).

Jonah 1:4-16 begins and ends the sailors' story. Theirs is a simple tale, a common one about a storm at sea. As normal for ancient mariners, they assume that the storm is of divine origin. What they suspect is in fact the case. God, who both initiates and then withdraws the wind, receives their grateful thanks (1:15-16). However, this simple tale of sailors on a dangerous sea functions as an episode in a far different drama, one involving God and Jonah. Yet these protagonists do not encounter one another directly in this episode.

The episode has several interwoven threads, each of which could provide the structure for an outline. Certainly we must take account of the fact that the storm powers the scene (1:4, 11, 13, 15). It provides the primary tension that must be resolved if the tale is to end safely. An outline might choose to focus on Jonah in the depths of the ship, making his words and actions carry the narrative. But in spite of Jonah's place in the story as a whole, 1:4-16 is really the sailors' tale. The outline below reflects the realization that for this brief moment, the sailors, not Jonah, are the main characters.

OUTLINE
Introduction, 1:4

Battling the Storm, 1:5-6

Divining the Cause, 1:7-10

Quieting the Storm, 1:11-15

Conclusion, 1:16

Jonah 1:4-16

EXPLANATORY NOTES

Introduction; Battling the Storm 1:4, 5-6

Jonah has made no oral response to God's commission. He has fled (1:3). Similarly, God reacts to Jonah's flight not with words but through action, hurling a great wind (1:4). This *great wind* causes a *great* storm (NASB; *mighty*, NRSV; *violent*, NIV). In Jonah 1:2, Nineveh is described as a *great* city. Here the action of God is described with the same adjective.

As elsewhere (1:2, notes), the word *great* pushes the imagination of the reader beyond the ordinary or normal. We are invited to picture a wind, a city (1:3), a fish (1:17), or even evil/anger (4:1) and then stretch our imagination still greater. Part of the humor in the story lies in the pictures generated by the word *great (gadol)*. The danger and the humor collide also in the response of the ship. The ship *thought itself* to be breaking up! (EFR; *threatened to break up*, NRSV, NIV).

Most contemporary readers do not anticipate experiencing humor in biblical narrative *[Comedy]*. We often find it difficult to imagine using humor to express the sacred and the serious. At the same time, we recognize the power of humor to engage the listeners. Hence, we should not be surprised that Hebrew narrative uses humor to captivate the readers. Because the humor in the biblical stories fit people long ago, we miss much of the laughter. Even when pointed out, we may not see the humor. Earlier readers likely would have sensed the combination of humor and pathos in sailors wildly hurling cargo overboard in response to a great wind that God has hurled at the ship, while the object of all the divine attention sleeps below the deck of a ship that thinks itself to be breaking up!

Be that as it may, the narrator states right up front that the sailors are terrified (1:5). This verb *fear (yara')* will follow the mariners throughout their adventure, till they are finally quieted so that they *revere* the LORD with the calming of the sea (1:16). Fear does not paralyze them. They frantically pray and hurl cargo.

Each prays to his individual god (1:5). We apparently are to imagine a diverse crew working this ship, a group with different religious and perhaps ethnic backgrounds. We do not know if each of them, prior to setting out to sea, has visited the appropriate sanctuary or shrine (cf. the whaling crew at Whaleman's Chapel in Herman Melville's *Moby Dick*). It is normal, however, for ancient mariners to attribute the weather to direct divine action, whether that weather be calm or storm. The sailors accompany their prayer with action. They match God's *hurling* with some of their own (1:5). They *hurl* cargo overboard to lighten the load, perhaps so the boat will ride atop the waves rather than be buried under them.

All the sailors frantically pray and work to save the ship and their own lives. But the one passenger, Jonah, is sleeping (1:5)! Jonah has continued his descent. First he has gone down to Joppa (1:3). Now he has gone down into the bowels of the ship. Nor is his descent over. He will go still farther down into the sea (1:15).

Jonah's sleep is not ordinary. The Hebrew word *radam* describes the very deepest sleep. Some sense in this action the first indication of Jonah's desire to die, which he pursues further in his choice to be thrown overboard and then finally confirms by his own words (4:3). Jonah is certainly headed downward, in the direction of Sheol. That imagery becomes even more explicit in his prayer from the fish (Jon. 2).

This Hebrew word *radam* can describe sleep that eventuates in death (Judg. 4:21). However, the narrator has not told us that Jonah seeks death, but only that he has fled from God's presence (1:3). A sleep of the type into which Jonah has fallen can be divinely induced as a prelude to divine action or revelation (Gen. 2:21; 15:12). Finally, we cannot know Jonah's intention. We can, however, say that the narrative draws the starkest possible contrast between the frantic action of the sailors and the completely passive action of Jonah. At first glance, it appears that the sailors are more in touch with reality than Jonah.

The captain finds Jonah asleep while others are trying to save the ship (1:6). His first question carries with it an accusatory tone: *"What are you doing sound asleep?" [Questions]*. The captain then directs Jonah with words having a familiar ring: *"Rise and cry out"* (1:6, EFR). These are the same Hebrew verbs found in God's original commission of Jonah (1:2). Not even in the most hidden part of the boat can Jonah escape instructions—if not God's, then the captain's. The captain hopes that *perhaps* an appeal to Jonah's deity will be the key to quiet the storm. The captain presumes neither on God's willingness nor ability to still the storm (similarly the king of Nineveh, 3:9).

The narrator tells us nothing of Jonah's response to the captain's command. Instead, the scene shifts suddenly to the sailors. Does Jonah rise and petition God as directed? The narrative gives the readers freedom to imagine Jonah's response as we choose, depending in large measure on each person's perspective of Jonah. Perhaps Jonah does pray. He seems to know what will be necessary to quiet the storm (1:12). But perhaps the narrator wants us to contrast the sailors' urgent appeals to their gods with Jonah's continuing dispute with his (Knight/Golka: 79-80).

Divining the Cause 1:7-10

The next scene still leaves the reader without direct access to Jonah's perspective on the ship and storm *[Narrator]*. Instead, we again join the sailors as they try to figure out the cause of the *evil* situation (1:7; *calamity*, NRSV, NIV). The narrator's repetition of the word *evil* reminds us that all the characters in the story find themselves confronting circumstances described as *evil* (1:3; 3:8, 10; 4:2). We dare not underestimate the experience of evil that pervades this narrative.

The casting of lots points to Jonah. Some have speculated on how this happens, but we know nothing about the process of casting lots in this situation (Stuart: 459-60). Immediately, the attention turns to Jonah, on whom the lot has fallen. Yet the ensuing dialogue is strange. The two parties to the conversation seem to talk past each other.

The sailors ask four or five questions. The first one goes to the heart of the sailors' concern: *"Tell us why this evil has come upon us"* (1:8). If answered, all the rest of the conversation could be omitted. This first question is actually missing in several ancient Hebrew and Greek manuscripts, which begin by having the sailors ask, *"What is your occupation?"* Perhaps these texts have dropped the first question because it adds a comic air to the exchange.

Following the crucial query, the sailors ask a rapid series of questions (1:8), ones normally asked upon first meeting a stranger (Wolff, 1986:114). Yet immediately after the exchange, we discover that the sailors already know Jonah, and that he has even told them the purpose of his trip (1:10). In response, Jonah answers only their last question, *"And of what people are you?"* (1:8). Perhaps Jonah is laughing at such an unusual barrage of questions. Jonah tells them that he is an *Hebrew*, a word used by foreigners to designate Jonah's ethnic group (e.g., Gen. 39:14; Exod. 1:16; 1 Sam. 4:9; 14:11).

Jonah then proceeds to answer a question that they have not asked, about his religion. He identifies his God, *"Yahweh, the God of the heavens"* (1:9, EFR). In the biblical material from the Persian period (538-336 B.C.), this title appears most frequently as a designation for the God of the Jews (as in Ezra 1:2; Dan. 2:37; Knight/Golka: 82). Jonah further identifies the LORD (Yahweh) as the one who *"made the sea and the dry land"* (1:9).

Some take this confession of faith to be hypocritical, empty words (Holbert: 67). After all, if Jonah really believes what he says about

God, then his sea voyage away from God becomes nonsense! Jonah's answer adds to the humor of the situation. Perhaps Jonah has realized all along that he cannot run away from the divine commission. Jonah later announces that he has known God's character before he ever left home (4:2). Be that as it may, Jonah's confession of faith admits that the sea will provide no escape.

However unusual the conversation between Jonah and the sailors, the effect is to increase their fear (1:10). We must note also that the narrator no longer refers to them as *sailors* (NIV; *mariners*, NRSV). Henceforth, they are *men* (1:10). We need to be careful not to overinterpret such changes, but something has happened in this exchange. Now Jonah deals not with sailors trying to do their job in the middle of a storm at sea, but with *men*, men whose fear has increased to terror (Wolff, 1986:116). The narrative escalates the emotional pitch by repeating the word *fear* twice and adding the word *great*. Their cry, *"What have you done?"* (1:10, NIV), gives voice to their terror (cf. the terror of the refugees from Egypt, trapped between the the sea and Pharaoh's army; Exod. 14:11).

This exchange concludes on a surprising note (1:10b). According to the narrator, the men know as much about Jonah as the reader knows.

Quieting the Storm; Conclusion   1:11-15, 16

After concluding that Jonah is the cause of the raging sea, the men turn to him for an answer that will quiet the sea (1:11). This time Jonah responds quickly and directly: *"Pick me up and hurl me into the sea"* (1:12, EFR). God has *hurled* wind (1:4); the sailors have *hurled* cargo (1:5). Jonah requests that one thing more be *hurled*—Jonah himself.

We do not know why Jonah concludes that such a toss will quiet the sea. The narrator has not told us. Not surprisingly, readers have interpreted Jonah's request in different ways. Some presume that Jonah's motivation remains unchanged from his desire to escape God's power and commission, even if escape brings his death. Thus Jonah has maintained a steady downward movement from his departure (1:3), to his deathlike sleep (1:5), to his potential drowning (1:12), to his anticipated death (4:2; Holbert: 69). Yet at this point in the narrative, others read Jonah as a person of faith, offering up his life for the innocent in a gesture of self-sacrifice (Stuart: 462-3).

There are other possibilities. Perhaps Jonah is neither a recalcitrant scoundrel nor a suffering servant, but a much more complex person, capable of mixed motives (Magonet: 86). After chasing him over the sea, God will not let the commissioned one (1:2) escape into death. As in the middle of the storm, so in the middle of the sea, perhaps Jonah knows himself in no mortal danger. If so, Jonah can quiet the sea for the terrified men and wait to see what God does next.

The *men* do not follow Jonah's instructions. In this narrative, not many characters take instructions well. Instead, they try to row to shore (1:13). That only increases the violence of the storm. For the third time, the storm has increased in velocity (1:4, 11). This time, however, the storm rages directly against the men (1:13). They have become the problem.

We are told why the men have chosen this course. They fear that in throwing Jonah overboard, they will be responsible for the death of an innocent man (1:14; cf. Deut. 19:8-13; 21:1-9; 2 Kings 24:4). They cry out, caught between the raging waters and possible divine rage over innocent blood. Another prophet, Jeremiah, warned Judah's officials about the danger of shedding his innocent blood (Jer. 26:10-15). In these narratives, men from diverse religious backgrounds worry about God's anger over shed blood. However confused they may be about the contest between God and Jonah, the sailors/men try to do what is right.

Their prayer concludes with a traditional doxology: *"You, O LORD, have done as it pleased you"* (1:14; cf. Ps. 115:3; 135:6). With that, the men give up and follow Jonah's instructions: they pick him up and hurl him into the sea (1:12, 15). The result is as Jonah has announced. The sea quits its raging.

This episode concludes with the sailors with quite a different attitude from the opening scene. As the drama begins, the *sailors*, out of fear of the storm, each cry out *to his [own] god* (1:5). Now they have become *men,* and their fear has been transformed.

The meaning of the word "fear" has grown (Magonet: 31-33). When a word or phrase has "grown" in the course of a story, the earlier use of the meaning has evolved through the narrative, becoming more complex or more intense. Here the word fear has grown from the panic of the sailors in 1:5 to a more complex and intense emotion in 1:16. It is probably not correct to say that the emotion has changed from fear to reverence, but has grown to combine anxiety with awe, apprehension with wonder. As 1:16 states the growth has combined complexity and intensity: *"the men feared the Lord even more."*

The text does not allow us to decide whether these non-Israelites have been converted. Some conclude that the men have added the LORD to the other gods they worship (Stuart: 464). Perhaps it is enough to say that this adventure has changed them, even if we do not know the extent of the transformation. We shall see a similar change in the inhabitants of Nineveh (3:5, 10). There too, we do not know the depth of their "conversion." Be that as it may, the sea is quiet, and the sailors' story is over. The *men* have experienced the powerful presence of God and acknowledged that experience.

THE TEXT IN BIBLICAL CONTEXT
Foreigners Acknowledge God

Several biblical texts narrate accounts of non-Israelites who come to acknowledge the presence and power of God. Numbers 22–24 tells of a non-Israelite prophet Balaam. Balak, the Moabite king, hired him to curse the Israelites so that the Moabites could defeat them. Balaam insisted that he could only pronounce what Yahweh commissioned him to say. He could not announce a curse on Israel against Yahweh's will: "If Balak should give me his house full of silver and gold, I would not be able to go beyond the word of the LORD, to do either good or bad of my own will" (Num. 24:13).

Foreigners frequently demonstrated more trust in the power of God than did Abraham. As a resident alien in Gerar, Abraham concluded that there was no fear of God in that place (Gen. 20:11). Therefore, he withheld from others the fact that Sarah was his wife, telling them instead that she was his sister. Operating under this assumption, Abimelech of Gerar took Sarah into his house. However, when informed by God in a dream that Sarah was married, Abimelech treated her with respect and demanded an explanation from Abraham (Gen. 20:1-18).

Balaam and Abimelech—among others such as Melchizedek, Jethro, and Rahab (Gen. 14:18-20; Exod. 18; Josh. 2)—are portrayed as taking the LORD more seriously than did many of Israel's so-called "heroes." The NT also observes people outside Judaism who appear as model figures in their reverence for God and obedience to God. Peter found such a person in Cornelius, a Roman army officer "well spoken of by the whole Jewish nation" (Acts 10:22). Sometimes these folks became a part of the community of faith. That seems to have been the case with Cornelius. Other "outsiders" remained as they were but exhibited respect for the LORD, the God of Abraham, Moses, Jonah, and Peter.

We do not know whether the men on the ship that sails from Joppa, eventually exchange their varied religious traditions for a single allegiance to the LORD, the God from whom Jonah has fled.

Nevertheless, the experience of these sailors suggests that we should treat with respect the "outsiders," those whose religious affiliation does not predispose them to acknowledge God's power. While not all outsiders may *fear* God, some may even teach us about God. Even if they do not worship the LORD as God, they may have more openness to the experience of God's unexpected presence and power than many "insiders."

THE TEXT IN THE LIFE OF THE CHURCH
God and Nature

Ancient Israel always struggled to understand how the LORD was the God of nature. Exodus, the key faith story in the OT, focuses not on the LORD as God of fertility, but on God's deliverance/salvation. The Exodus tradition established the LORD as the deity who directs history. Although the people at times ignored the LORD of history, the tradition remained firm in the witness that the drama of history must account for God's power and presence.

Nature was another matter. Israel matured among a people who worshiped Baal, the god of the thunderstorm. Baal's credentials as a god of fertility were longstanding, celebrated in Canaanite story and song. The LORD's relationship to fertility in the fields and safety on the sea apparently remained unclear, even in Israel. Hence, many chose to worship both the LORD and Baal, each as deities over a different aspect of their lives. The contest on Carmel between Elijah and the prophets of Baal is set within such a context (1 Kings 18).

This contest between the LORD and Baal was not primarily a matter of moral degeneracy due to Canaanite sacred prostitution. The issue was far more serious: Who was god over the fertility of the fields and flocks? Who was lord of the storms? The rain that fell with Elijah's petition (1 Kings 18) and the storm that raged on the sea at God's command (Jon. 1) proclaim the LORD as God of nature as well as history. In story and song, Israel repeated that affirmation, as in Jonah's words: *"I worship the LORD, the God of heaven, who made the sea and the dry land"* (1:9). In the lyric of the psalmist:

> O LORD God of hosts,
>   who is as mighty as you, O LORD?
>   Your faithfulness surrounds you.
> You rule the raging of the sea;
>   when its waves rise, you still them. (Ps. 89:8-9)

Knowing the Psalms that affirm the LORD's power over nature

does not banish all questions or concerns. Caught in a storm, some ancient Israelites may have acted like the sailors from Joppa and cried out to a host of divine beings, hoping to capture the ear of the one in charge. Natural disasters tested the faith of Jesus' disciples. In the midst of a storm at sea, their panic sounded like the Joppa sailors: "They went and woke him up, saying, 'Lord save us! We are perishing!'" (Matt. 8:25). In spite of questions and doubts, the account of the disciples in the storm on the sea, affirms again that the LORD is the God of nature.

We have more trouble than even our ancestors to identify God's presence in nature. The beauty of nature causes us to sing of the Creator, but we routinely declare storms and droughts as acts of nature, not acts of God. We ought not assign to God the apparent capriciousness of natural disasters. Yet our inability to speak of God's presence in nature—except in the beauty of the sunset, the mountains, and the flowers—shuts God out of a significant arena of life.

How can we learn from these sailors who experience God's power and presence at sea and on dry land? The confession of Jonah, *"I worship the LORD, . . . who made the sea and the dry land"* (1:9), interprets God's presence in a water world where the sailors struggle with storms as well as enjoy sunsets. Perhaps amid low-pressure areas and prevailing wind patterns, we too may find words that point to God's presence and power in all of nature, not just in the beautiful parts.

Under the Sea
Jonah 1:17—2:10

PREVIEW

This unit brings us to the best-known and most debated section of Jonah. Some of the controversy surrounding Jonah's sojourn in the *great fish* has proved to be intractable. The various disputants begin from such different assumptions. One side worries about protecting the inerrant truth of the Bible; the other side wants to preserve the integrity of academic study. Some, whose predisposition inclines them to treat all biblical statements as historical data, use the same eyes for reading about the fish swallowing Jonah.

Douglas Stuart (440) prefers to read Jonah as a historical report, although he avoids a direct discussion of the fish incident. Other interpreters assume that all biblical statements must be tested by the same rules of probability as any other statements claiming to be historical data. On the basis of such testing, Bruce Vawter (96-7) concludes that this is an exciting drama and not a historical account. Finally, we cannot prove whether or not this is a historical record of Jonah's undersea adventure. One suspects that if we could prove that, we would not be any closer to the truth of the story than we are now.

Jonah contains many features that raise historical questions. Some of the questions can be answered, but most cannot. We walk into a trap if we require historical verification before taking the story seriously as God's word. Many biblical narratives witness to God's dramatic work through people and events of history. But just as certainly, God's truth can be conveyed through parable and story that do not need historical verification to validate their worth.

Most scholarly debate has focused, not on the fish, but on the origin of the psalm in Jonah 2:2-9. Some scholars insist that the psalm is a later addition to the narrative; others conclude that it belongs to the original composition. This question too cannot be finally answered.

In the narrative, the poem is a song of thanksgiving where one would expect either a lament and/or a prayer of petition. Hence, many suggest that the psalm was inserted later, perhaps to cast Jonah in a more favorable light (Gunkel: 643; Simon, 1999:16). Others insist that the language and themes of the psalm connect so well with the prose narrative, that we need not assume that this was a later expansion of the story (Landes, 1967:3-31).

More recent emphasis on the literary character of biblical narrative has convinced many scholars to treat the psalm as an integral part of the story, without answering the question of exactly when the psalm might have been included (Ackerman, 1987:237). So far as we know, the text of both the synagogue and the church has always included this psalm. Therefore, we will look at the narrative in its final form and leave to others the final decision about the history of the psalm.

The unit contains a prayer by Jonah (2:1-9), bracketed by narrative statements describing God's instruction to the fish (1:17; 2:10). The prayer itself follows the traditional form of a psalm of thanksgiving. After a praise introduction, the psalm of thanksgiving describes a situation of distress and danger, followed by divine deliverance. In most thanksgiving psalms, the descriptions of both distress and deliverance use traditional poetic language rather than referring to specific events. The individual, after being delivered, recommits the self to God through offerings and vows, usually concluding with an expression of praise.

This unit has varied verse and chapter division. In Hebrew, verse 16 ends chapter 1, followed by 2:1-11. Thus, 2:1 in Hebrew appears as 1:17 in NRSV. Some versions use the Hebrew divisions (Tanak; NJB). This commentary, keyed to NRSV and NIV, begins the underwater scene with 1:17, followed by 2:1-10.

OUTLINE
Introductory Narration, 1:17

Prayer of Jonah, 2:1-10
    2:1   Introduction
    2:2-7 Report of Distress and Deliverance
    2:8-9 Praise and Promise

Concluding Narration, 2:10

EXPLANATORY NOTES

Introductory Narration 1:17

The adventure "On the Sea" (1:4-16) has begun with divine action. God has hurled a great wind on the sea (1:4). The drama "Under the Sea" begins similarly. This time, God designates (*appointed*, NASB; *provided*, NRSV, NIV) *a great fish* (NIV) to swallow Jonah. Once again, the narrative witnesses to God's presence in creation and power through nature. Here the fish plays the role of a divine agent. Notice that, like the wind, the fish is described with one of the story's most frequently used adjectives: *great* (*gadol*; cf. 1:2, 4, 12). God pursues Jonah "under the sea" in this scene as vigorously as God has stormed "on the sea" in the previous scene.

Prompted by curiosity, many readers wish for more information about the *fish* than the biblical narrative provides. We cannot even identify the species of the fish. The Hebrew text simply calls the animal a great *fish (dag)*. The Greek translation *(ketos)* means a "huge fish" or "sea monster." Most current readers picture a whale swallowing Jonah, a scene reinforced by the popular children's story, *The Adventures of Pinocchio*, by the Italian author Carlo Collodi. Earlier Christian artists portrayed a mythical sea monster rather than a whale (Snyder: 48; Limburg, 1990:22).

The purpose for the fish is more important than its species. Is the fish an agent of divine punishment, sent to devour Jonah? Or is the fish an agent of divine deliverance, sent to rescue Jonah from drowning? Either interpretation is possible. On one hand, the word *swallow (bala')* generally refers to a hostile action, often by God (e.g., Ps. 21:9/10 in Heb.). We might capture the hostility of that term by the English word *devour*. Yet the Hebrew narrative does not use a hostile word to designate the sea animal, simply calling it a *fish*, rather than a sea monster (cf. "Leviathan," Isa. 27:1).

We have no idea whether God even intends to punish Jonah. God's only expressed intention is for Jonah to go to Nineveh with a message of warning (1:2). It seems more likely that the fish here acts as an agent of divine deliverance, not punishment (Landes, 1967:10-3). Hence, it seems best to translate simply, *The LORD provided a great fish to swallow Jonah* (EFR).

Readers of the Hebrew text have noted that while the text uses a masculine form of fish twice (1:17; 2:10), in 2:1 (Heb.: 2:2) we find the feminine form of fish *(dagah)*. That change, not in our English translations, piques the reader's curiosity. Trible suggests that the feminine form elicits female imagery: "When Jonah prays from within the 'mother' fish, Jonah appropriately moves from death to life" (Trible, 1996:505).

The fish delivers Jonah from the land of the dead. In narratives from the ancient Near East, three days and three nights constitute the length of the journey from the land of the living to the land of the dead (Fretheim, 1977:97-8). It appears that, as he is hurled overboard (1:15), Jonah completes the journey to the land of the dead. By means of the fish, however, God turns the journey around. Instead, Jonah is brought from the land of the dead toward the land of the living.

Prayer of Jonah 2:1-10

2:1 Introduction

As noted in the Preview, this prayer of Jonah is a poetic psalm of thanksgiving *[Poetry]*. The flow of the psalm models closely the traditional movement of thanksgiving songs: distress, deliverance, praise, and promise. In language applicable to many different people and times, thanksgiving psalms describe the disaster that has occasioned the distress. If a thanksgiving psalm were specific to one situation, that detail would limit its usefulness to the worshiping community. Hence, these psalms describe distress in the language and/or metaphors of wasting disease (Ps. 32), violent enemies (Pss. 41; 118), the hand of death/Sheol (Ps. 116), as well as drowning (Pss. 42; 124).

We cannot know whether this prayer of Jonah is a traditional one not preserved in the Psalter (Stuart: 475), or an original one created out of traditional language (Magonet: 40-9). We can say that the psalm finds Jonah praying in words and phrases familiar to generations of worshipers in ancient Israel.

2:2-7 Report of Distress and Deliverance

This prayer begins by expressing the basic life experience that has generated a psalm of thanksgiving: distress, petition, divine deliverance (2:2). The opening verse directs our attention to God through a remarkable change in perspective. Jonah starts addressing an audience, both himself and us: *"I called to the LORD."* Suddenly the perspective changes. Jonah speaks not about God, but directly to God: *"You heard my voice."* Jonah's cry comes not so much from the belly of a fish as from *the depths of Sheol* (NIV/NRSV).

In the prayer, Jonah assumes that he has tangled directly with God. The danger of death, which the psalm describes, has come by divine action (2:3). Jonah has become one of earth's desperate suffering people (Knight/Golka: 96). As he replays the distress, Jonah recalls his own words telling of his separation from God: *"I am driven away from your sight; how shall I look again upon your holy temple?"* (2:4). The poem likens this distress to being buried under the huge primeval sea: *"The deep (tehom) surrounded me"* (2:5). Again, the phrases come from the common vocabulary of distress we see in the book of Psalms.

In summary, the psalm describes the distress as being drowned by God in the great cosmic sea. *God* is the problem, God's *waves* and *billows* (2:3). When one is buried by divine design, there can be no escape. The *bars* of Sheol lock the door (2:6). Jonah feels imprisoned in *the land* of the dead *forever*.

Even though the prayer portrays the disaster as terminal, the opening words of the psalm (1:2) have already reminded us that this is a thanksgiving song. The disaster that has prompted petition will produce divine deliverance. That in fact happens, though in this prayer Jonah first describes his deliverance (2:6), and then reports his petition (2:7).

The language of the poem in 2:6 recalls the previous prose: Jonah's choice has been to go *down* (1:3, 5). God's deliverance brings him *up*. As life drains away, Jonah *remembered the LORD* (2:7a). In the biblical tradition, "to remember" is not only to "call to mind," but to speak and to act. Jonah has assumed that he is cut off forever from the *holy temple* (2:4). That proves not to be the case. His petition reaches the sacred presence of God (2:7b).

Notice how once again the psalm switches perspectives, speaking first of God in the third person, then with God in the second person (*you*).

> As my life was ebbing away,
>   I remembered the LORD;
> and my prayer came to you,
>   into your holy temple. (2:7)

The recounting of danger and deliverance ends as it has begun, vacillating between God as a distant third person and as a present *You*.

2:8-9 Praise and Promise

After the experience of disaster and deliverance, the grateful person becomes a teacher in the community (Wolff, 1986:137). Hence, the song of thanksgiving ends with statements of praise and instruction. In this prayer, the delivered one admonishes the community to steadfastly maintain its relationship with God (2:8). The text uses a weighty Hebrew word *khesed*, meaning *true loyalty* (*grace that could be theirs*, NIV). *Khesed* reappears in 4:2, in the confession of faith, with Jonah describing God as *abounding in steadfast love/loyalty* (4:2).

Many note the irony: Jonah, the prophet who has fled from the presence of God (1:3), now speaks about *steadfast loyalty* to God. But are not the sailors the ones who have demonstrated true loyalty to God rather than Jonah? (Knight/Golka: 99). Jonah has not been guilty of worshiping idols, but neither can we say that Jonah has modeled true loyalty to God. Some hear self-righteous satire as Jonah contrasts himself with those others *who forsake their true loyalty*. For other readers, Jonah uses the traditional close of a thanksgiving psalm to instruct himself as much as others.

The psalm concludes with the customary promise to fulfill one's responsibility to God (2:9a). The promise is phrased in the traditional language of sacrifices and vows. Certainly this includes bringing one's offerings to God, but the traditional language refers to more. The grateful one promises to become once again a responsible member of the worshiping community. The rescued/saved member has been reincorporated into the community and promises to live out of that reality. This does not mean that Jonah has undergone a transformation in his basic character. In fact, events will prove that he has not (Magonet: 51-3). Yet it does mean that Jonah promises to fulfill his responsibility as a member of the community. And he will.

In many ways, Jonah's final exclamation of praise provides the key theme of God's action throughout the story: *"Deliverance belongs to the* LORD!" (2:9b). Here Jonah voices his own joy as the recipient of divine deliverance. He also defines the problem that will spark an intense dispute later in the story. In chapter 4, Jonah does not disagree with the affirmation that the LORD delivers. But the divine decision to save Nineveh enrages Jonah. Whoever declares *"Deliverance belongs to the* LORD*"* affirms both God's power and wisdom. Jonah will find himself happier with the divine power than with the divine wisdom.

Concluding Narration 2:10

God now speaks to the fish, which vomits Jonah out onto dry land. Many readers feel that the hypocrisy of Jonah's prayer of thanksgiving has as much to do with the vomiting by the fish as God's instruction (Trible, 1996:507). The phrases of Jonah's prayer mouth the right words, but his action betrays the piety of the phrases. The narrator, however, does not engage in such evaluation of the situation. Instead, we are simply told that God's decision lies behind this action as it has behind the wind (1:4) and the swallowing (1:17). We must not miss the narrative's reticence here. The narrative perspective keeps us as onlookers *[Narrator].* We have not been given God's perspective of the action on the sea (1:4-16) nor under the sea (1:17—2:10). We observe divine action. We can only guess at divine motivation.

THE TEXT IN BIBLICAL CONTEXT
Psalm of Thanksgiving

We have identified the prayer in Jonah 2:2-9 as a traditional psalm of thanksgiving. As such, it has a function in this particular story, but it also relates to a common genre of psalms present throughout the biblical tradition. Obviously, a song of thanksgiving is a responsive act, responding to God's delivering power (Westermann, 1989:166-200).

We find songs of thanksgiving scattered throughout the biblical narratives, in addition to several examples in the Psalter. Hannah expresses her joy through a psalm over God's deliverance of one whose barrenness exposed her to public ridicule as well as personal shame (1 Sam. 2:1-10). The Gospel of Luke is extravagant in its use of songs of thanksgiving, especially in the birth narratives of Jesus (Luke 1). The most intense joy expressed by God's people echos in psalms of thanksgiving. They acknowledge one of our deepest longings, that God would hear and answer the cries of those in danger.

Walter Brueggemann observes that the power of these praise songs does not lie only in their function as a grateful response to

God's deliverance. These psalms confess the world as an arena of divine transformation. They declare the provisional character of the present and look instead toward the new world carried on the wind of God's saving power. God remains active, and the future is wide open.

The formative power of the thanksgiving psalms goes even beyond the affirmation of God's transforming action in the world. These praise songs ignite the imagination of community. The poems invite the singer to imagine the world as God intends it, a world beyond illness and enemies, life without oppression and violence. These pictures not only judge the present world; they also energize the community to join God's transforming work toward a new order. The praise hymns of the church frequently have more power to free and energize the people than all the sermons of exhortation and admonition.

THE TEXT IN THE LIFE OF THE CHURCH

Jonah: Saint or Sinner?

Jonah in the belly of the fish has received some of the highest praise and most scathing criticism suffered by this much maligned and blessed prophet. For artists in the early church, the whole story focused in this event. For them, Jonah acted out the role of Christ, being buried for three days and then resurrected at God's command.

These early artists drew their pictures with an eye to the problems of their own time. The early Christians found the world to be a dangerous place, not unlike a stormy sea filled with monsters ready to devour them. For them, Jonah's experience ignited hope that, though monsters threatened to devour even them, all monsters remained under divine control. God only needed to speak, and they would be vomited out safely. John Calvin (91), while not necessarily sharing the artists' appreciation of Jonah, nevertheless celebrated this as a moment of resurrection, through which we can "be convinced of the restoration which God promises to us."

Others see this as the narrative's most strident satire (Holbert: 74). Jonah mouths all the right words, a prayer of thanksgiving, concluding with promise and praise. But the prophet's activities, both before and after his adventure in the sea, make a mockery out of his words. Rather than showing repentant gratitude, Jonah exults in his own piety in contrast to others, *"those who cling to worthless idols"* (2:8, NIV; Trible, 1996:508). The men on the boat, the citizens of Nineveh, all of them "pagans," live out the loyalty to God that Jonah's prayer admonishes, but that Jonah does not perform. Jonah's flight in chapter 1 is followed by his minimal prophetic performance in chapter 3 and his rage at God in the final scene (4:2). Many interpreters conclude that Jonah deserves much worse than he receives from God's hand.

How is it that Christians throughout the history of the church can listen to the same story of Jonah and experience him so differently? Like most individuals in the biblical narratives, Jonah must not be treated one-sidedly as saint or sinner. Jonah's actions do not always measure up to the words he professes. For a community of believers who put more stock in the actual "fruit of the Spirit" (Gal. 5:22-23) than in pious phrases, Jonah's disobedience, minimal effort, and anger do not endear him as a model figure.

Nevertheless, sometimes Jonah's words and deeds do match. We can read Jonah's request to be thrown overboard as sacrificing himself for the safety of others as easily as calling his action another cynical attempt to escape from God. We can hear the words of his prayer as a genuine expression of his faith, even if in other moments he acts to the contrary.

All of us are more like Jonah than we are different from him. History bears ugly scars as witness to the danger of branding people as all good or all evil. Efforts to deify some and demonize others create a climate that justifies the violent destruction of the "evil ones." The "evil Jonahs" become those who must be "purged from our midst" in the interest of peace and harmony. Both individuals and governments use elimination of the "evil ones" as vindication for their violence.

Part 2

The Unfulfilled Prophet

Jonah 3–4

Jonah 3:1-3a

The Recommissioning of Jonah

PREVIEW

The narrative brings us right back to where the drama began. We may or may not have returned to the exact geographical location. We do not know where this commissioning happened. Most locate this moment of the story in Palestine (Stuart: 481), but the narrator does not tell us. In terms of the relationship between God and Jonah, however, we have returned to the same spot. Much of what we find in this narration of Jonah's commissioning repeats verbatim the first such moment—most but not all.

Like Jonah 1:1-3, this unit divides in two parts, God's speech and Jonah's action. The content of God's speech echoes the first speech (1:2), with small but perhaps significant changes. Jonah's response to his second commissioning is obviously different from his action after the first.

OUTLINE

The Word from the LORD, 3:1-2
    3:1   Introduction of the Characters
    3:2   Divine Word

The Response of Jonah, 3:3a

EXPLANATORY NOTES

The Word from the LORD 3:1-2

The introduction of the characters happens with the exact words of the first commissioning (1:1), except for one change. Rather than introducing Jonah to us as the *son of Amittai*, the narrator reminds us that this constitutes a second commissioning: *The word of the LORD came to Jonah a second time* (3:1). Jonah finds himself still confronted with the same vocation. His attempt to flee from the urgency of his vocation has not succeeded. God addresses him again.

In many respects, God's commissioning speech re-echoes the first address (cf. 1:2; 3:2): *"Arise, go to Nineveh, that great city"* (EFR). Jonah's instruction and destination remain the same. But the reason for Jonah's trip to Nineveh has changed, or at least God's words do not repeat verbatim what was said before:

"Cry out against it; for their wickedness has come up before me." (1:2)
"Proclaim to it the message that I tell you." (3:2)

If the rest of 1:1-2 were not so carefully repeating things word for word, we might overlook the change as incidental. Hence, we must at least ask about the change in Jonah's instructions from God indicated by this different wording.

In the initial commissioning speech, God directed Jonah to announce disaster or judgment, to *"cry out against"* (1:2). In 3:2, Jonah is directed to speak the message as God instructs him. Gone is the evaluation of Nineveh as wicked. Gone also is any clear notion of the content of God's message to Nineveh. That has all been replaced by *"the message that I tell you."*

We may conclude that the message is not changed. Instead, Jonah's relationship with God is now changed. The words stress divine authority over Jonah (Trible, 1996:510). Jonah must now say only the words God directs (Wolff, 1986:139). Apparently, Jonah is now commissioned as God's mouthpiece more than as God's prophet. A prophet of God ordinarily had a certain amount of freedom to express God's word in ways and words fitting to each particular circumstance (Heschel, vol. 2: 206-26; von Rad: 70-9). The initial commissioning of Jonah has seemed to allow that freedom. But the command in 3:2, *"Proclaim to it the proclamation that I word to you"* (EFR), tightens God's instructions to the prophet.

Surprisingly, this second word from God leaves the exact content of the message more open than God's first address to the prophet. Rather than having Jonah *cry out against* Nineveh, God instructs the prophet to *speak to* Nineveh. The anger of God toward Nineveh is no longer expressed in the divine speech. Previously, that anger was quite clear: *"Their wickedness has come up before me"* (1:2). The anger may still be there. But God's words have a different feel. We wonder what exactly God will tell Jonah to say? We shall hear what Jonah does say in Nineveh (3:4), but we will not know for sure if he speaks *according to the word of the* LORD (cf. 3:3).

The Response of Jonah 3:3a

Jonah goes to Nineveh in accord with the *word of the* LORD. This marks a complete change from Jonah's response to the first commissioning. There the narrator tells us that Jonah flees *from the presence of the* LORD (1:3). Jonah's response this second time brings him into compliance with God's instruction.

Nevertheless, one thing has not changed. We still have not heard from Jonah. All we have is the narrator's report of Jonah's action. Some conclude that Jonah has changed. He now has become God's prophet in spirit as well as action (Calvin: 94). Yet Jonah has not repented in his prayer in the great fish (2:2-9). His prayer is one of thanksgiving, not repentance. Furthermore, his later action—in Nineveh and outside the city—suggests that any change in the prophet's attitude toward his vocation is at best partial (Stuart: 486).

Perhaps Jonah has simply acquiesced to God's inescapable power (Vawter: 104). Previously divine power has certainly stopped Jonah in midflight. On the other hand, some suggest that Jonah's decision to go to Nineveh this time comes from his own free choice (LaCocque, 1990:116). He may not have been motivated by any attitudinal attitude or coercion, but a simple decision to carry through the divine commission. Thus far, we do not know. We are not given Jonah's perspective on this recommissioning. Our perspective remains that of an onlooker *[Narrator]*. Jonah's thoughts and attitudes remain hidden from our sight. We know only that this time Jonah goes to Nineveh.

THE TEXT IN BIBLICAL CONTEXT
Commissioning the Prophet—Again

In many respects, Jonah's recommissioning is unique in the biblical tradition. To be sure, in the Bible we frequently find God working with a reluctant messenger. The narrative of Moses' commissioning displays God's incredible patience and persistence with one quite reluctant to accept his vocation. After addressing Moses' many objections to the call, God's patience eventually ran out. In anger, God appointed Aaron as Moses' spokesperson (Exod. 4:14-17).

Even then, rather than going directly to carry out his commission, Moses went back to ask permission from his father-in-law, Jethro (Exod. 4:18). The journey of Moses to Egypt was interrupted further by a strange attack in the night (4:24-26). After an initial and apparently unsuccessful attempt to carry out his commission, Moses turned to God, objecting once again to the whole enterprise (5:22-23). This resulted in still another divine commissioning of Moses (6:1-8).

God must commission and recommission Moses before the messenger finally obeys. In that narrative of the commissioning, the narrator takes us inside the interaction between God and Moses. We listen to the reasons for Moses' reluctance. We see God as both patient and impatient, insistent and adaptable.

Thus far in the narrative of Jonah, we are given no inside report on such a dialogue. We watch what happens and wonder. Suppose Jonah flees again. Will God renew the chase to bring the prophet once again face-to-face with his vocation? What prompts Jonah's response this time—fear, fatigue, interest? Whether it be the call of Moses or the commissioning of Jonah, the Bible provides remarkable stories of God trying to coax vocation out of those disinclined to cooperate.

THE TEXT IN THE LIFE OF THE CHURCH

Human Freedom and Divine Persistence

The sparseness of this narrative of Jonah's recommissioning leaves ample room for listeners to wonder. That space for interpretative imagination frequently prompts listeners to describe Jonah either as model figure or as antihero. Hence, some see in Jonah a model of free choice (LaCocque: 116) or restored faith (Calvin: 94). Others see him as parody of prophet (Miles) or forced into service by divine power (Vawter: 104).

God's brief recommissioning of the silent Jonah can function almost like a mirror. Christians find themselves reflecting on their personal or corporate experience of divine call and vocation. By not answering all our questions about divine call, the narrative invites the reader into conversation, asking each to struggle with an understanding of God's call. We search with difficulty for a way to articulate a theology of call that does justice both to the freedom of the individual and the insistence of God. Somehow we sense with Jonah, as LaCocque maintains, that the God who calls does not remove freedom of response from the called one.

Many have felt forced into a "church" vocation, trapped by a call "mediated" by family and friends. On the other hand, we affirm a theology of call that allows God the freedom to vigorously call leaders, insisting that they respond even against their initial reluctance.

Jonah 3:3b—4:11

The Drama on Land

PREVIEW

Following the recommissioning of Jonah, we find a unit parallel in important ways to the adventure on and under the sea (1:4—2:10). This time the action takes place on land, in and outside the city of Nineveh. Once again, the first scene involves Jonah in a setting with an international group of non-Israelites. The second scene finds Jonah alone with God. The balance in this narrative's structure displays the remarkable literary craftsmanship of this short story.

After the recommissioning, the narrative scene quickly changes to Nineveh. We are not told how Jonah reaches Nineveh or how long the trip takes. Through the perspective of the narrator, however, we find ourselves suddenly looking at the large city of Nineveh (3:3b) [Narrator]. This city and its immediate vicinity continue to be the location of the story until the end, though the action shifts outside the city for the second scene.

Even a quick reading can spot a literary division within this unit. The action opens in Nineveh proper (3:3b-10). There Jonah makes a brief appearance as a prophet of judgment (3:4). Then apparently Jonah moves to an unnamed spot outside the city, and that becomes the locale for a dialogue between God and Jonah (4:1-11). Exactly when Jonah leaves Nineveh depends on how we read 4:5 (notes). The narrative flow seems to support the generally held assumption that Jonah leaves town right after his prophetic announcement.

We can see other literary marks of this split in the unit. In Nineveh, the cast of characters includes Jonah and the Ninevites. Actually,

Jonah has an even smaller role here than in the parallel scene on the ship in chapter 1. The really prominent characters in this scene include the people, animals, and king of Nineveh. That changes with the scene in chapter 4. Once again, Jonah sits alone, not in a fish this time, but in a booth *east of the city* (4:5). In this isolated spot, Jonah argues with God instead of praying to God.

OUTLINE
In the City, 3:3b-10

Outside the City, 4:1-11

In these two units, the outline can be presented in chiastic format:

In the City, 3:3b-10
    Introduction, 3:3b
        Announcement of Disaster, 3:4
            Report of the Response, 3:5-9
        Action of God, 3:10a
    Conclusion, 3:10b

Outside the City, 4:1-11
    Introductory Narration, 4:1
        Dialogue: Jonah and God, 4:2-4
            Narration, 4:5-8a
        Dialogue: Jonah and God, 4:8b-11

In the City
Jonah 3:3b-10

PREVIEW
This episode is carried along by a traditional model of the prophetic task. This model constitutes one biblical paradigm of the successful prophet. In brief, the traditional prophetic success story includes three steps: (1) an announcement by a prophet of divine judgment or disaster, (2) response of repentance by the people, (3) forgiveness and/or restoration by God. Jeremiah lays out this prophetic ideal in a single sentence:

At one moment I [God] may declare concerning a nation or a kingdom that I will pluck up and break down and destroy it, but if that nation, . . . turns from its evil, I will change my mind about the disaster that I intended to bring on it. (Jer. 18:7-8)

This ideal prophetic success story forms exactly the outline of this unit. As we shall see, the narrative portrays this episode as not only mirroring the prophetic ideal, but as a phenomenal illustration of it.

The prophet, in this case Jonah, has a relatively minor role to play, to announce the disaster. The important moment in the flow comes as we await the response of the "nation" (Jer. 18:8; Jonah 3:5). The response of God follows consistently with the prophetic model. However, this story does not assume that God's forgiving response is automatic (3:9-10).

Once again, we will notice some of the special words that have reappeared throughout the Jonah story. Most conspicuous has been the word *great (gadol)*. Previously, we have encountered a great city (1:2; 3:2), a great wind (1:4, 12), and a great fish (1:17). In this scene, we find that if anything Nineveh has become even greater (3:3b). In addition, we meet all the inhabitants of Nineveh, from *great* to *small* (3:5).

Throughout the narrative, we have found repeated use of the word *call (qara')*. God calls Jonah (1:2; 3:2). The captain of the ship implores Jonah to call on God (1:6), which the sailors do (1:14). Jonah in distress eventually does *call* on God (2:2). In this scene, after God calls Jonah, Jonah calls out a word of judgment against Nineveh (3:4). In response, the citizens of Nineveh *call* a fast (3:5). This calling back and forth connects God, the prophet, and the sailors/citizens.

We have noticed another word featured throughout: *evil (ra'ah)*, used in a variety of ways. The narrator employs it to describe the problem in Nineveh that has prompted Jonah's call (1:2). In addition, the sailors use it to describe the calamity about to befall them due to the storm at sea (1:7-8). In this scene, the word is used again several times. The royal edict and the narrator describe the problem in Nineveh as *evil* (3:8, 10). The narrator uses *evil* to identify the action God plans against Nineveh. Calling God's action *evil* enlarges the use of the word in the narrative. It now directly describes an action of God.

In summary, just as various of the elements in this narrative are described as *great*, and all the parties *call* to one another, so all of the actors, including God, are in various ways involved in *evil*.

OUTLINE
Introduction, 3:3b

Announcement of Disaster, 3:4

Report of the Response, 3:5-9
   3:5   Response of the People
   3:6-9   Response of the King

Action of God, 3:10

EXPLANATORY NOTES

Introduction 3:3b

The scene begins with a description of the city of Nineveh. The city is described with terms that are even more grandiose than the single word *great (gadol)* used earlier (1:2; 3:2). Here the city is *great to God* (EFR), great even by God's standards. Such use of the word *God* frequently functions as the superlative (Wolff, 1986:148). The narrator emphasizes the awesome size of Nineveh, stating that it takes three days to walk across this *exceedingly large city.*

Some have preferred to understand this description of Nineveh in terms of importance rather than size (Stuart: 486-8). Importance no doubt comes as a corollary to size. However, as the translations indicate, the narrator portrays Nineveh as astonishingly large. In fact, this scene is basically about astonishment. Various attempts to tone the words down so as to make the whole situation more reasonable, undercut the amazement the narrator expects the readers to feel. The listener is not supposed to be trying to do arithmetic, but to be "lost in astonishment" (Wolff, 1986:148).

Announcement of Disaster 3:4

First of all, the narrator tells us that Jonah only *began to go into the city* (3:4a). Hence, we are probably right not to picture Jonah visiting throughout the city with various groups and officials (Stuart: 487-8). Instead, as text says, Jonah walks just one day into a city that would take three days to cross. He carries out his prophetic responsibility, but with only minimal effort. If we assume that Nineveh's government buildings are in the middle of the city, then Jonah does not even go that far.

Jonah's announcement consists of five Hebrew words: *"Just forty days, (and) Nineveh [will be] overthrown!"* (EFR). We find here an ever-so-brief announcement of disaster. Much of the traditional form and content of the prophetic judgment speech is missing (Westermann, 1967:129-94). There is no statement of the reason for the impending disaster, such as the *evil* in the city (1:2). Nor is there a call for repentance.

The announcement does not even identify the method or agent of this disaster. We may decide that the residents of Nineveh would presume that a god would cause the disaster; yet the announcement nowhere states that, nor exactly which divine being might be responsible. The citizens of Nineveh find themselves in a situation similar to the sailors on the sea, who faced a violent storm of unknown origin. Nineveh faces an unknown calamity of unknown origin (1:5).

Jonah's announcement contains yet another ambiguity. The language of the disaster echoes the traditional language about the destruction of Sodom and Gomorrah (cf. Gen. 19:25, 29; Deut. 29:23; Jer. 49:18; 50:40). The translations correctly indicate that we are to anticipate the destruction of Nineveh. However, the word *overthrown (hapak)* can also mean "alter" or "transform" (Wolff, 1986:149). Jonah does not intend it that way (4:2), nor do the Ninevites take it to mean "transform" (3:5-9). Some have wondered if the announcement actually contains a possibility that Jonah neither intends nor desires (Stuart: 489). Nineveh might be transformed.

We do not know for sure the origin of Jonah's five-word announcement (Trible, 1996:511). We know that God has instructed Jonah to speak the divine message as directed (3:2). However, we do not know if Jonah does as instructed or if this represents a condensed version, an unconditional announcement that Jonah wants to proclaim. In any case, it seems fair to conclude that Jonah's prophetic activity represents a minimal effort by a reluctant prophet (Ceresko: 583).

Report of the Response 3:5-9

3:5 Reponse of the People

Jonah's minimal effort achieves maximum results. In fact, the word *amazing* does not even sound adequate to describe the reaction of the people of Nineveh. Responding to the five-word announcement of disaster, the people *believe God*. They do not respond to Jonah by disagreeing or requesting clarification. They believe God, as did Abraham, awaiting the fulfillment of God's promise (Gen. 15:6), and Israel, following its deliverance from Egypt (Exod. 14:31). We are not told why they believe. The citizens of Nineveh do not have external verification of the danger as did the sailors at sea.

Here the narrator uses the general word for God, *'Elohim*. Up till now, the story has employed the particular name for Israel's God, *Yahweh*. The LORD (as most versions translate *Yahweh*) has commissioned Jonah (1:1; 3:1). The LORD has controlled the storm at sea (1:4) and the fish under the sea (1:17; 2:10). The sailors appealed to the LORD for mercy and turned to the LORD in worship (1:14, 16). However, the citizens of Nineveh turn more generally to *God*. We can only wonder if that relates to Jonah's abbreviated announcement of disaster. He does not name the LORD as the agent of the coming calamity.

Although Jonah's announcement does not invite such a response, the people of Nineveh *call* a fast. The publicly proclaimed fast functions as a ritual of repentance and mourning. The ritual involves abstaining from food and also acting out signs of humiliation, such as wearing clothes of dishonor *(sackcloth)* and sitting in a place of shame *(in the ashes)*.

A community would re-enact such a ritual of shame as an expression of intense sorrow for sin. The Day of Atonement, a special day of confession and repentance, has become part of the regular Jewish calendar (Lev. 16:29-34). The people hoped that, through such an intense ritual of confession, they would be cleansed of their sin and forgiven by God (Lev. 16:30).

Special fast days were sometimes called and observed in ancient Israel or among their neighbors, to show repentance, avert disasters, and/or express grief. Jeremiah (36:6, 9) mentions a fast when Nebuchadnezzar threatens Judah. Zechariah (7:3-7) refers to fasting in mournful memory of Jerusalem falling to the Babylonians. Joel (1:2-4, 13-14) called for fasting when the people faced a devastating plague of locusts. In Esther (4:3, 16; 9:31), fasting is part of the effort to avert destruction of the Jews.

We do not know what Jonah anticipates from his five-word announcement delivered some place partway into the city. The response, however, exceeds the hopes and dreams of the most optimistic prophet. Everyone in Nineveh, from most important to least, from oldest to youngest, from biggest to smallest—all of them respond with the ritual of confession and repentance (3:5b). As for Jonah himself, he has disappeared from the scene, apparently going outside the city to watch what happens (4:5).

3:6-9 *Response of the King*

It is difficult to interpret the response of the king. On one hand, this king's behavior appears exemplary. Jeremiah could only wish that the king of Judah would have responded half as well as the king of Nineveh. In response to Jeremiah's call for repentance in the face of disaster, the people proclaimed a fast (36:5-10). But King Jehoiakim burned the prophet's written announcement piece by piece (36:23-24) and ordered Jeremiah and his scribe, Baruch, arrested (36:26).

By contrast, the narrator provides a ponderous picture of the king of Nineveh rising from the throne, removing his royal robes, putting on the clothes of repentance, and sitting in the ashes of shame (3:6). Then the scene takes a comic turn. The king, after conferring with his advisers, proclaims a ritual fast, like the one already called for and carried out by the people. Yet the king goes the people one better. He includes the entire human community and also the animals! (3:7). The king directs that everyone abstain from food and even from water. He declares that the people be dressed in the traditional clothes of shame and confession; the animals shall be clothed in sackcloth of confession as well! (3:8).

Some read this royal proclamation as a portrayal of an exemplary king. It may be that the narrative laughs a bit at the king's ponderous piety. The people have already done what is necessary. The king's action adds little but extravagance to the simple confession and ritual by the people of Nineveh.

Nevertheless, the king's proclamation does explicitly set out the purpose and hope for the ritual of confession and fasting. He directs everyone to *"turn from their evil ways and from . . . violence"* (3:8b). Once again, we meet the word *evil (ra'ah)*. First God (1:2), and now the king, describes the way of life in Nineveh as *evil*. In a poetic two-part statement, the proclamation supplements the description of *evil* with the word *violence [Poetry]*. Indeed, the stories and pictures about Assyria as an empire and Nineveh in particular emphasize that this was a violent people *[Nineveh]*.

The king directs the people to *call* out to God (cf. the sailors, 1:14). He gives voice to the hope inherent in the ritual of confession and repentance. Perhaps God will *repent* and *turn from* anger, so that Nineveh will not perish. We are not used to thinking of God as repenting *(nakham)*. More commonly, the translations say *relent* (NASB), *change his mind* (NRSV), or *have compassion* (NIV). In general, *nakham* designates a situation in which one regrets and repents of an action committed or planned (Wolff, 1986:154). In the prophetic literature, it normally refers to the decision of God to forgo a previously anticipated action of judgment in response to prophetic intercession (Amos 7:3, 6) or community confession (Jer. 18:8; cf. 36:7).

The royal proclamation does not presume on God's decision. Instead, it introduces the hope for divine compassion with a dramatic *"Who knows?"* (3:9). The desire that drives the king's command to his people repeats the ship captain's command to Jonah, *"So that we do not perish"* (3:9; 1:6). Through the ritual of fasting and shame, the Ninevites have symbolically touched death (Ackerman, 1987:239). By acknowledging the possibility of death, the Ninevites pray for life.

Action of God 3:10

The hope of the people of Nineveh becomes God's decision. Motivated by their act of turning away from *evil*, God *repents* or *relents* from the intended *evil*. The *evil* (*calamity*, NRSV; *destruction*, NIV) that God has planned will not happen.

Obviously, we find here two different nuances for the word *evil* (*ra'ah*). With regard to the Ninevites, *evil* refers to their violent and wicked actions. Yet the same word describes God's intended action of judgment. In one sense, these are two different things, human wickedness and divine judgment. However, they both participate in the web of violence and destruction that consumes the earth. The Ninevites decide no longer to initiate and or augment violence. God responds by withholding divine judgment that, though it would accomplish justice, would do so at the cost of more violence. With an emphatic summarizing sentence, the narrator declares that God *did not do it*.

The story of God's case against Nineveh is over. The tension that drove the narrative from the first sentence is now resolved: *"Go at once to Nineveh, . . . and cry out against it"* (1:2). The prophetic task has been successfully completed: (1) prophetic announcement of disaster, (2) the response of repentance, and (3) the action of divine forgiveness (Jer. 18:7-8). The final statement, *[God] did not do it*, provides the period at the end of the narrative. For God and for Nineveh, the story is over. For Jonah, it is not over!

THE TEXT IN BIBLICAL CONTEXT

The Sign of Jonah

The Gospels of Matthew and Luke refer to the "sign of Jonah" (Matt. 12:38-42; 16:4; Luke 11:29-32). These NT references to the "sign of Jonah" have stimulated the imagination of the Christian community. Quotations like Matthew 12:40 are in part responsible for the use of Jonah as prototype of Jesus in early Christian art: "For just as Jonah was three days and three nights in the belly of the sea monster, so for three days and three nights the Son of Man will be in the heart of the earth." However, the emphasis in NT references to the "sign of Jonah" directs our attention more to Jonah in Nineveh (Jon. 3) than Jonah in the great fish (Jon. 2).

According to Luke and Matthew, Jesus referred to the "sign of Jonah" in announcing judgment on "this generation" (Luke 11:29). Luke pictured the preaching of Jesus as similar to the preaching of Jonah in Nineveh. Jesus' presence and message constituted a call for repentance in "this generation" just as surely as did Jonah's proclamation in Nineveh.

Indeed, with the Jesus event, "this generation" even had "something greater than Jonah" happening in their midst, making the call to repentance more clear and more urgent (Luke 11:32; cf. Matt. 12:41). Yet there was a difference between Nineveh and "this generation." Most of Jesus' hearers failed to repent in response to his proclamation. Thus Nineveh's repentance stands as a condemnation of the refusal of "this generation" to respond in the same way.

In Matthew's Gospel, the comparison of Jonah and Jesus is similar to that in Luke, but a bit more complicated. In Matthew, Jesus' opponents demand a sign, a request designed to discredit Jesus (Matt. 12:38). Jesus refuses their demand except for the "sign of Jonah." Nor does Matthew tell us exactly what constitutes the "sign." However, the narrative is clear that God will validate Jesus' ministry in a way reminiscent of the validation of Jonah's ministry (Gardner: 206). Just as God delivered Jonah from death in the belly of the fish, so God will deliver Jesus from the "belly/heart" of the earth (Matt. 12:40). The Ninevites, who did repent from Jonah's preaching, will judge those who refuse to repent and acknowledge the person and work of Jesus. After all, with Jesus, "this generation" encounters "something greater" as they hear a prophet greater than Jonah, and a sage wiser than Solomon (Matt. 12:41-42).

The NT church found in the repentance of Nineveh an amazing story. Regrettably, this story of repentance was not duplicated in their day, even though their "generation" was confronted with One even greater than Jonah. The "sign of Jonah," in whatever way that is to be interpreted, remained both as a warning and a hope. *Evil* persists in each generation, as does the call for repentance. People do respond to the call, often people whom we would not expect to answer. Others do not respond.

THE TEXT IN THE LIFE OF THE CHURCH
Divine Freedom and the Promise of Forgiveness

According to the narrative, the citizens of Nineveh (and their king) understood both the reality of judgment and the possibility of forgiveness. The Ninevites did not presume on divine forgiveness. They did not even presume that their repentance would result in forgiveness. Indeed, the text carefully protects God's freedom to decide.

Both the Jewish and the Christian community have continued to live between the promise of forgiveness and divine freedom to decide such matters. The Jewish calendar has embodied the repentance-forgiveness theology in its most sacred day, Yom Kippur (Day of Atonement), when the story of Jonah is read (Simon, 1999: vii). The prayers of Yom Kippur lead the community in confession and assurance of divine forgiveness. Nevertheless, the prayers recognize that the response of God to the petition remains a divine decision, not guaranteed either by the correctness of the ritual or even the sincerity of the petitioner.

Sometimes Christian theology has emphasized the assurance of forgiveness and sometimes divine freedom. The early Pietists and Anabaptists lived out the conviction that the prophetic paradigm holds true for individuals as well as peoples/nations: announcement of God's word, repentance from sin, and forgiveness by God. In Crefeld (Krefeld), Germany, John Lobach (1683-1750) described his conversion to Pietism in such a way:

> In this was my heart touched by the word of the loving God. . . . I began to confess with a sorrowful heart all the sins which I had ever committed. I experienced then finally a living solace and assurance in my soul, . . . that Jesus would cleanse me from all sins. He would grant me the Holy Spirit to assure me of the inheritance of the saints. (Durnbaugh, 1986:195-6)

The Pietists and Anabaptists used this threefold promise as a theological model for relationships between church members as well as with God. Using Luke 17:4 as his text, Alexander Mack asserted,

> Without the admission of the sin, there is no forgiveness of sin, not even by God. Just so must believers be minded that if the sinner admits his sin, he must be forgiven. (Durnbaugh, 1986:337)

For the most part, the early Pietists and Anabaptists expressed the conviction that upon hearing the word of God preached, and upon confession of sin, the individual or the community would be forgiven. There was little talk of the freedom of divine sovereignty expressed in the king of Nineveh's declaration: *"Who knows? God may relent and change his mind"* (Jon. 3:9).

Nevertheless, the Pietists and Anabaptists did not lose sight of the fact that fundamentally, forgiveness rests in freedom of divine decision. In 1744 the anonymous writer of *A Humble Gleam* placed God's decision to forgive at the beginning of the process of hearing and repenting rather than at the end: "No beginning of true conversion occurs without the finger of God appearing, . . . so that the words of God may penetrate the heart" (Stoffer: 93-4). Christians, especially in the believers church tradition, continue to emphasize both sides of the theological equation: (1) affirming that all who hear and repent will be forgiven, and (2) cautioning against a theology that makes divine forgiveness the automatic result of correct ritual. Finally, the king of Nineveh is correct: *"Who knows? God may relent . . . so that we do not perish."*

Outside the City
Jonah 4:1-11

PREVIEW

After Jonah 3:10, the scene abruptly shifts. The narrator turns our attention to Jonah, who is situated east of Nineveh, waiting to see what will happen to the city (4:5). This scene is the only one not initiated by God's action or word. In terms of the narrative tension established by the instruction of God in chapter 1, the story ends with chapter 3. The evil in Nineveh that has come before God (1:2) has been dealt with by the prophet more or less as commissioned. The city and God have turned away from evil (3:10).

Jonah, however, has leftover agenda. This episode opens with Jonah's problem and closes with God's response. Whether God's response adequately deals with Jonah's concern or further exacerbates the problem depends on the reader's decision. Throughout the story, the narrator has kept the readers involved with the people in the drama. No place is that more true than in the concluding episode. In fact, the narrative ends with God's question: *"And should I not be concerned about Nineveh?"* (4:11). The answer to that question remains the responsibility of the reader. As we shall see, either a "Yes" or a "No" leaves us with difficulties.

This is the first time in the narrative that the two main characters have entered into genuine dialogue. God has spoken to Jonah (1:2; 3:2), and Jonah has acted in response (1:3; 3:3a, 4b). Jonah has prayed to God (2:1-9), and God has acted (2:10). Here, finally, the two protagonists directly engage one another, in a fashion. The initiative lies with Jonah, and God basically answers with questions. God opens the final speech with a statement (3:10), but that only serves to set up the question that constitutes the heart of God's last word. A narrative unit that has begun with God's word of instruction (3:2) ends with a divine question (4:11). With 4:11, the story may end for God and Jonah, but not for the readers. We are left to answer God's final question, not quickly or naively, but while aware of both the anguish of Jonah and the compassion of God.

In this episode, the combination of narration and dialogue makes it difficult to develop an outline. Nevertheless, exactly this juxtaposition drives the narrative to its conclusion. Hence, an outline will serve best that displays the movement from narration to dialogue, then back to narration, concluding with a final dialogue between Jonah and God. The reader will notice that a statement about or by Jonah opens each narration and dialogue. All the other episodes have belonged to God. This one, however, is Jonah's.

OUTLINE
Introductory Narration, 4:1

Dialogue: Jonah and God, 4:2-4

Narration, 4:5-8a

Dialogue: Jonah and God, 4:8b-11

EXPLANATORY NOTES

Introductory Narration 4:1

The decision of God and Nineveh to turn away from *evil* has caused *great evil* to come upon Jonah. By translating *ra'ah* as *displeasure* (NRSV, NIV, NASB), the English versions lose the convergence of the two key words that have led us throughout this narrative: *evil* and *great*. At this point, the narrator merges the two words: *great evil* comes upon Jonah. Indeed, Jonah burns with anger.

At this point Jonah is directly involved in the web of *evil* that has connected the various characters in the drama. The narrative has used *evil* in a variety of ways, from the wickedness of Nineveh (1:2; 3:8), to the catastrophe facing the sailors at sea (1:7-8), and the judgment/disaster that God plans to bring upon Nineveh (3:10). But despite each different nuance, *evil* carries pain, suffering, and even violence. Heretofore in the narrative, the *evil* has been dealt with so as to promote life on land and on sea, for the people and for the animals.

Jonah, however, feels left out of that resolution. In a sense, the *evil* that has touched all the characters now burns in Jonah. At this point, many readers find it easy to condemn Jonah. Can he not see the magnificent drama that has played itself out? The sailors frantically cried out to any God and finally turned to the worship of the LORD. Nineveh, the city of *evil*, has turned around. God has decided not to carry through the divine intention of judgment/evil. *Evil* that has come before God and affected God's own intentions, has been resolved in peace. How can Jonah not rejoice?

We usually find it easy to rebuke someone who is angry. Anger brings its own condemnation. In the shadow of God's compassion, how much more should we denounce Jonah's anger! Such quick censure of Jonah may be premature. We may not take Jonah as seriously as his situation warrants. God does not dismiss Jonah as easily as we tend to. Perhaps first we should hear what the angry prophet has to say.

Dialogue: Jonah and God 4:2-4

Jonah opens the dialogue by addressing God; the narrator says he *prayed* (4:2). At last, Jonah explains his initial refusal to accept the divine commission. It seems that Jonah has already anticipated the outcome of the adventure in Nineveh. All along, Jonah has understood God. From song and sacred liturgy, Jonah has been taught that compassion, mercy, and unending love lie deepest in the divine soul.

Jonah quotes back to God a traditional doxology of divine compassion: *"You are a gracious God and merciful, slow to anger, and abounding in steadfast love, and ready to relent from punishing"* (4:2). These words sound familiar, even to current listeners. With some variations, they appear as a common doxology in Psalms and in prophetic and narrative literature (Ps. 86:15; 103:8; 111:4; 145:8; Exod. 34:6; Num. 14:18; Nah. 1:3; Neh. 9:17, 31). Only in Joel 2:13 do we find the doxology including the final phrase *(relent from punishing)* as found in Jonah 4:2. In Joel, the doxology functions as the basis for a prophetic admonition:

> Return to the LORD, your God,
>   for he is gracious and merciful,
> slow to anger, and abounding in steadfast love,
>   and relents from punishing. (Joel 2:13)

Nineveh has met the conditions that Joel set out, and God has acted accordingly. Everything has gone as Jonah has expected, and that has become Jonah's problem.

Frequently interpreters have concluded that Jonah does not want to be shown as a false prophet, one whose announcements do not come true (Deut. 18). But deciding between true and false prophets does not seem to be the issue here (Simon, 1999: x). Neither the narrator nor Jonah focuses on Jonah's personal life and vocation. Even more commonly, Jonah is accused of being a narrow nationalist, unable to handle a God who loves "Gentiles." However, the opposition between Jews and Gentiles does not seem inherent in the story (Bickerman: 27-8, Clements: 18-20). That antagonism seems more a product of church interpretation.

Throughout the narrative, one of the key words is *evil*. The way in which God deals with wickedness in Nineveh has brought *evil* to Jonah (4:1). Jonah has feared all along that God would let compassion override justice. The problem for Jonah is not that Nineveh is Gentile, but that Nineveh is evil. God knows it, and Israel bears the scars of Nineveh's evil. God's compassion in the light of Nineveh's evil is precisely what Jonah will not condone (LaCocque, 1981:84).

Jonah's problem is the reverse of Job's. The suffering of Job, the world's most righteous man (Job 1:1, 8), caused him to wonder if justice was absent in God's actions. For Jonah, the opposite is the case. The pardoning of the wicked causes him to raise the same question (Freedman: 30-1). For both Job and Jonah, life is not worth living if God is not fair (Job 3; Jon. 4:3). God's action makes a mockery of earnest human effort toward justice (Eagleton: 243). Hence, Jonah shouts the ancient doxology of assurance as a complaint against God.

Jonah is not the only prophet to ask God to take him out of his misery. Most early listeners to this story would remember that Elijah addressed God with a similar request: "It is enough; now, O LORD, take away my life, for I am no better than my ancestors" (1 Kings 19:4b). Elijah's request came because he had been unsuccessful in calling Israel back to the worship of the LORD. Ironically, Jonah's request came after he had been magnificently successful in calling Nineveh to worship God. Indeed, Jonah's situation now displays the same mixture of irony and tears that has accompanied the prophet throughout the narrative. Hopefully, the reader can see both the humor and the tears and not just one or the other.

God does not take on the agenda Jonah has set out in his complaint (Trible, 1996:519). Instead, God responds to Jonah with a question: *"Is it right for you to be angry?"* (4:4). Is God asking for information with this question? *[Questions]*. Is this a rhetorical question that presumes the answer no? We often read it that way. Later in this episode, Jonah will actually answer a similar question with yes (4:9). Does the question have an accusatory edge, the counterpoint to Jonah's accusation? That decision rests in the hands of the reader. A question requiring such reader involvement marks this as a didactic question. In fact, all of God's questions to Jonah throughout this scene aim to teach.

Narration   4:5-8a

God's question to Jonah receives no reply. Twice before, when God has addressed Jonah directly, there is no verbal reply (1:3; 3:3a). On those two occasions, Jonah has departed: once in disobedience (1:3), the other in compliance (3:3a). This time Jonah says nothing and apparently does nothing. We can only wonder how Jonah feels while being addressed by God's didactic question in the midst of his anger.

Instead of an immediate response from Jonah, we find a narrative comment that he has gone *east of the city* and built himself a booth, *waiting to see* what will happen (4:5). Some scholars treat this as an action that Jonah does at that moment, assuming the dialogue in 4:2-4 may have occurred in Nineveh (Fretheim, 1977:122-3). Many, however, agree that this is a flashback, with the narrator inserting a comment to inform us of something that has occurred earlier: Jonah has left and has situated himself to watch the city from the east. At other times in this narrative, we have encountered such sudden scene shifts and received delayed information (as in 1:7, 10). Here the information serves to abruptly close off the initial dialogue between Jonah and God.

Jonah has built a booth. Many have suggested that Jonah's booth is inadequate, perhaps a few stones and dead leaves (Stuart: 504). The narrative, however, does not describe the construction. God's control of nature eventually provides more relief than Jonah's booth, but we need not assume that Jonah is a poor builder or has inferior materials. Instead, the narrative tells us that Jonah has built a sacred booth, one that is traditional in his religious heritage. The narrator describes Jonah's booth by using the same word *(sukkah)* that identifies the shelters built for the Festival of Booths/Tabernacles/Ingathering (esp. of the vintage; Lev. 23:39-43; Neh. 8:13-18). This autumnal harvest festival commemorated God's protection of Israel in the wilderness. Perhaps Jonah's concern also involves divine protection. For him, it requires divine destruction of Israel's enemies (LaCocque, 1990:152).

God acts, not to destroy Nineveh, but to provide protection for Jonah (4:6). Once again, God uses elements of nature. At sea, God has hurled a wind and instructed a fish (1:4, 17; 2:10). On land, God appoints a bush. We do not know what kind of bush any more than we know the identity of the fish. Whatever kind, the bush has a specific purpose: to provide shade for Jonah's head and to *save him from his evil* (4:6, EFR; *discomfort,* NRSV, NIV). Jonah's construction provides *shade* (4:5). God's construction has a dual function: *shade* and *deliverance.* The plant will do for Jonah what his ceremonial booth cannot. The plant will save Jonah from the *evil* that has overcome him.

The plant transforms Jonah's *great evil* (4:1, EFR) into *great joy* (4:6b, EFR; *very happy,* NRSV, NIV). The narrator does not tell us exactly what has happened to accomplish this transformation. We see it only from the perspective of an onlooker *[Narrator].* Why does this enable Jonah to move from suicidal depression to ecstasy? Perhaps the plant satisfies Jonah's selfish concern for his own comfort, as some suggest (Burrows: 97). More likely, Jonah experiences God's plant as a reaffirmation of the divine promise of protection, symbolized by his sacred booth. In building a sacred booth celebrating God's protection of Israel, Jonah remembers God's justice in the past, and longs for it in the present: Jonah is *waiting to see what would become of the city* (4:5). In the plant, Jonah rejoices over God's response.

God has not finished appointing. God *appointed* a worm to destroy the plant, and the sun and wind to *beat down* on Jonah (4:7-8). The worm attacks the plant, and the sun and wind attack Jonah. The narrator tells us that the plant withers, and Jonah grows faint, asking once again to die (4:8a). God's appointments have taken Jonah from depression to ecstasy and back to suicidal depression. This time, the desire for death has a physical as well as a psychological cause. According to the narrator, Jonah asks his life *(nepheš)* to expire!

Dialogue: Jonah and God 4:8b-11

Jonah's oral request to die reiterates and adds urgency to the statement of the narrator (4:8b; Alter, 1981:77-8). God rejoins the conversation by repeating the divine question: *"Is it right for you to be angry?"* (4:4, 9a). God's inquiry is not an exact repetition. This time God specifies Jonah's target of anger: *"about the bush."* The narrative attention has shifted from events in Nineveh to Jonah's location *east of the city*. Destruction has not come on Nineveh, but does threaten Jonah—through the worm on the plant and through the heat. So we are not surprised by Jonah's reply, *"Yes, angry enough to die"* (4:9b).

God's action and question have served to reinforce Jonah's anger at divine injustice. Now Jonah's own experience with destruction at the hands of God has convinced him that God is not just (Fretheim, 1977:126). His physical weakness and his theological rage prompt Jonah to a new stance in the dialogue. Jonah answers God directly, *"Yes, angry enough to die."*

God, however, does not intend the episode with the bush to be vindictive, but to be instructive (4:10-11). The plant has come to Jonah as a gift from God, not as something Jonah has earned (4:10). Jonah has become deeply attached to a plant that appears one day and is gone the next. The Hebrew word behind *are concerned* refers to "sympathy," "compassion," "mercy." Jonah has been moved to tears over the bush. His tears over the plant establish "compassion" as a legitimate reason for saving a creature from destruction (Ceresko: 584).

Of how much more value is the *great city* of Nineveh (4:11). Here God uses a typical argument from lesser to greater (cf. Matt. 12:9-14; Wolff, 1959:853). God's argument concludes with at least a smile, if not laughter. Nineveh is quantitatively great, a population of greater than 120 thousand, plus *many animals* (4:11). However, their quality does not match their size. God says the Ninevites do not know *"their right hand from their left."* Whether we take that as a reflection on their wisdom or uprightness does not matter. People and animals, whoever they may be, call forth God's compassion.

Some interpreters seek to limit the reference of those who do not *"know their right hand from their left"* to mentally deficient adults or young children. Phyllis Trible correctly notes that any such limitation lacks evidence in the text (1996:523). The direct and only antecedent of this phrase is *"more than a hundred and twenty thousand persons."*

At this point, God does not even make repentance a qualification for divine compassion. By stating that they do not *"know their right hand from their left,"* God may even be admitting that Nineveh's repentance cannot be trusted (Freedman: 31). Instead, God's answer asserts the supremacy of compassion, even if that puts at risk the neat coherence of God's world (Heschel, 2:67). Justice provides fairness and coherence in the world. Divine compassion can undermine that coherence and thus sometimes even feel unfair. Which do we prefer?

THE TEXT IN BIBLICAL CONTEXT

The Concluding Question

Many readers conclude that the narrator invites us to side with God over Jonah (Ackerman, 1987:242). That may be true in part, but this ought not to override the fact that the story ends with a question and not with a statement. Only Nahum has a similar ending (3:19). In Nahum, the concluding dirge against Nineveh makes the final question rhetorical: "For who has ever escaped your [Nineveh's] endless cruelty?" Jonah 4:11 allows us to wonder whether this prophet is yet convinced. The cry for divine justice runs deep in the biblical tradition and the human soul.

The prophetic tradition frequently pictures God internally at war between compassion and justice. God instructs the prophet Isaiah to preach in such a way as to prevent Israel from turning to God and being healed (Isa. 6:10). Repentance might short-circuit justice. In Hosea, God struggles with the same problem, but from a different side. For Hosea, God's urge to compassion cannot be denied even at the cost of justice (Hos. 11:9).

The NT church affirmed that in Christ divine compassion and love has become God's way of relating to humankind in the world (1 John 4:7-12). God's free act of reconciliation (Rom. 5:6-11), breaks even the required connection between repentance and forgiveness! While we were still weak, while we were still sinners, Christ died for us (5:6, 8).

Nevertheless, the cry for justice cannot easily be set aside. Faced with oppression, persecution, and even martyrdom, the early Christians envisioned an end, a final judgment, when God would bring justice (cf. Rev. 4–10). With Jonah's perception, the absence of justice leaves him caught in an ocean of evil. Can a speech of repentance, no matter how sincere, or a moment of fasting, no matter how earnest, erase the violence and death that Nineveh has visited on Israel, Judah, and other vulnerable people? *[Nineveh].* Where amid the compassion God has showed toward Nineveh do we find fairness for the victims of Assyrian violence?

In the same dialogue, God's speech raises the question of whether repentance is required for compassion. Jonah insists that repentance is not sufficient for sinners to receive forgiveness. By ending with a question, the narrative allows the listener to feel Jonah's anguish in an unfair world, as well as God's deep compassion for all people and animals. We do not understand Jesus' parable of the laborers if we easily dismiss the request for fairness, coming from workers who have labored all day (Matt. 20:1-16).

THE TEXT IN THE LIFE OF THE CHURCH

Mystery of Divine Compassion

The Christian church must never ignore the cry for justice. Many Christians, however, have sought to live out the divine *yet* as stated by Abraham Heschel (2:67) at the conclusion of his comments on Jonah: "Yet, beyond justice and anger lies the mystery of compassion." The mystery of compassion often appears as nonsense in a world more comfortable with retributive or even distributive justice. Uriel Simon forcefully states Jonah's concern: "What remains of the rule of law when iniquity that merits annihilation can be wiped away by a few days of penance" (1999:35). *Yet,* beyond justice lies the mystery of compassion.

Christians in the believers church tradition have struggled with the mystery of compassion as their faith and practice has developed. Although emerging as a persecuted minority, they insisted that justice in history must be left to God. The faithful were called on to suffer as did Christ (cf. Menno: 42-50). At all costs, they should avoid taking up the sword, even for justice.

Extending that affirmation, the church has sought to witness not only to Christ's suffering and patience, but also to the mystery of divine compassion. This happened early as Anabaptists and Pietists extended hospitality to many different refugees fleeing religious and political oppression (Graber: 165). Such expressions of compassion have steadily gained more organizational visibility, undergirded by Matthew 25:40: "Truly, I say to you, as you did it to one of the least of these my brethren, you did it to me" (RSV; Eller: 128-34).

This kind of life and practice has always been controversial. Some have wondered if the mystery of divine compassion has been replaced by a doctrine of Christian service. If so, the church acts as a humanitarian relief organization, sometimes more universal or efficient than private or governmental relief, and frequently as a competing organization. In compassion as in service, we may lose our center as a community that in awe worships the mystery of divine compassion.

Others suggest that the concern for compassion has muted the cry for justice in places where fairness needs to be the primary concern. Victims of evil and violence receive food, clothing, and Band-Aid care rather than justice.

The church must ever discern how to live faithfully out of God's final question: *"Should I not have compassion on Nineveh?"* (4:11, NASB). Yet the church must do so without belittling the anguish of Jonah when, beyond anger and justice, lies the mystery of compassion.

Outline of Jonah

The Unfulfilled Prophetic Mission	**1:1—2:11**
The Commissioning of Jonah	1:1-3
The Word from the L<small>ORD</small>	1:1-2
Introduction of the Characters	1:1
Divine Word	1:2
The Response of Jonah	1:3
Statement of Flight	1:3a
Detail of His Action	1:3b
The Drama at Sea	1:4—2:10
On the Sea	1:4-16
Introduction	1:4
Battling the Storm	1:5-6
Divining the Cause	1:7-10
Quieting the Storm	1:11-15
Conclusion	1:16
Under the Sea	1:17—2:10
Introductory Narration	1:17
Prayer of Jonah	2:1-10
Introduction	2:1
Report of Distress and Deliverance	2:2-7
Praise and Promise	2:8-9
Concluding Narration	2:10
The Unfulfilled Prophet	**3:1—4:11**
The Recommissioning of Jonah	3:1-3a

The Word from the LORD	3:1-2
Introduction of the Characters	3:1
Divine Word	3:2
The Response of Jonah	3:3a
The Drama on Land	3:3b—4:11
In the City	3:3b-10
Introduction	3:3b
Announcement of Disaster	3:4
Report of the Response	3:5-9
Response of the People	3:5
Response of the King	3:6-9
Action of God	3:10
Outside the City	4:1-11
Introductory Narration	4:1
Dialogue: Jonah and God	4:2-4
Narration	4:5-8a
Dialogue: Jonah and God	4:8b-11

Esther

Esther: The Orphan Queen

OVERVIEW

The Orphan Queen

The biblical book of Esther narrates the dramatic story of a woman unexpectedly thrust into a royal role in ancient Persia. Esther, not born into palace life, has grown up as one of the least among those in the realm—vulnerable in three ways. In a culture where family provides protection and identity, Esther is an orphan. In a culture defined and controlled by men, Esther is a woman. In the powerful Persian Empire, Esther is a Jew. The story of how this Jewish orphan woman becomes the decisive royal figure in all the realm has thrilled and perplexed readers for as long as the narrative has been retold.

As one would expect for a culturally vulnerable person, the events that define Esther's life are not of her own choosing. After dismissing Queen Vashti, the Persian king appoints a royal search committee to choose a new queen. Under the coaching of her cousin Mordecai and the royal eunuch Hegai, Esther appears as a candidate before King Ahasuerus. She wins the king's favor and becomes Queen Esther. Thrust into the middle of court intrigue and ethnic tension, Esther as queen finds herself nearly as vulnerable as she has been as an orphan.

While the book narrates the story of an unusual woman living in an ancient culture, Esther actually struggles with problems facing minority and/or subordinate persons or groups living in many times and cultures. Sidnie Ann White reminds us that subordinate communities, lacking political, economic, religious, and cultural standing, must decide how to gain whatever control they can over their own lives (1989:167). To gain some measure of security and satisfaction, minorities must always make their way within the majority culture in order. This has been the Jewish struggle throughout the ages. Living as a minority community, dependent on the attitude and actions of the majority, has kept Jews always in a precarious position.

Controversy and Concerns

The narrative of Esther has aroused as much controversy as any biblical book. Interpreters have questioned almost everything about it, including the moral character of its main figure, the significance of its theology, and the quality of its values.

The absence of any direct mention of God has troubled readers. In biblical narratives like Joseph (Gen. 37–50) and Ruth, God appears as a quiet, background presence, not actively intervening in the course of events, as we find in other biblical narratives such as Exodus and Joshua. Unlike any other biblical story, however, the Hebrew narrative of Esther lacks any explicit mention of God.

To be sure, not all versions of Esther lack mention of God. The narrative of Esther preserved in an ancient Greek translation (the Septuagint) not only names God, but portrays an active divine role. Even in the Hebrew version of Esther, some interpreters have insisted that God is indirectly mentioned. Several readers point to Esther 4:14, Mordecai's only direct speech to Esther: *"For if you keep silence at such a time as this, relief and deliverance will arise for the Jews from another quarter."* These readers suggest that *another quarter* indirectly refers to God.

Other interpreters have focused on Esther's call for a fast (4:16). In some biblical texts, a fast implies a prayer of confession and/or intercession, whether or not God is explicitly mentioned. Be that as it may, the absence of the divine name from the narrative of Esther makes the book unique in the Bible, and for some readers raises questions about its spiritual value.

Some readers object to the story on ethical grounds, pointing specifically to the glorification of violence: *So the Jews struck down all their enemies with the sword, slaughtering, and destroying them, and did as they pleased to those who hated them* (9:5). Most readers remember that Esther is not the only biblical narrative that seems indifferent to or even rejoices in acts of violence. The so-called conquest narratives in the OT (Josh., Judg.) and the apocalyptic narratives in the NT (Rev.) portray violence exercised either by God or at God's command. In Esther, nevertheless, the story not only uses violence as acceptable defense in conflict; it also seems to glorify the slaughter.

While some readers lift up Esther as a model and hero, others believe Vashti provides a more exemplary model than Esther (Wyler: 111-35). Vashti refuses to cooperate with the king's command that she appear at the banquet to show off her beauty. By contrast, Esther accommodates herself to the royal ethos, using her beauty and shrewdness to win the security she seeks for her people. Esther's effort does not gain independent stature for her. As the story concludes, it is Mordecai rather than Esther who stands next to King Ahasuerus (10:3). Taken altogether, this prompts some readers to be carefully selective in referring to Esther as a model for women or men.

Luther's well-known comment about Esther has struck a chord in many readers: "I am so hostile to it that I wish it did not exist." Regrettably, much of Luther's objection to the narrative came from his antagonism to Judaism. For a variety of reasons, the book's inclusion in the canon (the accepted, authoritative books of the Bible) was in dispute well into the fourth century. Under the influence of Augustine, meetings of the Western (Roman) church at Hippo (393) and Carthage (397) affirmed its canonicity. But official acceptance has not quieted the controversy that continues to accompany the story of Esther.

Different Versions of Esther

In the Christian community, the Protestants and Roman Catholics have used different versions of the narrative of Esther. The ancient Jewish and Christian communities had available several different editions of the narrative. Only two, however, are still in use, and a third has been partially preserved on an ancient manuscript.

The Protestant churches have generally translated Esther from the Hebrew version handed down by the Jewish rabbis in the Masoretic Text (MT). Hence, Protestant Christians have joined the Jewish community in using the Hebrew narrative as their canonical version of Esther. In the MT, the narrative is shorter than its Greek counterpart. It lacks any direct reference to God. The MT version does not have any of the several prayers found in the Greek edition of Esther. This Hebrew text of the narrative (as translated in NRSV OT) will serve as the primary basis for this commentary.

Roman Catholic and Eastern Orthodox Christians employ a Greek edition of the story of Esther. This Greek text, known as the

Septuagint (LXX), also goes back to an original Hebrew text. The LXX and the MT are similar in the parallel parts. Yet as far as we now know, neither is derived from the other. Instead, they represent two separate versions preserved by the Jewish and Christian communities.

Unlike the MT, the LXX emphasizes the religious piety of Mordecai and Esther. For example, in Esther 4 the Greek version of Esther contains two lengthy prayers, one by Mordecai and one by Esther. In his prayer, Mordecai professes God as Creator and Sovereign, and affirms his own innocence in the conflict with Haman. Then he addresses God with a prayer of petition: *"Spare your people! For men are seeking our ruin and plan to destroy your ancient heritage"* (4:17f, JB; cf. 13:15, NRSV Apocrypha, in Addition C).

In her prayer, Esther voices her faithfulness to God: *"Nor has your handmaid found pleasure from the day of her promotion until now except in you, Lord, God of Abraham"* (4:17y, JB; cf. 14:18, NRSV Apocrypha, in Addition C). She also petitions God both in behalf of her people and for herself: *"Save us from the hand of the wicked, and free me from my fear"* (4:17z, JB; cf. 14:19, NRSV Apocrypha, in Addition C).

Beyond the prayers, the Greek version expands the Esther narrative in other ways as well. In Esther 3, the LXX includes the letter of King Ahasuerus authorizing the extermination of the enemy people as identified by Haman (cf. 13:1-7, NRSV Apocrypha = Addition B). The MT only states that the king wrote such a letter (3:12). Similarly, in Esther 8 the Greek version provides a text of the royal letter announcing Haman's execution and informing all citizens that the Jews have the right to exterminate those who seek to destroy them (cf. 16:1-24, NRSV Apocrypha = Addition E).

A third version of the Esther narrative has been preserved in Greek on an ancient manuscript usually called the Alpha Text (AT). Many scholars believe the AT represents the most ancient version of Esther (Clines, 1984:71ff.). This old version, though similar to the MT and the LXX, differs from both in some passages, and in other passages agrees with each one against the other. For example, the AT has no suggestion that Persian law is irrevocable, an element used by the king in the canonical versions to explain why he cannot simply cancel Haman's decree to destroy the Jews. The AT also does not connect Esther with the Festival of Purim. This suggests that in some communities, the story of Esther may have existed independently of that holiday.

Many interpreters have insisted that the (Greek) LXX version of Esther represents an effort to supplement the story, to bring it more in line with normative theology in Scripture. From this reasoning, they conclude that the Hebrew text (MT) is the more original. The (Greek) Alpha Text cautions us not to draw any quick conclusion that either the Jewish/Protestant or Catholic/Orthodox version of Esther should be assumed as more "original." Apparently the story was retold in slightly different ways in various ancient Christian and Jewish communities (Dorothy: 437-8).

A Festival Novella

The narrative of Esther exhibits the customary characteristics of the Hebrew novella *[Novella]*. The narrative plot is centered in the tension between Mordecai and Haman, especially in the royal decree Haman obtains to authorize the annihilation of Mordecai and his people (3:9-11). As it develops, the plot is resolved through a dramatic reversal. Haman, the one who has sought the destruction of Mordecai and the Jews, is himself executed—not only Haman, but his sons and hundreds of others are also killed (7:10; 9:6-15). Plot reversals shape distinctive features of the Esther narrative. Thus Haman goes from high office to the gallows, Vashti from queen to commoner, Esther from orphan to queen, and Mordecai from national enemy to honored royalty.

While sharing the narrative features common to Hebrew short story *[Short Story]*, the novella of Esther is both longer and more complex than many biblical short stories, such as Ruth and Jonah. The length itself affects the narrative features. The story contains more characters, and the reader sees them involved in a wide variety of situations. This allows for more development of the major characters.

For example, the reader first meets an obedient Esther as a contrast to Vashti, the disobedient queen. Thus we expect Esther to be submissive, and for a time she appears as such (Gunn/Fewell: 79). As the narrative develops, however, a different Esther emerges. She not only takes control of her life, but also exercises political power in behalf of others. By the end of the story, Esther appears as skillful and also as ruthless, requesting from the king an additional day to kill *enemies* in the capital city (9:5, 13).

Scholars frequently discuss whether this novella can appropriately be called a historical account (Clines, 1984a: 256-61). The narrative of Esther is set in the Persian Empire and reflects the character and life of that kingdom. Besides reflecting the opulence of the royal palace and banquets, the narrative uses distinctively Persian terms for specific objects and government officials.

Most interpreters agree, however, that the narrative itself frustrates attempts to extract a historical account of that era. Besides lacking external evidence for the names of the characters and events portrayed in the story, the narrative focuses on internal palace intrigue. It thus encourages the reader not to insist that the details be verified as historical data.

The character of Esther reflects the problem of trying to turn narrative details into historical data. According to the Greek historian, Herodotus, Amestris was the wife of the Persian king Xerxes. While one might wonder if the name *Esther* is a variation of *Amestris*, the latter was a Persian woman, not a Jewish orphan. Some have suggested that Amestris was actually Vashti, but that creates as many difficulties as equating Amestris with Esther (Clines, 1984a: 258-9).

Rather than a historical account, the narrative of Esther provides us an example of a festival novella. While the Alpha Text (see above) may indicate that the story was not always connected with the Festival of Purim, both the Hebrew and Greek canonical editions make that connection explicit and intentional. According to 9:26, the festival was named Purim after the term *Pur*. This refers back to 3:7, where *the lot (Pur)* was cast to determine the date of the annihilation of the Jews. The festival narrative connects Purim with the celebration that concludes with the annihilation of the enemies of the Jews and also insists, *"Never . . . should the commemoration of these days cease among their descendants"* (9:28).

As a festival narrative, Esther shares some similar characteristics with the Exodus story of the plagues in Egypt (Exod. 7–11). The account of the plagues provides the narrative grounding for the festival of Unleavened Bread and Passover, presented in Exodus 12: "This day shall be a day of remembrance for you. You shall celebrate it as a festival to the LORD; throughout your generations you shall observe it as a perpetual ordinance" (Exod. 12:14).

In the NT, Matthew 1 and Luke 2 function as a festival narrative for Christmas, and the Passion narrative (Mark 14–16 and parallels) for Easter. Unlike Exodus 12:14 and Esther 9:28, the NT narratives do not have any statement directing the establishment of Christmas and Easter celebrations. Nevertheless, these narratives all share a similar function in the life of the community of faith.

Meaning and Message

Athalya Brenner (1995:79) observes that the narrative of Esther is not a morality tale. In fact, few if any Hebrew stories can be reduced to the level of merely teaching a moral, intending to instruct readers on model behavior. The Esther novella seems unique in the absence of a moral to the story. Esther's commitment to help her people at the risk of her own life is seemingly the only dimension of this narrative that readers have found worthy of imitation. Granting that emphasis, the story of Esther points to other concerns and issues worthy of attention by the interpreting community of faith *[Interpreting Community]*.

Leadership has always proved to be a difficult undertaking. In this narrative, the designated leader, King Ahasuerus, fails at nearly every turn. Perhaps surprisingly, Ahasuerus does not fail because he is arbitrary and despotic. He consistently and unreflectively takes the advice of his counselors. Decisions resulting from his consultations range from frightening to funny. On advice of counsel, he deposes Queen Vashti, issues an order of annihilation of the Jews, and authorizes an elaborate display of honor for Mordecai. Ahasuerus fails because he is so dependent and disconnected from the significance of events in the palace.

Leadership by other royal figures in the novella appears equally ambiguous. Vashti decides to directly refuse a royal command, perhaps grounded in her conscientious objection to the public display of beauty demanded by the king. Vashti disappears from the story. In his dispute with Haman, Mordecai tries to exercise control over events through his adopted daughter, Esther. She takes the responsibility he gives her and carries it out, not as Mordecai directs, but in her own way. Both Haman and Esther seek to direct the course of events by manipulating the king. Esther succeeds; Haman fails.

What constitutes *good* leadership? The narrative does not answer that question. Ahasuerus "surrendered effective power" to those who knew how to use his love of honor, anxiety about events, and desire to be generous (Fox, 1991:1730). Esther and Haman become almost indistinguishable in their exercise of political manipulation, except that one works for good and the other for evil—a difference that does matter. Jon Levenson (14) observes that the story of Esther reflects the biblical tradition's long-standing skepticism about political power in general and royal politics in particular.

Perhaps, as Levenson suggests, the biblical tradition generally lifts up the value of a small-village form of social organization. Nevertheless, circumstances require Christians to function in a wide variety of political contexts, compelling them to use skills appropriate to the different situations. There is no single political strategy called for in every situation. The Gospels show Jesus as one who approached political power in a variety of ways, ranging from direct address to giving up his life.

Some strategies appropriate to one situation, such as noncompliance, may in other circumstances be ineffective and even counterproductive. Other options, such as skillful political maneuvering, may be effective but can be employed for evil even by good people. Esther employs her political skill to deliver the Jews from annihilation. Then she goes on to use her influence to prolong the slaughter of the *enemies*. A similar situation occurs in the biblical story of Joseph. Joseph used his political skill to save Canaan and Egypt from famine, but did so with an economic plan that enslaved the Egyptian people (Gen. 47:20-21).

On one hand, this narrative features the political strategies required of a minority in an alien setting. Esther, however, is not only the story of an ethnic (Jewish) minority. As the title of the novella makes clear, this is a story about a woman. The novella cannot be read without reference to issues of gender: the role of women and their options in social and political contexts. The narrative features two women, Vashti and Esther. The crisis is initiated by the decision of one and resolved by the determination of the other.

The story requires us to consider ways in which "women achieve their goals, especially in situations where they have little power" (Bellis: 216). Action in the political arena is inevitable even by those who, like Esther, prefer to avoid it. Faithful action cannot be reduced to a single good strategy. The success of women in the social and political realm is especially difficult in cultures where men have decided who has access to the political arena, and also what strategies are available and permissible.

The vagaries of royal politics constitute the stuff of this story. God is not mentioned, at least not directly. Nevertheless, David Clines correctly writes that Esther cannot be read simply as a story of human foibles and political cunning (Clines, 1984a: 270). The narrative does not see the world as a place where God intervenes to reverse misfortune, nor as a place where God is absent or uninterested. In Esther, the drama of life is the realm where God's will works itself out in the course of human events and in cooperation with all those of goodwill.

Michael Fox notes that a "coincidence is a miracle in which God prefers to remain anonymous" (Fox, 1991:241). In the book of Esther, God remains anonymous. That is precisely the arena of service for persons of faith. They need a stance of profound faith so that they can act in anticipation of the coming reign of God, even in the face of circumstances that seem to deny God's presence. This is all the more true in a world where God chooses to remain anonymous.

Finally as Adele Berlin writes, the story of Esther expects us to laugh (2001:xvi-xxii). The narrative shares many of the features of a comedy, including exaggeration, caricature and irony. She goes on to observe that the threatening world at the beginning of the narrative is inhabited by an improbable cast of incompetent characters given to excessive food and drink. The eventual failure of Haman's evil plans is clear from the very beginning (2001:xvi-xxii). The comedic dimensions do not reduce the value of the narrative. Instead, they remind us to avoid obsessive preoccupation with problems and threats, for the earth is the Lord's and all that is in it, the world, and those who live in it (Ps. 24:1).

A Glance at the Whole

In spite of the complexity of the Esther novella, Susan Niditch (1985) has pointed to the traditional and relatively simple movement that characterizes the literary flow or plot. The narrative movement from problem to action to resolution is a common feature of folk literature within and outside the Bible *[Narrative Structure]*.

Although Esther contains several different subplots, the dominant plot originates in the tension created by the clash between Mordecai and Haman. That clash between two royal officials results in a decree of annihilation against the Jews (3:12-14). In due course, that decree is resolved by a counteredict (8:9-17) and the slaughter of enemies of the Jews (9:11-16). As Niditch points out, this traditional pattern of plot frequently ends with the violent destruction of those who plotted violence against others (Niditch, 1985:40).

The novella of Esther, however, gives evidence of another equally familiar but more complex literary structure—*chiasm*. In a chiastic structure, the reader can see specific moments in the narrative balanced by a corresponding moment later in the story *[Narrative Structure]*. In strict chiasm, all moments have their counterpart except one; only the central turning point in the story does not have a balancing or corresponding element. Seldom do we find such rigid chiasm in Hebrew narrative.

Jon Levenson (8) has observed in Esther not strict chiasm but rather a symmetrical chiastic flow. This chart shows corresponding elements left and right, with the turning point centered:

Greatness of Ahasuerus (1:1-8)	Greatness of Ahasuerus and Mordecai (10:1-3)
Two Banquets of the Persians (1:1-8)	Two Banquets of the Jews (9:20-32)
Esther Identifies Herself as a Gentile (2:10-20)	Gentiles Identify Themselves as Jews (8:17)
Elevation of Haman (3:1)	Elevation of Mordecai (8:15)

Anti-Jewish Edict (3:12-15) Pro-Jewish Edict (8:9-14)
Fateful Dialogue: Fateful Dialogue:
  Mordecai and Esther (4:1-17)   Ahasuerus and Esther (7:1-6)
Esther's First Banquet (5:6-8) Esther's Second Banquet (7:1-6)

Parade of Honor for Mordecai (6:1-13, turning point)

The use of such literary symmetry, while not rigid, generates movement in the narrative and directs the reader to the turning point in the story. According to this chiastic outline, the plot turns on the nighttime insomnia of the king and the resulting parade honoring Mordecai. Indeed, the speech of Zeresh, Haman's wife, reinforces this moment as pivotal: *"If Mordecai, before whom your downfall has begun, is of the Jewish people, you will not prevail against him, but will surely fall before him"* (6:13).

We have looked at two different literary patterns present in Esther: chiasm and folk literature. The chiastic structure furnishes us with a sense of the narrative's symmetry. The traditional folk literature pattern of plot (problem-action-resolution) will be employed in this commentary. It features the flow of the narrative that is most obvious to the listener.

An Outline of the Major Units

The story line of Esther follows events, plots, and plans in the Persian royal palace. The opening scene, 1:1—3:6, contains two distinct but interwoven threads: the crisis in the royal household prompted by the disobedience of Queen Vashti, and the clash of two royal courtiers, Mordecai and Haman. Of the two, it is the clash of the courtiers that provides the primary tension in the narrative. Nevertheless, the appointment of a new queen furnishes the seeds for the eventual resolution of the crisis. The long opening scene concludes with the decision of Haman to *destroy all the Jews* (3:6) as a way of avenging Mordecai's refusal to show him honor.

The second scene, 3:7—7:10, narrates events in the palace resulting from the crisis. Thus 3:7 opens with a temporal statement: *In the first month* (Mar.-Apr.). Throughout this scene, we find similar temporal statements marking the transition from one episode to another. The first episode features the plots of the two opposing courtiers: Haman and Mordecai (3:7—4:17). Each of them approaches different members of the royal family, enlisting their support to destroy the other. The second episode similarly opens with a temporal phrase: *On the third day Esther put on her royal robes* (5:1). This episode narrates Esther's initial intervention in the crisis. It concludes with Haman convinced that he will be victorious (5:9-14).

Continuing the second scene, the pivotal third episode (6:1-13) again opens with a temporal remark: *On that night the king could not sleep* (6:1). The king's inability to sleep results in a parade honoring Mordecai. With that, Haman's wife, Zeresh, becomes convinced that Haman has lost. The fourth episode (6:14—7:10) confirms Zeresh's fear. Beginning with a hurried temporal remark, *While they were still talking* (6:14), this scene marks Esther's second and decisive intervention. It concludes with the execution of Haman (7:10).

The third and final scene, 8:1—9:32, with the edict authorizing the destruction of the Jews, resolves the narrative's opening crisis. Beginning again with a temporal phrase, *On that day,* chapter 8 features Esther's second audience before the king. This meeting successfully resolves two matters. The king gives Jews the right of self-defense against all enemies, and he elevates Mordecai to the royal position previously held by Haman. The ninth chapter, beginning with *Now in the twelfth month,* narrates the Jewish action against their enemies and presents the institution of a festival, Purim, commemorating the victory.

In an epilogue (10:1-3), Esther fades from view. Ahasuerus and Mordecai stand side by side: *For Mordecai the Jew was next in rank to King Ahasuerus.* Confirming the victory of Mordecai over his rival, this epilogue informs the reader that Mordecai is both powerful and popular.

These three scenes and the epilogue lead to the following outline of the book of Esther:

Scene 1: Tension in the Royal Court, 1:1—3:6
   1:1—2:20 Episode 1: Conflict in the Royal Family
      Deposing of Vashti, 1:1-22
      Selection of Esther, 2:1-20
   2:21—3:6 Episode 2: Conflict Among the Royal Courtiers
      Conspiracy Against the King, 2:21-23
      Conflict Between Courtiers, 3:1-6

Scene 2: Action and Counteraction, 3:7—7:10
   3:7—4:17   Episode 1: Haman Versus Mordecai
      The Plot of Haman, 3:7-15
      Response of Mordecai, 4:1-17
   5:1-14   Episode 2: Esther's First Intervention
   6:1-13   Episode 3: Royal Decree Honoring Mordecai
   6:14—7:10 Episode 4: Esther's Second Intervention

Esther Overview

Scene 3: Resolution and Celebration, 8:1—9:32
    8:1-17 Resolution of the Crisis
    9:1-32 Institution of Purim

Epilogue: Ahasuerus and Mordecai, 10:1-3

Scene 1

Tension in the Royal Court

Esther 1:1—3:6

Esther 1:1—2:20

Episode 1
Conflict in the Royal Family

Deposing of Vashti
Esther 1:1-22

PREVIEW

The opening scene introduces several of the themes and threads found throughout the narrative. Even a quick reading reveals that Esther is a book of banquets. The book opens with royal banquets and closes with the feast of Purim (9:16-32). In fact, the word *feast* (*mišteh*) occurs as many times in Esther as in all the rest of the OT. In the style of the royal chronicle, this chapter reports not only two banquets given by the king, but also mentions a third: *Queen Vashti gave a banquet for the women* (1:9). The banquets listed in this opening chronicle place the story in the royal palace. That palace casts its shadow over the entire book.

Not only does the story take place inside or in the shadow of the palace; royal action and inaction also constitute a major theme. All five major figures have a royal role: King Ahasuerus, the queens Vashti and Esther, and the courtiers Haman and Mordecai. The centrality of this theme can be seen in the repeated use of the Hebrew

Esther 1:1-22

root for *royal, m-l-k* (as in *malak*, reign; *melek*, king; *malkah*, queen), 250 times in 167 verses (Berg, 1979:59).

Given a royal setting, the reader is not surprised to encounter traditionally royal issues. Immediately we meet the question of obedience to a royal command. Queen Vashti disobeys a direct command of the king (1:12). That creates a crisis of royal proportions. Indeed, readers find obedience and disobedience a constant thread throughout the story. Direct disobedience and unreflective obedience always create problems in this story. The effective leader will discover a strategy to unite disobedience and obedience so the two work with each other toward a single goal.

A feature of Esther's literary style becomes evident in this opening scene: word pairs, triads, and parallelism. Duplications and parallelism, such as *official and ministers, Persia and Media* (1:3), characterize this prose so much that it makes the story difficult to read in a language unaccustomed to such a style. This literary technique may serve not only to set the story in the royal palace, but also to keep it there by using the customary style of royal language (Levenson: 11). In content and style, the book asks the reader to think royal.

OUTLINE

The narrative begins with an introduction to the Persian king, Ahasuerus (1:1), and follows by chronicling what appears to be his favorite activity: preparing and participating in banquets (1:2-9). These banquets, however, take an unexpected and angry turn when the queen refuses to participate as she is directed (1:10-12). The king presents the problem to his advisers. Consistent with their advice (1:13-20), he deposes the queen and reaffirms not only his own dominance, but that of every man in every household (1:21-22).

Introduction, 1:1

Chronicle of the Banquets, 1:2-9
    1:2-8   The King
    1:9   The Queen

Disobedience and Its Consequences, 1:10-22
    1:10-12   Disobedience of Vashti
    1:13-22   Consequences
        Consultation with Advisers, 1:13-20
        Royal Edict, 1:21-22

EXPLANATORY NOTES

Introduction 1:1

The Hebrew name *Ahasuerus* does not appear as such in the list of Persian kings outside of the Bible. Nevertheless, scholars have identified Ahasuerus with the Persian king whom the Greeks called Xerxes I (486-465 B.C.). The note that this is *the same Ahasuerus that ruled from India to Ethiopia* (1:1) serves to distinguish this king from another that might come to the mind of early readers—perhaps the one mentioned in Daniel 9:1, the father of Darius. Already with Cambyses (530-522), the Persian Empire stretched from India to Egypt. Yet there is no evidence of 127 political divisions in the empire, as mentioned in 1:1. The Greek sources mention twenty to thirty districts; Daniel 6:1 speaks of 120.

Chronicle of the Banquets 1:2-9

The list of banquets begins with the king giving a banquet for *all his officials and ministers* (1:3). The description of this banquet emphasizes a party that exceeds all imaginable criteria for extravagance. The feast lasts six months, during which the king deliberately displays the wealth of the empire (1:4).

In spite of the opening words, *when these days were over* (1:5, NIV), the second banquet in verse 5 seems to blend into the 180-day party. The grammar of verse 6 suggests that the description of the extravagance in decorations and the authorized indulgence in alcohol relates to the 180-day party for the *officials and ministers* (1:2-4) as much as or more than to the seven-day party for *all the people*. That is also suggested by the closing statement in verse 8: *The king had given orders to all the officials of his palace to do as each one desired*. The first banquet is for the *officials* (1:3), the second for *all the people present in the citadel of Susa* (1:5).

Whether this extravagance relates to the first banquet (1:3-4), the second banquet (1:5), or both, it sets the tone for the royal administration. The account seems to focus less on food at these affairs and more on drink. According to the Jewish historian Josephus, protocol may have dictated that everyone drink along with the king (*Antiquities,* 11.188). Here, however, the king puts no restraint on the consumption of alcohol.

Apparently men and women could and did attend the same parties in Persia. But in this story, the queen gives her own banquet *for the women in the palace* (1:9). The banquet is not described except for identifying its place and its class of guests. The short statement about the queen's banquet serves as a contrast to those given by the king. The reader is apparently to imagine the king's banquets as unrestrained male drinking parties. Narratively, the statement about the queen's banquet establishes a distance between the king and queen, which will only grow wider.

A long narrative introduction is unusual for Hebrew narrative [*Characteristics of Hebrew Narrative*]. Indeed the whole of Esther features much more description than one expects in biblical narrative. As such, Adele Berlin observes that "the story of Esther is conveyed by 'telling' rather than by 'showing'" (Berlin, 2001:xxv). Most commonly in the Bible, a reader learns about the characters by watching them speak and act, i.e. showing. In Esther, the narrator tells the reader about the characters, often including thoughts and feelings, i.e. telling. Esther's "telling" mode has the affect of keeping the reader more distant from the story (Berlin, 2001:xxvi). One is not only outside looking in, but being told by the narrator what the room looks like and why the people act as they do. The "showing" style of most Hebrew narrative invites the reader to more active participation by imagining the scenes and making ones own discernment about motivations and feelings.

Disobedience and Its Consequences 1:10-22

1:10-12 Disobedience of Vashti

The Septuagint version of Esther ("Different Versions," in Overview) presents the seven-day royal banquet for all the residents of Susa (1:5) as part of the royal wedding, when Vashti is to be proclaimed queen (cf. 1:5, 11, NRSV Apocrypha; Levenson: 46). If so, the king's command for Vashti to appear may be less arbitrary. Nevertheless, in the Hebrew text, the scene appears to be a large party drinking without restraint. Then the king orders the eunuchs to bring Vashti so she can *show . . . her beauty,* as he has shown off his wealth (1:4, 11).

Currently, most readers sympathize with Vashti. Some even empathize more with Vashti's refusal to be a part of an outrageous banquet scene, than with Esther's subsequent joining with and deferring to the king, who gave these parties (Beal: 88-96). That has not always been the case. In the past, some Jewish interpreters understood Vashti as the evil granddaughter of Nebuchadnezzar, the Babylonian king who destroyed Jerusalem. Christian tradition has at times employed an allegorical interpretation, in which Vashti was symbolic of the disobedient synagogue, then replaced by

Esther, representing the obedient church.

Informed of Vashti's refusal to come, the king burns with rage. The twofold repetition of the king's rage emphasizes its intensity (1:12).

1:13-22 Consequences

Following the statement of rage, the king takes an action that typifies his behavior in this story. He consults his advisers. In spite of possessing absolute power, almost never will Ahasuerus make his own decisions. Characteristically, he will ask others what he should do and immediately implement their advice. Therefore, the counselors, courtiers, eunuchs, and women actually control the direction and fate of the empire (Brenner, 1995:76).

In this episode, the king turns to *sages* versed in *the laws* (1:13). The words themselves suggest that these men are astrologers (Moore, 1971:8). The king asks them *what is to be done* to Queen Vashti because of her disobedience (1:15). *Memucan* answers for *the sages*. He insists that as word gets out concerning this act by the queen, it will encourage deviant behavior by others. Women throughout the realm will disobey their husbands. According to the sages, Vashti's action threatens the social fabric of the entire empire, causing all the women *to look with contempt on their husbands* (1:17). The advisers fear an almost immediate revolution, beginning with the aristocratic women (1:18).

Memucan counsels that the king depose Vashti and replace her by one *better than she* (1:19). He also proposes making the king's action imperial *law* so it cannot be altered or rescinded, and so Vashti can *never again* come before the king (1:19; cf. 8:8). Though not found outside of biblical tradition, the nonrevocable Persian law plays a major role in this narrative (cf. Dan. 6, Daniel defying an unchangeable Medo-Persian ban on prayer). This theme of inviolability of Persian law intensives the danger to victims of an edict (in this case, women of the empire) and the difficulty that can face the king, who is rendered powerless to correct a bad law.

The leading royal adviser, Memucan, identifies the wider purpose of this edict against Vashti—no longer called Queen Vashti. With this royal decree, *all women,* regardless of their station in life, will realize that they must honor their husbands (1:20). In ancient royal social structure, there is not a social contract as we have come to understand it, no common set of rights and expectations. The monarch establishes rights and expectations. The royal advisers decide that this single action by the queen will destroy the entire social matrix.

Conversely, a single royal edict will preempt the developing catastrophe!

This speech provides a marvelous example of the frequent use of comedy throughout Esther *[Comedy]*. The narrator describes the royal advisers as *wise,* and yet they provide foolish counsel for the king. Danger does loom for the empire, yet it comes not from the women, but from within the palace itself (2:21-23).

The narrative maintains its comic edge in reporting the king's response: *This advice pleased the king* (1:21). In the repetitive language style of the royal chronicle, the narrator states that a letter goes out to every province, in every language, informing everyone of the king's action. Because of this law, every man *should be master in his own house*—except the king, as we see, who is not able to master anything, let alone his own house, now or later.

A final phrase in 1:22 has created difficulties in both translation and interpretation, that *every man . . . speak according to the language of his people* (RSV). The NIV inserts it before *be ruler over his own household.* The NRSV follows the (Greek) Septuagint and drops it, suspecting that the Hebrew text accidentally recopied the earlier phrase *every people in its own language.*

THE TEXT IN BIBLICAL CONTEXT

Israel in the Persian Empire

Various biblical texts reflect the tradition's deep ambivalence about Persia and the Persian occupation of Israel. On one hand, Cyrus the Persian liberated Israel from the violent oppression of Babylon. Isaiah poetically describes the liberation by Persia, using messianic language.

> Thus says the LORD to his anointed, to Cyrus,
>   whose right hand I have grasped
> to subdue nations before him
>   and strip kings of their robes,
> to open doors before him—
>   and the gates shall not be closed:
> I will go before you
>   and level the mountains. (Isa. 45:1-2)

In the same light, the Chronicler sees the action of Persia as fulfilling Jeremiah's announcement of Babylon's destruction and Israel's restoration (Jer. 29:10):

> In the first year of King Cyrus of Persia, in order that the word of the LORD by the mouth of Jeremiah might be accomplished, the LORD stirred up the spirit of King Cyrus of Persia. (Ezra 1:1)

In Ezra, the Chronicler goes on to report the edict of Cyrus that allowed the Jewish exiles to return to Judah and rebuild the temple in Jerusalem. It was the policy of Cyrus and Persian rulers who followed him to allow displaced peoples throughout the empire to return to their home areas and reestablish their patterns of life and worship. This pattern of partial local autonomy in the social and religious realm came with required loyal allegiance to the Persian Empire. While much more benevolent than Babylonian rule, Persia, nevertheless, maintained firm political control of the empire.

The Jewish community located in Israel and the Jews dispersed throughout the empire learned to live as an ethnic minority. Yet their situation was fraught with danger. The stories preserved by the Jewish community record tensions that arose often between the Jews and other groups in the empire, as in the narrative of Daniel and the Persian Emperor Darius. According to the story, Daniel had become an important government official (Dan. 6:2). But other officials sought to destroy him. Without letting Darius know the real intent of their request, these officials obtained an irrevocable royal edict outlawing prayer "to anyone, divine or human, for thirty days, except to you, O king" (6:7). Anyone caught disobeying that edict would be thrown into a den of lions.

Like the story of Esther, the Daniel narrative portrays the Persian monarch as naively used by evil advisers. For the most part, the biblical narratives set in the Persian period do not see the empire itself as evil, although they do report periodic clashes with the Persian authorities. The texts reserve their harshest criticism for the Babylonians who preceded the Persians, and for the Greeks who followed them. In contrast to its picture of Persia, the Bible portrays Babylon not in terms of one or two diabolic public officials, but as an empire that sought to destroy the Jews.

While the Persian period did not see Israel restored to the political greatness of the Davidic period, it did allow the religious development of Judaism. During this time, Judaism was allowed to unite all Jews dispersed throughout the world in a single religious tradition.

THE TEXT IN THE LIFE OF THE CHURCH

The Fabric of Society

The fear of social chaos expressed by the royal advisers and the king seems oddly familiar. They conclude that the social fabric of the Persian Empire is fragile enough that a "misstep" by the queen will cause irreparable damage. Similar concern about the social fabric has continued to provoke action, sometimes within the church, and occasionally against the church.

In the monarchies of the ancient world, the king and queen have a direct influence on the character of society. Hence, the "wise" advisers to the king worry that an act by the monarch can be construed as acceptable behavior for any and all subjects of the realm. The character of Western society is defined not directly by the dictates and behavior of a monarch, but by what has been called a *social contract*, a blend of legal statutes and social customs that transcends any moment and yet evolves over time. The social contract is influenced both by the common behavior of the people and by the actions of the officials.

Nevertheless, many "elders" of society past and present express the fear that the social fabric is quite fragile, just a step from disintegrating into chaos. According to the Gospel accounts, fear by the "elders" of social and political chaos played a role in the crucifixion of Jesus (cf. John 11:48-50).

Worry about social chaos has made governments in North America and elsewhere reluctant to grant military exemption to those whose religious commitment prohibits participation in war. At times of national military emergency, most officials worry that any dissent will undermine the social solidarity that they deem necessary. Government officials have sought by law to control not only the behavior of dissenting Christians, but also their beliefs. One suspects that a Persian law requiring allegiance to the husband as master of the house would be no more successful than contemporary attempts to coerce conscience. Nevertheless, the perceived threat of social chaos can tempt a government to try legal action to compel many kinds of social conformity.

The church has always acknowledged the importance of a stable social environment. Social chaos threatens the church as well as the other social institutions. Hence, the church regularly affirms its support for a stable social structure. While affirming the need for social stability, the Christian community has also recognized that a social environment can become stagnant and oppressive. The right kind of change keeps society vibrant and healthy. Yet in every age some changes in the social milieu lead toward a more just and robust global community, and other innovations threaten to destroy the fabric of social existence.

Even faithful disciples will disagree on which changes cooperate with God's work in history. Some, such as the Amish and Old Order Brethren, have felt that any dilution of the rural family-centered social organization of previous generations will ultimately destroy both the people and their faith. Others have observed that faithful Christians have and can adapt to a wide variety of social patterns throughout the centuries and around the world. Perhaps most problematic are those folks, like the king's advisers, who dramatically overreact to any perceived threat and try to coerce what they believe to be a divinely sanctioned social organization.

Selection of Esther
Esther 2:1-20

PREVIEW

The process of selecting a queen invites the reader to observe the rituals and customs of the royal court in the ancient Orient. The emphasis on cosmetic and dietary detail reminds us that concerns about such matters have a long history for both women and men. Step by step, the selection process works itself out until Esther is chosen. At the conclusion, the palace celebrates with a great banquet, another in a series of banquets/feasts in the story.

Many interpreters point to elements of this narrative reminiscent of other stories from the ancient Orient about ordinary young women who become queen, such as *A Thousand and One Nights*. In that classic story, the king established a testing process to select a queen. He directed his advisers to bring a different woman into his chamber every night. The following morning, the king ordered each woman executed. Finally, Scheherezade, the daughter of a royal courtier, was brought to the king. Night after night, she held the king's attention by telling him story after story. Each night she stopped just before the end of the story, leaving the conclusion until the following night. Her ingenuity kept her alive and won her the royal crown.

The narrative of Esther's rise contains some similar elements: an Oriental palace, a woman who was the *(adopted) daughter* of a royal courtier, a king who calls the prospective queens one by one into his presence, and a harem with a eunuch who oversees the women. Those common elements set both stories in the same world, the royal court of the ancient Orient. Such similarities, however, do not provide reason to suggest that one of the stories is dependent on the other. Esther's rise from obscurity to prominence connects not only with royal traditions of the ancient Orient, but also with a distinctive biblical tradition: a person of low estate or difficult circumstances who rises to a position of prominence. This includes such people as Joseph, Ruth, and David.

The story of Esther's selection as queen is interrupted by an aside about Mordecai that provides important information connecting this narrative to specific threads of the biblical story (2:5-7). These verses ground this narrative in the great story, the ongoing narrative of God's people. The narrator does not want the story of Esther read as an isolated incident of Jews living in Persia. These notes about Mordecai and Hadassah/Esther link the tensions that erupt in Persia to long-standing antagonism between Esther's ancestors and their neighbors.

OUTLINE
Introductory Comment, 2:1

Proposed Search Process, 2:2-4
    2:2-4a Proposal by Royal Advisers
    2:4b   King's Acceptance

Introduction of Mordecai and Esther, 2:5-7

Selection of a Queen, 2:8-17
    2:8-11   Gathering the Candidates
    2:12-14   The Standard Procedure
    2:15-17   Selection of Esther

Concluding Banquet, 2:18
Concluding Comment, 2:19-20

EXPLANATORY NOTES

Introductory Comment 2:1

In the half episode that has led to the dismissal of Vashti, the king begins with a banquet and concludes in anger (1:1-21). This half episode moves the opposite way, from anger to banquet.

Throughout the whole story, quick emotional shifts characterize King Ahasuerus. As we see, the king seldom initiates action, preferring instead to consult first with his advisers (1:13-20). Indeed, the actions he initiates flow from his emotions. Ahasuerus quickly acts against Vashti out of anger (1:12), and he chooses Esther just as quickly out of love (2:17). Later in the narrative, he will honor Mordecai (6:1-11) and condemn Haman (7:7-9) with a quick emotional decision. Esther will carefully plot her approach to Ahasuerus, aware that his emotional reaction cannot be predicted (4:11).

We are not told how long King Ahasuerus remains angry about Vashti. However, the queen is deposed in the third year of his reign (1:3), and the selection of the new queen does not occur until the seventh year (2:16). Jon Levenson (54) suggests that there may be a hint of humor in what seems to be a long period of anger, after which the king *remembered Vashti* (2:1). The use of the word *remember* (*zakar*) often signals a positive emotion, such as affection or compassion. The emotional outbursts and unexpected royal responses signal that we should expect humor and satire in this narrative *[Comedy]*.

Proposed Selection Process 2:2-4

Characteristically in this king's court, the royal advisers propose each course of action. Whether it be deposing Vashti (1:15-20), choosing a new queen, or dealing with allegedly subversive groups (3:8-11), the king consults with his advisers. Each time, as here, he takes their advice without question. When the king acts deliberatively, Ahasuerus implements the advice of counsel.

Just as deposing Vashti was a political event, so choosing a new queen will happen through a political search process. The advisers propose gathering *all the beautiful young* women to the *harem*, (literally, *the house of women*). Although most readers assume that the women brought to the kings are to be *virgins*, the Hebrew word (*bethulah*) indicates their age more directly than their sexual experience. They are young.

The advisers propose a structured approach to recruiting the candidates. Commissioners are to be appointed in each province. These commissioners are to gather all (2:3), not just some, of the beautiful young women of the realm. These are to be brought to *the women's house* in the palace and placed under the direction of Hegai, the king's eunuch. The text identifies two basic criteria for the women: *young* and *beautiful* (2:3). The narrative allows the reader to speculate about how many qualified women might be found in all the Persian provinces!

This proposal *pleased the king, and he did so* (2:4b).

Introduction of Mordecai and Esther 2:5-7

The narrative introduces Mordecai and Esther with images quite different from those describing the king and queen. The extravagant pictures of the oriental royal court of Ahasuerus and Vashti contrast dramatically with the painful language of Israel's exile. Mordecai lives as a Jew in Susa, a child of the Babylonian exile.

After Judean King Jehoiakim's death in 598 B.C., the Babylonian army under Nebuchadnezzar captured Jerusalem (597) and dispersed to various parts of the empire much of Jerusalem's population, especially Jehoiachin/Jeconiah's government and business community (2 Kings 24; 1 Chron. 3:16). Another rebellion, a decade later, brought Babylon back to destroy the city and disperse still more of the population (587/6; 2 Kings 25).

The narrative identifies Mordecai as *one who had been carried into exile* (2:6, NIV). Scholars have tried various explanations for the 110+ years from the Exile (597), when this deportation with *Jehoiachin/Jeconiah* happened, to the reign of the Persian king Xerxes (486-465), the presumed time of this story. One of those proposals is most clearly reflected in the NRSV translation of 2:6. The traditional proposal suggests that Mordecai's great-grandfather *Kish* was a member of the Exile generation. This allows three generations from the Exile to Xerxes. It is doubtful that any proposal will successfully put all the elements of the story of Esther into an exact historical time frame (Berlin, 2001:25).

The introduction of Mordecai and Esther does not focus on the exact date, but on their roots and circumstances. Mordecai's ancestors come from the tribe of Benjamin, the same tribe as Israel's first king, Saul. The text later connects Haman to one of ancient Israel's most bitter enemies, the Amalekites, against whom Saul fought (3:1). Hence, according to this narrative, Israel's ancient antagonisms can follow them even into distant lands, erupting many generations later.

Esther, whose Hebrew name is *Hadassah*, has lost both mother and father. Mordecai has *adopted* Esther, his cousin, the daughter of his uncle. We have little if any information about adoption in ancient Israel. Adoption is attested in the social practice of ancient Babylon and may have been accepted by the Exiles as they dealt with their social problems in new ways as a dispersed minority (Clines, 1984a: 287). Translated more literally, the text says, *Mordecai took her to himself as a daughter* (2:7). This may be language indicating adoption, but not necessarily. Mordecai may have simply provided informal assistance to an orphaned cousin.

Selection of a Queen 2:8-17

2:8-11 Gathering the Candidates

Esther 2:8 returns the reader to the ongoing narrative, the selection of a queen. In 2:7 the narrator has told us that Esther fits the criteria of beauty. Hence, as we should expect, Esther is one of many taken to the *women's house* and placed under the supervision of Hegai, the royal eunuch. Kristen de Troyer (50) suggests that being put under Hegai's care, with all the attention to beauty and diet, prepares the girls to become women.

In the *women's house*, for reasons the story does not explain, Esther becomes a favorite of Hegai. He provides Esther with the best attendants and accommodations. Consequently, Esther moves rapidly to join the elite group of women being prepared for an "interview" with the king.

Along with her beauty and attractive presence, the narrative presents Esther as compliant, following the instructions of both Mordecai and Hegai. At the behest of Mordecai, she does not reveal her ethnic identity (2:10). The narrator later reminds us that Esther has concealed her Jewish identity (2:20). The reader does not know what if anything the royal court knows indirectly about Esther's Jewish identity, either before or after her selection as queen. On one hand, we are not told that Jewish ethnicity would disqualify her or even hinder Esther's selection. Nevertheless, it is seldom an advantage for a minority person to reveal their ethnicity. In this story, concealing this information from the king heightens the drama at a decisive moment when the identity is revealed (8:5-6).

2:12-14 The Standard Procedure

The narrative pauses to inform us of the procedure leading up to the "interview." It begins with a year's treatment, using specific cosmetics. Then the woman is readied to go to the king. She can ask for whatever she wants to take with her to the royal chamber. In the evening she goes from the *women's house* to the *king's house* (2:13, EFR). In the morning she comes *back*, but not to the same house. Instead, she goes to a *women's house* presided over by the eunuch *(Shaashgaz)* in charge of the concubines (secondary marital associates). Each woman in that house is at the pleasure of the king.

The transformation of the girls into women and then into concubines is defined by, and presided over by, the men of the palace. The women are passive, permitted only to ask for what they want to take with them for their night in the *king's house*.

2:15-17 Selection of Esther

If the standard procedure in the *women's house* defines the women as passive, Esther is as compliant as the other women, perhaps more so. When it comes her turn to go the *king's house*, she asks for nothing except what Hegai recommends. The narrator allows us to sense Esther's obedience in several ways. Her compliance here stands in direct contrast to Vashti's disobedience; it also contrasts with the moment in chapter 4 when Esther herself will take charge of the action (4:16). In addition, Esther's deferral to Hegai serves as an initial illustration of her political acumen. Admired by Hegai, and indeed by all who see her (2:14), Esther lets Hegai decide what she should take into the *king's house*. Hegai provides her with "the right stuff."

The narrative does not allow us to follow Esther into *the king's house*. We find out only the result: *the king loved Esther more than all the other women* (2:17). Esther has won the favor of everyone else; likewise, she wins the king's favor and love. The crown now is set on Esther's head. The narrator adds emphasis and closure: Esther has replaced Vashti. The difficulty caused by Vashti's disobedience has been resolved.

Concluding Banquet 2:18

From beginning to end, this narrative moves from one banquet to another. The story opens with feasts given by the king (1:1-8), and the mention of a banquet by Queen Vashti (1:9). This dinner, though given by the king, is called *"Esther's banquet."* As we shall see, when Esther first takes the initiative, she orders a fast rather than a feast (4:16). Later she will ask for two royal banquets (chaps. 5, 7), and finally the Jews will have their feast (8:17).

Besides the banquet, the king proclaims a holiday throughout all the provinces. The narrative does not tell us what the proclamation of a holiday might involve except to mention the king's generosity. Different translations include *remission of taxes* (Hebrew Targum, RSV) and *amnesty* (LXX) as a part of the royal wedding holiday. Examples throughout the ancient Near East suggest that this kind of holiday might add such elements as release of prisoners and exemption from military service (Levenson: 63).

Concluding Comment 2:19-20

Esther 2:19 has long puzzled interpreters. The queen has been chosen, so there is no need for a second gathering of young women. Michael Fox treats this as a parenthetical reference to a part of the selection process whereby the women were moved to a second harem (Fox, 2001:38). The Greek versions of Esther omit the phrase.

The second phrase in the verse, *Mordecai was sitting at the king's gate*, appears also in two verses later (2:21). This raises a possibility that the entire verse resulted from a copying error. Be that as it may, both here and in verse 21, *sitting at the king's gate* designates Mordecai as a royal official. The text does not identify Mordecai's position. Because he later becomes an informer, some have speculated that Mordecai was a secret-service official (Berlin, 2001:31). The significance for the narrative lies not in Mordecai's exact office, but in Mordecai, like Haman, being an official in the royal government.

Esther 2:20 reiterates Esther's secret, her Jewish identity. This secret plays a role in the tension of the plot in relationship to the royal edict mandating the annihilation of the Jews, in 3:13. But with each reading, this verse serves as an all-too-familiar reminder that minority status usually proves an economic and social liability. Such prejudice always brings tragedy, and sometimes horror.

THE TEXT IN BIBLICAL CONTEXT

From Insignificance to Importance

The journey from insignificance to importance appears as a recurring thread in the biblical tradition. As the first epistle of Peter declares, such experience comes as a gift of God, not only to an individual, but to the whole people: "Once you were not a people, but now you are God's people; once you had not received mercy, but now you have received mercy" (1 Pet. 2:10).

The biblical story of Esther has frequently been related to the narrative of Joseph (Gen. 37–50). The connections are wide-ranging, and clearly visible in this thematic element—the rise from low estate to prominence. Joseph, after being threatened with death by his brothers, was sold to the Ishmaelites/Midianites. Then he was taken to Egypt, where he was resold to Potiphar, an Egyptian royal official (Gen. 37:25-36).

The LORD was with Joseph, and he rose to become the head steward of the household. Potiphar's wife, however, accused Joseph of sexual assault, and he was thrown into prison (Gen. 39:6-20). Eventually, the God's gift of discernment enabled Joseph to come to the attention of Pharaoh. The king of Egypt elevated this Hebrew servant/prisoner to be second only to himself: "You shall be over my house, and all my people shall order themselves as you command; only with regard to the throne will I be greater than you" (Gen. 41:40).

The story of Joseph is not the only biblical narrative of a Hebrew who arose from obscurity to become an official in a royal court. A variation on that same theme is found in the story of Daniel. The first six chapters tell of Daniel and his friends living in Exile, following the destruction of Jerusalem by the Babylonian King Nebuchadnezzar. Because of their beauty and intelligence, a group of young men, including Daniel, was chosen to be attendants in the palace (Dan. 1:3-7).

Acting on their commitment to remain true to their religious piety, these Exiles chose to disobey royal decrees that required them to compromise their faith. Daniel was thrown into a den of lions (Dan. 6), and three of his colleagues were cast into a furnace of blazing fire (Dan. 3). All of them survived because of God's protection. Shadrach, Meshach, and Abednego were promoted to official positions (Dan. 3:30). Daniel was lauded by the king and prospered even into the Persian Empire (Dan. 6:28).

The story of Ruth has some of the same elements. This Moabite widow defied her mother-in-law's directive that she remain in her homeland. Instead, she accompanied Naomi to Bethlehem. She lived there as a foreigner and a servant (2:10; 3:9). Through a combination of divine providence and human initiative, she obtained life-sustaining grain for both women and became the wife of Boaz, a prominent man in the village. Boaz himself declared Ruth to be a woman of character (3:11). The women of the village equated Ruth with great women of tradition, proclaiming her more valuable than seven sons (4:11-12, 14).

Esther rises from obscurity to become the queen of Persia. Her story is distinctive. Nevertheless, she has other brothers and sisters in the Bible with similar life stories, people of faith who found themselves with low status in a foreign land but then rose to positions of power, prominence, and prosperity.

THE TEXT IN THE LIFE OF THE CHURCH

Heroes of Faith

The stories of heros of the faith who rise to positions of prominence and prestige are retold in part to inspire the next generation. Perhaps the best-known biblical recitation of such heros appears in Hebrews 11, where the author lists some of those whose life has witnessed to the faith as fulfilled in Jesus. Less well-known is the hymn in honor of ancestors found in Sirach (Ecclus.) 44–50, in the Apocrypha. This hymn, included in the Bible used by Roman Catholics, lists primarily religious and political leaders from Noah to Zerubbabel.

The different lists throughout the biblical tradition raise the question of who should be included. Whose stories from our denominational and local history should be remembered and retold as heroic? Older documents have listed mostly men whose work has been visible and celebrated. Only recently have we recognized the heroic work of women. In the North American church, we have mostly listed our own kind, not recognizing or remembering the work of other Christian heros.

Not all Christians would develop a list that mostly consists of political leaders, such as that found in Sirach 44–50. In the believers church tradition, many have been reluctant to applaud members who have taken an active role in public and economic life, preferring instead to thank God for those who have distinguished themselves in religious and service occupations. Some Christians would also hesitate to include many of the people found in Hebrews 11, such as Gideon, Samson, and Jephthah (Judg. 6–8, 11, 13–16), because they made their name through military leadership. They might wish to omit David because of events surrounding his marriage to Bathsheba (2 Sam. 11).

Indeed, the selectivity inherent in each list of heros bears witness to values of the listing community rather than providing full access to the ancestors who have been the most influential or faithful in the past. Christians' preference for particular heroic figures generally allows them to remain within their faith comfort zone.

Nevertheless, stories like Esther can remind listeners that God's presence and power accompany those who by choice or chance venture into unfamiliar and dangerous territory, perhaps even territory into which one ought not venture. To be queen of Persia may be a danger for soul as well as body. Yet even there, nothing "in all creation will be able to separate us from the love of God in Christ Jesus our Lord" (Rom. 8:39).

Esther 2:21—3:6

Episode 2
Conflict Among the Royal Courtiers

PREVIEW

The first episode (1:1—2:20) has introduced the readers to King Ahasuerus and newly crowned Queen Esther. In this episode (2:21—3:6), we learn about the conflict between the primary antagonists, Mordecai and Haman. Both episodes feature tension in the royal court. The initial tension has arisen in the royal family itself: Queen Vashti refuses to obey an order of the king. In this episode, the clash occurs between two royal courtiers, originating with the king's decision to elevate Haman to a preeminent position in the court. For his part, Mordecai refuses to acknowledge Haman's preeminence in the way the latter considers appropriate. Their conflict escalates toward violence.

While each episode (1:1—2:20; 2:21—3:6) is distinctive, both feature similar elements and together establish the explosive tension that drives the remainder of the narrative. In both episodes, the subordinate person (Vashti, Mordecai) disobeys an order of the superior. This disobedience elicits rage and retaliation. Ahasuerus has deposed Vashti and chosen another. In addition, the king has issued an order designed to establish, by royal fiat, a master-subordinate relationship between husbands and wives.

Similarly, Mordecai disobeys Ahasuerus by not bowing to Haman, whom the king has elevated to first among royal courtiers (3:1-3). Like his king, Haman explodes in anger. Vashti's disobedience to the king has resulted in the loss of her crown; Mordecai's disobedience to Haman threatens an even greater catastrophe. The narrator informs the reader that Haman's anger leads him to plot the extermination of *all the Jews, the people of Mordecai* (3:6).

The narrative flow itself serves to increase the tension in this episode. Two seemingly unrelated incidents are placed one right after the other. Although not directly related, their position next to one another creates a narrative dissonance that will exist until it reemerges as the king struggles with insomnia, later in the story (6:1). In the first incident, Mordecai discovers a plan to assassinate the king and reports the plot to Queen Esther. The king executes the conspirators (2:21-23). Then the narrative immediately reports that King Ahasuerus promotes Haman, setting *his seat above all the officials* (3:1). The incongruity between the loyalty of Mordecai and the elevation of Haman underscores the antagonism between the two, a hostility that quickly becomes dangerous.

OUTLINE

Conspiracy Against the King, 2:21-23
    2:21   Conspiracy
    2:22   Mordecai's Report
    2:23   Royal Response

Conflict Between Courtiers, 3:1-6
    3:1   Promotion of Haman
    3:2   Action of Mordecai
    3:3-6   Response
        Of the Royal Servants, 3:3-4
        Of Haman, 3:5-6

EXPLANATORY NOTES

Conspiracy Against the King 2:21-23

2:21 Conspiracy

The narrative does not tell us what angers Bigthan and Teresh. The Greek version of the story asserts that Mordecai's position in the royal administration prompts their anger (2:21, NRSV Apocrypha). In the Hebrew narrative, however, we learn only that these men, who guard the entrance to the royal apartments (the threshold), become angry. Clines (1984a: 292) notes that anger lies just beneath the surface throughout the narrative.

Previously, King Ahasuerus has become angry when Queen Vashti refused to present herself at the royal feast as the king demanded (1:12). Haman becomes angry when he feels slighted by Mordecai (3:5). Later, the king will again erupt in anger when he interprets Haman's action as an assault on the queen (7:8). Anger spews out frequently in this carefully controlled royal administration, and it seldom leads to constructive action. Whatever the aggravating circumstances, Bigthan and Teresh consider themselves provoked enough that they conspire to *assassinate (lay hands on)* the king.

2:22 Mordecai's Report

This brief verse looms large in the context of the entire narrative. Haman will persuade the king of the disloyalty of an unnamed people (Mordecai's people). However, coming in the narrative just before Haman's charge of treason, this statement establishes the loyalty of both Mordecai and Esther.

In addition, 2:22 reestablishes the connection between Mordecai and Esther. The narrator's brief statement does not reveal how Mordecai gets word to Esther. Apparently, at this point at least, Esther is not at all hesitant to convey the information to the king, a reluctance that emerges later (4:11). The narrator simply states, *He [Mordecai] told it to Queen Esther, and Esther told the king*.

We must not miss the final phrase in this brief narration: Esther conveys this information about the conspiracy *in the name of Mordecai*. These words become crucial in a later scene where the king is reminded of Mordecai's loyalty (6:2). Levenson (64) suggests that this phrase has a second function. It reveals that the king has some knowledge about the connection between Esther and Mordecai, even though Mordecai has insisted that Esther keep her identity a secret (2:10). Mordecai's Jewish identity is well-known in the palace. He has told the royal courtiers *that he [is] a Jew* (3:4).

2:23 Royal Response

In retaliation for their conspiracy against the crown, Bigthan and Teresh are executed. This establishes another element that reappears throughout the narrative, the legal custom of direct retaliation *(lex talionis):* "If any harm follows, then you shall give life for life, eye for eye, tooth for tooth, hand for hand, foot for foot, burn for burn, wound for wound, stripe for stripe" (Exod. 21:24-25). This narrative extends the law of retaliation another step. Conspiracy to take life constitutes sufficient cause for retaliation (cf. false witnesses receiving what they schemed to do to the accused; Deut. 19:16-21; Susanna 61, in the Apocrypha). Retaliation against those conspiring to take life justifies the attack of the Jews against those *who had sought their ruin* (9:2)—a dimension of the story that troubles many readers.

The narrative explicitly notes that the conspiracy against the king and its outcome are written in the royal record. That entry will play a significant role in the eventual downfall of Haman and the elevation of Mordecai (chaps. 6–9).

Conflict Between Courtiers 3:1-6

3:1 Promotion of Haman

Immediately after Mordecai's action to thwart the assassination plot, the narrative records the king's promotion of Haman to the preeminent position in the royal administration. The absence of royal acknowledgment of Mordecai's loyalty and the immediate and unexplained promotion of Haman creates a tension in itself.

In addition, this short note adds still more tension to the narrative. According to 3:1, Haman is the *son of Hammedatha the Agagite*. The term *Agagite* recalls the encounter between Saul and the Amalekites (1 Sam. 15). Saul defeated and "utterly destroyed all of the people with the edge of the sword" (15:8). But he spared the life of the Agag, the king of the Amalekites. The memory of antagonism between the Mordecai's people and Haman's ancestors precedes even Saul's action against the Amalekites. At Moses' behest, Joshua fought off Amalek's attack on the Israelites as they journeyed from Egypt to Canaan (Exod. 17).

The story of Israel's wilderness journey provides still other notes about the Amalekites. Balaam, the seer from the east, was called by Balak of Moab to deliver an oracle concerning Israel. Among other matters, Balaam announced, "First among the nations was Amalek, but its end is to perish forever" (Num. 24:20). Finally, in his farewell speech, Moses admonished Israel to "blot out the remembrance of Amalek from under heaven: do not forget" (Deut. 25:19).

Whether or not the narrator intends the tension between Mordecai and Haman to serve as the next chapter of this long-standing feud, it connects this one moment (Esther 3:1) to the whole history of Israel. The reasons for the antagonism between Mordecai and Haman belong to this story, and also to a much larger drama of antagonism between ancient Israel and those who seek to destroy them.

3:2 Action of Mordecai

Mordecai, refusing to follow the practice of his fellow courtiers and the command of the king, does not bow down to Haman, the one who has been elevated over them. No reason is given for Mordecai's refusal. The narrative's reticence in this regard has prompted a wide variety of suggestions by readers past and present. Some ancient interpreters insisted that Mordecai appropriately refuses to bow down before one who is wicked. Others have suggested that Haman claims a special relationship to the gods, and so bowing down to him would be idolatry. Recent interpreters use the ancient enmity between the Israelites and the Amalekites as the reason for Mordecai's action (Berlin, 2002:34-36; Fox, 2001:45-46).

A Greek version (LXX) reports a prayer by Mordecai in which he says: "O Lord, that it was not in insolence or pride or for any love of glory that I did this, and refused to bow down to this proud Haman; . . . I will not bow down to anyone but you, who are my Lord" (13:12-13, NRSV Apocrypha, in Addition C; cf. Dan. 3). This Greek text seems to assume that such action is forbidden. Yet in other biblical texts, bowing before another person is not prohibited (Gen. 23:7; 27:29; 1 Kings 1:31).

Although the text does not state a reason for Mordecai's refusal, it does present a framework within which Mordecai's decision is understandable: the collective memory of Israel, common political rivalries, and Jewish religious piety. The text and its interpreters have suggested all of these as possible factors in Mordecai's crucial decision not to bow down to Haman.

Response 3:3-6

3:3-4 Of the Royal Servants

Other royal officials recognize that Mordecai's refusal will cause trouble. They ask Mordecai for an explanation: *"Why did you disobey the king's command?"* The narrative records no response from Mordecai. In fact, the narrator reports that the courtiers talk to Mordecai day after day, but he *"would not listen to them."* Mordecai's fellow courtiers themselves escalate the tension by telling Haman. They apparently want to see who will win this conflict in the royal court.

At this point, the narrative seems to present Mordecai's decision as a battle for ascendancy and power in the royal court—a frequent enough struggle in any administrative organization. Readers may choose to posit religious piety or practice as the motivation for Mordecai's disobedience, but the courtiers interpret it as a power struggle.

3:5-6 Of Haman

Haman erupts in rage when he sees Mordecai's refusal to honor him. This is the second incident of disobedience in the story. Both generate rage. The first, Vashti's refusal to present herself at the king's command, has provoked royal rage (1:12).

In that case, the king's counselor's advises the king to see Vashti's disobedience as an attack on the social fabric of the empire. While Haman does not turn to counselors for advice, he also decides to deal with Mordecai's disobedience as an element in a much larger danger. Knowing that Mordecai is Jewish, Haman sets out to destroy all the Jews *throughout the whole kingdom of Ahasuerus.*

Haman's plot repeats some of the language with which this episode has begun (2:21). As Bigthan and Teresh *became angry* at the king, similarly Haman becomes *enraged.* Both Haman and these two courtiers seek *to lay hands on* the one they have identified as the enemy. The two courtiers are executed when their plot is reported to the king. This repetition of language suggests that the same destiny may await Haman.

THE TEXT IN BIBLICAL CONTEXT

Choosing Disobedience

Disobedience to authority has a long history in the biblical story. Jon Levenson (68) points to that tradition, comparing the actions of Vashti (Esther 1) and Mordecai with those of Joseph in Egypt. Day after day, Potiphar's wife tried to persuade Joseph "to lie beside her" (Gen. 39:10). He would not consent. In retaliation, Potiphar's wife accused Joseph of assault, sending him to prison.

Levenson suggests that the several connections between the narrative of Joseph in Egypt and Esther in Persia make Joseph's no to Potiphar's wife a particularly apt comparison with Mordecai (and Vashti). Indeed, the strain of such disobedience runs deep in the Bible, from Rahab in Jericho to Paul in Caesarea.

According to the biblical narrative, Joshua sent two spies to Jericho to observe the lay of the land before Joshua leads the people across the Jordan River (Josh. 2). The two spies spent the night in the home of a prostitute, Rahab. The "king of Jericho" learned of this infiltration and ordered her to turn the spies over to him: "Bring out the men who have come to you, who entered your house, for they have come only to search out the whole land" (Josh. 2:3). Instead, Rahab hid the men and in the night let them down over the city wall. The narrative does not report the king's reaction to Rahab's act of disobedience. Later, Joshua sent the two spies back to help Rahab and her family escape from the city (Josh. 6:22-25).

The book of Acts reports that Paul was frequently in trouble with authorities, trouble that occasionally landed him in prison. Unlike Mordecai's one act of defiance, much of Paul's ministry, as recorded in Acts, placed him at odds with civil and religious authorities. He was imprisoned in Philippi (Acts 16) and threatened in Ephesus, where a mob dragged his traveling companions Gaius and Aristarchus before the town clerk (chap. 19). In addition, Paul was beaten and chained in Jerusalem (chaps. 21–22), held for trial and imprisoned in Caesarea (chaps. 23–24), and eventually came to live under house arrest in Rome (28:16).

Various religious and political leaders accused Jesus of religious blasphemy and conspiracy against the government. According to the Gospel writers, his refusal to say more than the enigmatic "You say so" (Matt. 27:11) amazed and confused the authorities. The Roman rulers responsible for jurisdiction in Jesus' trial interpreted their situation in a way similar to King Ahasuerus dealing with Vashti and Haman with Mordecai. They feared that failure to act against the accused would ripple throughout the kingdom, potentially undermining civil order (cf. Matt. 27:24; John 11:48). Jesus was executed. The writer of Hebrews proclaims that with Jesus' sacrifice of himself, the old order disappeared and a new order was established (Heb. 10:9-10).

THE TEXT IN THE LIFE OF THE CHURCH

Mixed Motives

The text does not say why Mordecai refuses to bow down to Haman, generating a conflict that will escalate toward disaster. Experience suggests that no action of a person or group can be reduced to a single motive, such as merely self-interest or purely religious faithfulness. Christians act and have acted in response to the prompting of the Spirit, but seldom only for that reason. Issues of individual or group interest and preference affect our decisions to act as Christians. This mixture of motives is frequently more visible to others than to the actor.

In the early 1880s, a significant schism occurred in the group known as the German Baptist Brethren. Various religious and theological differences were lifted up by different disputants, including changes in church polity, respect for traditional practices of faith and life, and understandings of the church's authority. Each faction had articulate and forceful leaders who gathered the attention and agreement of various groups in the church. By the mid-1880s, the movement had split into three major Brethren groups.

What caused the split? Perhaps it was prompted by genuine disagreement over substantial issues of faith and practice, or by cultural changes that drew Brethren in different directions, or by articulate individuals who sought to exert their leadership. Most historians looking at the developments suggest that all these elements, and perhaps others we can no longer identify, played a role in the conflict. Converging factors provoked the participants to take a position of absolute opposition, even to dividing the church.

This fracture within the believers church tradition serves as an example of schism that has plagued the Christian church at all levels and eras. Many of the same observations about multiple causes and motivations characterize the split between the Eastern (Orthodox) and Western (Roman) churches in the eleventh century, and the sixteenth-century split of the Western churches into Catholic and Protestant. Disputes over distinctive convictions of Christian faith and practice have played a role in all such divisions, but other factors have affected the course of events as well: personality conflicts, struggles for power, economics (church taxes), and so on.

We search in vain for an event in the life of the church or of individuals that can be attributed to purely religious motives. This seems to be true whether one examine Paul's mission to the Gentiles as vigorously debated at the Jerusalem Council (Acts 15), Luther's ninety-five theses posted on the Castle Church door at Wittenberg (Oct. 1517), or more recent actions. It seems unlikely that we can establish the faithfulness of Christian action solely on the purity of motives among individuals or groups, whether that be Mordecai, the apostle Paul, or Martin Luther. We witness a miracle when God takes our complexly motivated actions and moves us a step closer toward the society of divine shalom (wholeness/peace).

Scene 2

Action and Counteraction

Esther 3:7—7:10

Esther 3:7—4:17

Episode 1
Haman Versus Mordecai

PREVIEW

In the previous chapters, the narrative has carefully established the story's characters and tension. Four major characters figure in this palace drama: King Ahasuerus, Queen Esther, and two royal officials, Haman and Mordecai. The king has appointed Haman to head the government. Haman's appointment produces conflict with Mordecai (and surprises most readers). Mordecai is the one who has saved the monarch from a conspiracy by officials plotting to assassinate the king. In response, Mordecai openly refuses to acknowledge the primacy of Haman. At this point in the story, Haman has the ear of the king, while Mordecai is allied with the queen.

In the second scene (3:7—7:10), the drama plays out the consequences of these tensions and alliances. In the first episode (3:7—4:17), the tension explodes between the courtiers, Haman and Mordecai. Haman decides on a strategy to destroy not only Mordecai, but also Mordecai's people, the entire Jewish population (3:7-15). In response, Mordecai turns to his ally in the royal household, the queen.

In this episode, we find more than just the opposing strategies of two antagonistic royal officials. Esther emerges as the key figure in the drama. In the first scene (1:1—3:6), Esther has appeared as a one-dimensional figure, a character type more than a fully developed person [Character Types]. Esther has obediently done as she is told by her adoptive father, Mordecai, and by the palace officials into whose care she was placed. Indeed, Esther has functioned exactly as she is described: *the girl . . . fair and beautiful* (2:7). Now in this episode, Esther shows herself to be more than just a dutiful daughter. The unit concludes with a revealing statement: *Mordecai . . . did everything as Esther had ordered him* (4:17).

OUTLINE

Plot of Haman, 3:7-15
   3:7   Casting the Lot (Pur)
   3:8-9 Speech to the King
       Description of Danger, 3:8
       Request, 3:9
   3:10-11 Response of the King
   3:12-15a Issuing an Edict
   3:15b   Concluding Note

Response of Mordecai, 4:1-17
   4:1-3 Ritual of Mourning
   4:4-5 Response of Esther
   4:6-17 Mission of Hathach
       Inquiry and Report, 4:6-9
       Dialogue: Esther and Mordecai, 4:10-16
   4:17   Concluding Note

EXPLANATORY NOTES

The Plot of Haman   3:7-15

3:7 Casting the Lot (Pur)

There is much that we do not know about this verse. Some ancient texts actually place it later in the story, after Haman has obtained permission to issue a decree of annihilation. In that location, casting the lot more clearly functions to establish the day of the execution of the decree. In part because the text uses a Babylonian word, *Pur*, as the term for *lot*, many interpreters have suggested that the verse arose as a later editorial remark to more closely tie the story to the festival of Purim.

Difficulties with this verse go beyond placement and origin. The reader is not told who actually casts the lot or why, but simply that *they* cast a lot *before Haman*. We also have no idea what device might be used to obtain an answer. Finally, we do not know the precise answer provided by casting the lot.

The Hebrew text says that the lot falls on *the twelfth month, the month of Adar* (Feb.-Mar.), without any reference to a day of the month (3:7, NIV). Other ancient manuscripts identify a day, but those versions differ between the thirteenth and fourteenth day of Adar. Correcting to *the thirteenth of Adar* (3:7, NRSV) is consistent with the date given later in the story (8:12; 9:1, 17).

Although many questions about the origin and meaning of this verse cannot be answered with any certainty, its presence provides an interesting and somewhat mysterious introduction to Haman's plan. By casting a *lot,* a day is chosen. Readers are left to wonder what that day will bring.

3:8-9 Speech to the King

Haman's speech to the king moves seductively from a simple observation to a self-serving lie (Fox, 1991:47-8). Haman begins with an accurate observation: *"There is a certain people scattered and separated among the peoples in all the provinces of your kingdom"* (3:8).

After that, Haman's statements becomes progressively less accurate and more dangerous:*"Their laws are different from those of every other people"* (3:8). To be sure, the Jews have *some* practices and religious laws different from other people, but Haman's overstatement makes it sound dangerously disloyal. Then Haman speaks a lie to reinforce the subversive character of this unidentified people: *"They do not keep the king's laws."* From this, Haman draws a troubling conclusion: *"It is not appropriate for the king to tolerate them"* (3:8).

With that preparation, Haman turns from analysis to petition (3:9). He asks the king for a decree authorizing the destruction of this unnamed group. Haman adds a financial incentive as further inducement, enticing the king to grant his request. According to Clines (1984a), Haman's bribe amounts to two-thirds of the total annual income of the entire Persian Empire!

With his petition, Haman has successfully turned a dispute between two courtiers into a national emergency: *"It is not appropriate for the king to tolerate them."* We recall that King Ahasuerus did exactly the same thing when Queen Vashti disobeyed him (1:10-21). Like Haman here, Memucan, speaking for the royal advisers in the Vashti incident, insisted that the queen's disobedience would have negative consequences for the whole empire.

3:10-11 Response of the King

Before speaking, the king symbolizes his response to Haman's petition by action. He hands his signet ring to Haman (3:10). With this ring, Haman has the power to act on behalf of the king (cf. 3:12; 8:2, 8; Gen. 41:42). The narrator signals the importance of this action by stating Haman's full name and adding an ominous descriptive clause: *Haman . . . the Agagite, enemy of the Jews* (3:10, EFR; 3:1, notes).

The king's speech confirms his bestowal of the signet ring (3:11). Haman, whom the narrator identifies as *an enemy of the Jews*, has obtained authority to do with the Jews as he deems necessary. Though King Ahasuerus grants Haman's request, the king's response to the bribe is less certain (cf. 4:7, mentioning the bribe). Some translations make it clear that the king refuses the money: *"Keep the money"* (NIV). Other versions, however, maintain the ambiguity found in the Hebrew text: *"The money is yours"* (EFR; cf. NRSV, *"The money is given to you . . . to do with them . . ."*). This way of translating the king's response suggests that Haman is free to do with his money as he chooes, perhaps even giving it to the king.

Does King Ahasuerus know that *the Jews* are the people Haman describes as seditious? In his petition to the king, Haman does not identify the group. Not even the Greek version of the story, which supplies a text of the royal edict, indicates the name of the "treasonous" people. The Jews are not identified until Haman's subsequent annihilation decree (3:13). There is no indication that the king chooses to investigate the allegations made by his premier.

3:12-15a Issuing an Edict

The language and procedure used in this edict echo the style of the one issued after Vashti's disobedience (1:21-22). Both edicts are sweeping in scope. The first says, *Every man should be master in his own house* (1:22). The second orders people *to destroy, to kill, and to annihilate all Jews, young and old, women and children* (3:13). The distribution of both edicts is similarly global: *to all royal provinces, to every province in its own script and to every people in its own language* (1:22); *to every province in its own script and every people in its own language* (3:12).

The edict of annihilation is issued on the thirteenth day of the first month, Nisan (3:12, Mar.-Apr.). Levenson (73) notes the irony of this date. The date of issuance (thirteenth of the first month) is the day before the beginning of Passover, the festival commemorating Israel's deliverance (Lev. 23:5). In the Hebrew text, the edict designates the day of destruction as the thirteenth day of the month of Adar, exactly eleven months later (3:13). As the story develops, we shall see a new drama of Passover (deliverance) reenacted in the eleven months between Nisan 13 and Adar 13. As in the Exodus drama, here in Esther a potentially disastrous day will become a festival day.

3:15b Concluding Note

The concluding note emphasizes the effect of this decree on the palace and the population of Susa. The food and drink consumed inside the royal palace contrast with the dismay and confusion in other sectors of the city. The narrator does not elaborate on the confusion in the general population. Some interpreters have assumed the confusion was limited to alarm among the Jewish citizens. Others, however, note that Esther does not portray the Gentile population as anti-Jewish, and insist that the edict makes no sense to anyone except the one who has written it, Haman.

The entire incident reaffirms the picture of King Ahasuerus as impulsive and incompetent, but not malevolent (Talmon: 442-3). Nevertheless, if the edict is carried out as Haman plans, the Jews will be destroyed. Any such distinction will not matter to the victims.

Response of Mordecai   4:1-17

4:1-3 Ritual of Mourning

The narrative focus switches from Haman to Mordecai. Mordecai has responded to the news about *all that had been done* with a ritual of mourning, sackcloth, and ashes. This ritual is an appropriate response not only to the death of a loved one, but to any news of tragedy or impending tragedy (cf. Gen. 37:29; 2 Kings 18:37). The ritual of sackcloth and ashes was not exclusively a religious rite (cf. Gen. 37:34; 1 Kings 20:31-32), although in the biblical narratives it is frequently associated with confession in worship, either personal or corporate (1 Kings 21:27-28; Neh. 9:1; Jon. 3:5-6). In his stories about the Persian court, the Greek narrator, Herodotus, tells about individuals who sought royal attention and response by coming to the palace gate in a show of grief (Berlin, 2002:44-45). The action by Mordecai seems to have more in common with a ritual of tragedy than with a religious ritual of confession and petition. Still others see Mordecai's action as part of a hidden religious dimension in the story.

Mordecai is not alone in his response to the edict. Throughout the realm, Jews react similarly (4:3). They mourn in sackcloth and ashes, and fast and weep. The sound of their weeping echoes Mordecai's loud and bitter cry. Listeners to Mordecai would hear both the cry of one wronged (Neh. 5:1) and an appeal for help (2 Sam. 19:24, 28). His behavior does elicit a response from Queen Esther.

4:4-5 Response of Esther

Those who serve Esther apparently know of her connection with Mordecai, because they bring the information to her. The narrator does not tell us how it can be that Mordecai, the population of Susa, and the Jews throughout the realm know about the impending tragedy, while Esther knows nothing. Of course, we are not certain how much the king actually knows.

Esther acts immediately with what she intends as a helpful response. She sends Mordecai proper clothing, so that he may get rid of the sackcloth. When Mordecai refuses her offer, Esther directs (Heb.: *commands/orders*) a messenger to find out what is going on. She sends *Hathach, one of the king's eunuchs.*

4:6-17 Mission of Hathach

Hathach finds Mordecai in the main square of the city and brings back to Esther several items of information:

1. The events that have happened to Mordecai. (4:7a)
2. The sum of money Haman has offered the king. (4:7b; cf. 3:9, 11)
3. A copy of the edict authorizing the annihilation of the Jews. (4:8)

In addition, Mordecai demands (Heb.: *commands, orders*) that Esther intervene with the king.

Mordecai's demand initiates a dialogue between the queen and her erstwhile benefactor, Mordecai. In sending Mordecai clothing (4:4), Esther has already become more assertive than she appeared when she first became queen: *for Esther obeyed Mordecai just as when she was brought up by him* (2:20). This time, however, Esther's response to Mordecai, through Hathach, is not simple compliance.

Esther describes for Mordecai the reality of the royal court (Bellis: 214). She reminds him that, as everyone in the country knows, a person entering the inner court without invitation risks death (4:11). Furthermore, for a month Esther has not been invited into the king's presence. Esther has no reason to assume that she will suddenly be received with favor by the king. The narrator does not explain how it can be that everyone in the palace and the provinces knows about this constraint, but that Mordecai appears to know nothing of it, or perhaps thinks that Esther can appeal to the king anyhow.

As the exchange between Esther and Mordecai becomes increasingly intense, the messenger, Hathach, virtually disappears. To be sure, the narrator does not bring Esther and Mordecai face-to-face—not yet. Mordecai gives his reply to *them* (4:12-13), and Esther simply speaks *in reply* (4:15).

Mordecai begins his speech by asserting that Esther is in mortal danger regardless of what she decides in reaction to this royal edict (4:13). The reader cannot be sure that the queen is actually in the same danger as other Jews. Mordecai has earlier insisted that Esther hide her Jewish identity (2:10, 20). Yet in 2:22 (notes) the narrator has shown that the king knows of a connection between Esther and Mordecai (cf. 3:4). In 4:4 Esther's attendants know of her connection with Mordecai. While the king knows that Mordecai is a Jew (6:10), the narrator has not revealed what the king knows of Esther's identity. Not until 7:3-4 does Esther reveal her Jewish identity directly to the king.

At this point, however, Mordecai is engaged in an argument that often encourages overstatement rather than precision. He declares that if Esther decides to remain passive, help *will rise for the Jews from another quarter,* and Esther and her *father's family will perish* (4:14). Then Mordecai quickly switches his tone from threat to encouragement: *"Who knows? Perhaps you have come to royal dignity for just such a time as this"* (4:14b).

Whether or not Mordecai's insubordination is justified in defying Haman and disobeying the King's command (3:3), he has set in motion a potential slaughter that he cannot stop. Will Esther be able to take advantage of her royal position to defuse the situation?

Interpreters have long discussed whether Mordecai's speech implies divine intervention and/or assistance if Esther refuses to act (4:13-14). Many have taken the phrase *from another quarter* (Heb.: *maqom*) as a veiled reference to God, as in later Jewish literature, which often avoided speaking the holy name. Other readers suggest that *"Who knows?"* may be a reference to God, comparing this text to Jonah 3:9: "Who knows? God may relent and change his mind, . . . so that we do not perish" (cf. Jer. 29:23; Eccles. 6:12). Either phrase (or both) may allude to God, but we cannot know for sure. The Greek version tells the story with God actively present and with Mordecai praying, "You know all things, . . . O Lord" (13:12, NRSV Apocrypha, in Addition C). But the Hebrew text allows readers much more room to wonder.

Esther responds to Mordecai with assertive instruction: *"Go, gather all the Jews . . . in Susa"* (4:16). She directs Mordecai to call all of the Jewish community to *fast*. The Greek version of the story understands Esther as calling the community not just to fast, but also to prayer. It thus incorporates prayers of petition by both Mordecai and Esther (chaps. 13-14, NRSV Apocrypha, Addition C). The Hebrew text, however, mentions only fasting.

For her part, Esther declares that she will defy the law and go to the king: *"If I perish, I perish"* (4:16). Esther's words echo those of Jacob when he agreed to allow Benjamin to accompany his brothers to Egypt: "If I am bereaved of my children, I am bereaved" (Gen. 43:14). The phase signals a letting go—whether out of resignation or courage, the listener must decide.

4:17 Concluding Note

The episode closes with a statement indicating that this has now become Esther's story: *Mordecai then went away and did everything as Esther had ordered him.* Chapter 4 begins with Mordecai initiating the action. At the end of the chapter, the situation is quite different. A Jewish orphan woman with no inherent power of her own has taken charge. She now instructs Mordecai and is prepared to risk death in behalf of her people.

THE TEXT IN BIBLICAL CONTEXT

Women in Danger

In ancient Israel, the social position of women was similar to that of most other women in the ancient Near East (Meyers: 1988). The records and narratives feature men in the public realm: religious, political, economic, and social. Women apparently functioned more frequently in the less-public realm. Calling the women's domain "private" or "domestic" must not imply that women were less influential than men, especially in the agrarian village of ancient Israel (Meyers, 1999).

In royal society, nevertheless, women in the public realm frequently found themselves at a disadvantage and sometimes in danger. Whether in the sanctuary or law court, the narrative and legal literature portrays the woman primarily as a dependent, permitted to act independently only when the lack of a male required a woman to assume a role, for example, as a landowner.

The family formed the basic social unit of ancient society, a realm where women seem to have had much power, directly influencing not only the family, but also community life (Meyers, 1999:111-6). In the Decalogue, the woman was to be equally honored with the man (Exod. 20:12//Deut. 5:16). In village life, a distinction between public and private domains may not be helpful, especially if such identification implies strong separation of realms and subordination of the "private" realm.

Even so, while women had a central role in the family in both the agrarian and royal society, they faced constraints and dangers men seldom confronted. The biblical stories illustrate the danger to women when circumstances or decisions place them in the public arena. Infertility and famine set Sarah in alarming circumstances (Gen. 13; 16). The mysterious death of Judah's sons nearly cost Tamar her life (Gen. 38). Men could misuse sex, endangering or even abusing women, as in the stories of Dinah (Gen. 34), Bathsheba (2 Sam. 11), Tamar (David's daughter, 2 Sam. 13), and Esther. Famine and death proved perilous to Naomi and Ruth (Ruth 1–3).

Mary, Jesus' mother, found herself in crisis because, though engaged, she was pregnant outside of marriage (Matt. 1:18-25; Luke 1:26-56; 2:5). In virtually every such biblical narrative, we find the woman in some degree of danger caused or intensified by her gender.

Obedience to Mordecai has thrust Esther into the public realm in a foreign country. That in itself signals danger. Mordecai asks Esther to act in a way (going directly to the king) that she realizes would increase the danger for anyone in the palace. Recognizing the danger of simply being a woman in the public realm, the biblical narratives tell stories of women required to act carefully, creatively, and quickly. While possessing few options and uncertain power, they acted to achieve their goals, saving the lives of themselves and others. Ruth risked her life on a threshing floor to obtain an heir for her mother-in-law. Mary, finding herself pregnant, ran to Judea and the protection of Elizabeth. Now Esther decides to go the king: *"If I perish, I perish"* (4:16).

THE TEXT IN THE LIFE OF THE CHURCH

For Such a Time as This

Feasts and banquets carry the narrative of Esther along, from the king's ostentatious banquets with which the story opens to the concluding celebration of Purim, a festival to be kept *throughout every generation* (9:28). Chapter 4 stands in dramatic contrast to the food fest found in the rest of the story. This moment in the narrative prompts fasting, not feasting, thus becoming the narrative moment that changes the course of the story.

Esther 3:7—4:17

Mordecai cannot change the course of events. His conflict with Haman has set in motion a tragedy that he has no power to avert. Control of the future seems to lie in the hands of an incompetent king who authorizes an edict of annihilation, and in the hands of an evil premier who issues the decree. Mordecai turns to Esther, demanding that she do something.

The narrative provides no previous evidence that Esther is capable of dealing with the catastrophic disaster that lies eleven months ahead. We have been introduced to her as a Jewish orphan, a pretty woman who has become queen on the basis of her beauty and obedience. She hides her Jewish identity at the request of Mordecai. Later, that same Mordecai turns to Esther to deliver the Jewish people, whom Mordecai then identifies as *her people* (4:8). Esther responds to the emergency. In so doing, she changes disaster into deliverance.

Mordecai's speech suggests that when person, position, and circumstances all come together, an individual can make a decisive difference. Such moments, which Mordecai calls *for just such a time as this*, Paul in Galatians 4:4 calls "the fullness of time" (cf. Eph. 1:10). Faithful action in the fullness of time changes everything for all time and people. Generations have retold the biblical story as the great drama of opportune moments. Thus we remember Moses, the fugitive shepherd, called to bring his people out from Egypt (Exod. 3:12). We remember the baby born in Bethlehem, named Jesus, "for he will save his people from their sins" (Matt. 1:21).

This convergence of person, position, and circumstances, which some call coincidence or fate, Christians recognize as Providence. Whether named (in the Greek version of Esther) or unnamed (in Hebrew), the eyes of faith discern the hand of God, providing unexpected and often danger-filled opportunities for people to redirect the course of events away from death and toward life.

Therefore, it is not surprising that Mordecai's phrase, *for just such a time as this* (4:14), has been lifted up frequently in pulpit and classroom. Indeed, the phrase has entered popular discourse even where reference to the book of Esther has disappeared. Politicians declare themselves the right person *for just such a time as this*. Some teachers recount history as the story of great individuals who have made a difference because they were available *for just such a time as this*. Elders urge children to consider that they too might be chosen *for just such a time as this*, whatever the time or circumstances.

Some individuals may hear this phrase as encouragement. Others may find it oppressive, laying a responsibility on them that they cannot or will not accept. Mordecai loads just such a responsibility onto

Esther. The witness of the biblical tradition encourages us to remember that God not only opens up special moments and opportunities, but also accompanies us through the danger or difficulty. Though individuals can and do make a difference, the outcome of the drama does not rest on any one person's shoulders, and no one walks alone into *such a time as this.*

Esther 5:1-14

Episode 2
Esther's First Intervention

PREVIEW

In the next three episodes (5:1—7:10), the plans of the two courtiers work themselves out. Haman has obtained from the king a decree authorizing the annihilation of the subversive people (3:8-11), and Mordecai has obtained from the queen a commitment to intervene in behalf of *her people* (4:8). Their own destiny now basically lies outside the control of the two courtiers whose antagonism has initiated the crisis. The clock is running toward the moment when the decree of annihilation will be carried out. Meanwhile, the queen has assumed the responsibility of persuading the king to revoke that irrevocable decree.

An important shift in the book occurs in the previous chapter (4:1-17). The story has presented Esther as a beautiful and compliant woman. While undoubtedly still beautiful, now she has seized the initiative. Her decisions and conduct will drive the action of the story forward, defining the course of the plot. While Esther has moved into that position in response to a challenge by Mordecai, the narrator notes the new relationship between the two: now Mordecai follows Esther's instructions (4:17).

From this point forward, another and less visible woman will also play a key role in the narrative. Zeresh, the wife of Haman, enters the story in this episode. Initially, she instructs her husband on the next steps he should take concerning Mordecai (5:14), counsel he eagerly embraces. Later she will inform him that his cause is lost (6:13). While it is the men who initiate the conflict, the women to a considerable extent control the resolution.

OUTLINE

Intervention by Esther, 5:1-8
    5:1-2   The Approach
    5:3-5a   The Dialogue
    5:5b-8 The Banquet

Decision by Haman, 5:9-14
    5:9-10a   The Problem
    5:10b-14a The Counsel
    5:14b   The Response

EXPLANATORY NOTES

Intervention by Esther 5:1-8

5:1-2 The Approach

Mordecai has suggested that Esther may have come to *royal dignity for just such a time as this* (4:14). Therefore, *on the third day* (end of fast, 4:16), Esther dons her royal robes. No one can overlook the social location of this episode since 5:1 has a sixfold repetition of the Hebrew root for *royal (m-l-k): royal robes, king's palace, king's hall, king, royal throne,* and *palace* (cf. 1:1-22, Preview). Esther finds herself right in the midst of a *royal* setting.

Esther stands in the *inner court* (5:1), presumably the palace area that houses the royal apartment and the *throne* room. She apparently does not enter the throne room itself. However, in the moment the king sees Esther, *she won his favor* (5:2). The mysterious, magnetic presence that Esther brings with her, captivates the king, exactly as when Esther first entered the royal world (2:9, 15, 17). The king immediately extends to her *the golden scepter*. Using a literary style that conveys deliberate caution, the narrator concludes with the statement, *Esther approached and touched the top of the scepter*. Esther's fear will likely not become reality (4:11). She will not die for an unlawful approach before the king, at least not immediately.

5:3-5a The Dialogue

The dialogue between the king and Esther preserves the royal formality established by Esther's approach. The king speaks first, asking two questions: *"What is it. . . ? What is your request?"* He adds an offer to grant her any request up to and including half the empire (5:3; cf. 5:6; 7:2; Mark 6:23). Esther's response seems as surprising as the king's offer. She asks for a banquet! More specifically, Esther asks for a dinner for three: the king, the queen, and Haman. The reader suspects that the queen has not fully answered the king's query: *"What is it, Queen Esther? What is your request?"*

Interpreters, both Jewish and Christian, have struggled to explain Esther's petition for a banquet. Why does she not forthrightly state her request for the king to set aside the annihilation decree? Some have suggested that Esther's anxiety and timidity cause her to postpone the dangerous petition. Others propose that Esther intends to use wine to increase her chances of success. In fact—typical of the reticence characteristic in Hebrew narrative—neither Esther nor the narrator explains her request [Characteristics]. Although the reader can hear Esther's words and see her actions, the text provides no access to her thoughts and strategy.

The king immediately grants Esther's initial request (5:5a). It is clearly less costly than the offer he has made. Like Mordecai earlier (4:17), King Ahasuerus acts in response to Esther. Esther has become the one setting the agenda and directing the action.

5:5b-8 The Banquet

The king and Haman attend Esther's dinner. This banquet carries quite different overtones from earlier ones, the ostentatious royal feasts with which the narrative begins (1:1-9), and the wedding feast at Esther's marriage to the king (2:18). Although the wedding feast was called *"Esther's banquet,"* that banquet was *for* Esther. This banquet is *by* Esther.

This is not the first small dinner party in the story. A royal dinner for two followed the decree of annihilation. That scene is incongruous and unsettling, given the confusion in Susa over the decree (3:15). Esther's banquet for three also seems incongruous, with an ominous feel about it. The reader knows that Esther has asked to dine with the enemy (Haman). This dinner setting calls to mind the ancient tradition of the dangerous banquet—a dinner invitation in which hospitality and frivolity cover the danger that attends the meal. In this case, we cannot be sure who is in greatest danger—Esther, Haman, or perhaps even the king.

The king interrupts the flow of wine at the banquet by reiterating his offer to Esther: *"What is your petition? It shall be granted you. And what is your request?"* (5:6). Apparently the king shares the readers' sense that Esther has not yet voiced her real request. In response, Esther requests yet another banquet! She adds that *tomorrow* she will, in fact, make known her request (5:7-8).

Many readers have found this second postponement even more difficult to understand. Recognizing that Esther has already drawn the king into his most comfortable ambience, a dinner, some interpreters attribute this further delay to Esther's anxiety and loss of nerve. However, neither the words of Esther nor comments by the narrator provide even a hint of Esther's motivation or strategy. We know only that she asks for another banquet, promising a further word at that time. Whatever the reason for a second banquet, the postponement increases tension in the narrative. Each day's delay brings the decree of annihilation that much closer to fulfillment.

The narrator does not report the king's response to Esther's request. Nevertheless, the initiative for action in the narrative now rests with Esther. We anticipate that Ahasuerus will again agree to her request.

Decision by Haman 5:9-14

5:9-10a The Problem

The dinner has not turned out to be dangerous for anyone. Haman leaves the dinner overjoyed. The Hebrew text uses words that express deep and intoxicating joy. Yet suddenly Haman's mood changes—from ecstacy to anger (5:9). He comes past Mordecai, who overtly expresses his disdain for Haman by not rising or trembling before him. Levenson notes that at this point, Mordecai has escalated their conflict (Levenson: 92). Earlier he refused to bow before Haman (3:2); now Mordecai does not even acknowledge Haman's presence. Barely controlling his fury, Haman continues home (5:10a). This brief narrative sequence reveals the laceration in Haman's life. Disdain from Mordecai cuts deep into the joy of Haman's royal position and honor.

5:10b-14 The Counsel and the Response

The scene shifts from the royal palace to the home of Haman. After gathering together his friends and family, Haman details his accomplishments (5:11). In direct speech, however, Haman admits that all the honor in his life is effectively negated by his shame from the presence of *the Jew Mordecai* (Klein: 166). That humiliation, overshadowing all the royal honors, including dinner with the queen, has seized control of Haman's thoughts, emotions, and actions. He appears paralyzed by the problem of Mordecai.

In response to the "Mordecai problem," Haman mirrors the procedure of his king. Like Ahasuerus, Haman turns to others for counsel. Zeresh, his wife, apparently takes the lead, recommending that Haman build a gallows and convince the king to execute this adversary. With that accomplished, Haman could go to the queen's next dinner in the same frame of mind as when he left the last dinner, intoxicatingly happy (5:9, 14). Haman's response to his wife's counsel mirrors his king: *This advice pleased Haman* (5:14; cf. 1:21; 2:4).

The proposed instrument of execution is huge, about eighty feet (24 meters) high. Although the Hebrew text calls it a *stake*, many readers picture a gallows. The reference is probably to a pole on which the dead body is impaled, an act of humiliation and shame. This would balance the shame Haman has felt at Mordecai's refusal to acknowledge his royal position. Later, in an ironic twist, each of Haman's sons will be impaled on a stake after they have been killed (9:10, 13; cf. 2 Sam. 21:9).

THE TEXT IN BIBLICAL CONTEXT

The Dangerous Banquet

The tradition of the dangerous banquet appears in the literature of Israel's neighbors as well as in the Bible. In Egyptian literature, the god Set invited his brother, Osiris, to a banquet. As a part of the games played at the feast, Set lured Osiris into a box, then nailed the box shut and threw it into the Nile River.

The chronicles of David's reign describe a dangerous banquet between long-time enemies. In 2 Samuel, the narrator relates that following Saul's death, David made a covenant with Abner, Saul's military chief (2 Sam. 3). Abner represented the elders of the northern tribes, Israel. This covenant effectively made David king of the northern tribes (Israel) as well as the southern tribes (Judah). David sealed the covenant with a banquet, inviting the political and military leadership of the north. Abner departed in peace (3:21). But this peace accord between David and his former enemy enraged Joab, David's own military chief, who sent a messenger to Abner and brought him back to Hebron. Joab took Abner aside "to speak with him privately," then murdered him (3:26-27). The banquet of peace turned out to be a deadly dinner.

The Christian church annually remembers the dangerous banquet in the life of Jesus, a meal that tradition calls "the Last Supper." The danger that attends this meal, briefly mentioned in Luke (22:21-23), is a significant feature of the narration in Matthew (26:20-25), Mark (14:17-21), and especially John (13:21-30). According to the synoptic Gospels, this banquet of betrayal was a Passover meal, the festival that reenacts Israel's deliverance from danger and death.

THE TEXT IN THE LIFE OF THE CHURCH

Obsessions

According to his own words, Haman lacks only one thing—Mordecai's respect. That one missing element becomes the defining dimension of Haman's life. He enjoys the splendor of riches, the esteem of family, the honor of a royal position. Wealth, family, royal honor—none of that counts for anything beside the humiliation that comes from Mordecai's disdain. How can it be that one who has almost everything, becomes obsessed by the one thing lacking?

The biblical narrative portrays Saul as similarly afflicted. This handsome man of the tribe of Benjamin, who "stood head and shoulders above everyone else" (1 Sam. 9:2), was anointed as ruler over his people (1 Sam. 10:1). In the course of events, Saul became obsessed with the popularity of David, the best friend of his son Jonathan. David, Saul's palace musician, twice became the object of a spear thrown by Saul. Both times Saul missed. Even after David twice spared Saul's life and was embraced by Saul, David recognized that he was not safe from Saul's jealous anger: "I shall . . . perish one day by the hand of Saul" (1 Sam. 27:1).

The first biblical story of human interaction reminds us of the danger of such obsession. In the garden of Eden, God gave the man and the woman permission to eat of every tree but one. Predictably, they become obsessed by the forbidden tree, the one tree whose fruit they were not to eat, "the tree of the knowledge of good and evil" (Gen. 2:17). Their obsession led to disaster.

In their book about hospice care, *Final Gifts*, Maggie Callanan and Patricia Kelley talk about the strange conspiracy that can arise between the ones near death and their family. The family who becomes obsessed with their own need to keep their loved one alive may lose an important moment together. In the final weeks and days, they may forfeit the chance to do the work of letting go. The compulsion to prolong breath may increase suffering and generate anger.

Indeed, obsession with life as they have known it may prevent the family from growing in faith.

The same thing happens in many settings. Governments become consumed by the one community in their country that they cannot control. Pastors become preoccupied with the one voice of dissent within the congregation. Children desire only the toys that they do not have. Family members become consumed with the need to prolong the life of the dying. The histories of society, the church, and our families remind us of how valuable is the counsel of the psalmist: "Those who seek the LORD lack no good thing" (Ps. 34:10).

Esther 6:1-13

Episode 3
Royal Decree Honoring Mordecai

PREVIEW

This episode provides a narrative interlude between the two dinners attended by King Ahasuerus, Queen Esther, and Haman. The first dinner, given at the request of Esther, has ended without a clear resolution of Esther's original but unexpressed petition (5:1-8; cf. 4:8). Haman has left the dinner happy, but both the king and queen recognize that the dinner itself has not exhausted Esther's petition. There will be another dinner (6:14—7:10). The purpose and outcome of that dinner remain for later. Meanwhile, the narrative does not rest, and neither does the king.

Chapter 6 provides the most obvious example of narrative irony, a literary feature that characterizes the entire book *[Comedy]*. After a sleepless night, the king inquires of Haman: *"What shall be done for the man whom the king wishes to honor"* (6:6)? Haman misreads the purpose of the king's question. This miscalculation results in an outcome exactly the opposite of Haman's intention. It is important that we carefully read the king's speeches in verses 3 and 6. The king's word choice makes possible Haman's miscalculation and sets up the ironic conclusion.

As the episode draws to a close, the pace of the narrative increases dramatically. Haman *hurried* home (6:12) but does not even have opportunity to conclude his conversation with his wife before the story itself hurries on (6:14). From this moment, the story moves quickly to the decisive scene, the downfall of Haman.

In "A Glance at the Whole" (Overview), we noted the chiastic symmetry found in the narrative of Esther. This chiasm points to Esther 6 as a key moment of transition in the story. Haman's fortunes suddenly turn, and he finds himself bestowing honor on Mordecai, the one person who has refused to honor him. Haman's wife gives voice to the reversal about to befall Haman and Mordecai.

OUTLINE
The Bestowal of Honor by the King, 6:1-12
    6:1-2   Introductory Note
    6:3-9   The King Takes Counsel
        Dialogue with Advisers, 6:3-5
        Dialogue with Haman, 6:6-9
    6:10-11 Decision and Implementation
    6:12   Concluding Note
The Advice from Haman's Wife, 6:13

EXPLANATORY NOTES

The Bestowal of Honor by the King 6:1-12

6:1-2 Introductory Note

The episode opens with King Ahasuerus mysteriously unable to sleep. The Greek editions of the story (as in LXX) attribute this insomnia to God (6:1, NRSV Apocrypha). The Hebrew text, however, provides no explanation. Whatever the cause, the king's sleeplessness proves to be a blessing for Mordecai. Indeed, this entire interlude depends on coincidence—or Providence.

The king decides to pass nighttime hours listening to a reading of the royal annals. Royal records such as these are kept to chronicle the events of a king's reign (cf. 1 Kings 14:19; Ezra 4:14-15). The reader cannot be sure whether the king expects this reading to provide entertainment or sedation. Regardless of the intention, the reading furnishes a timely item of information. An entry in the royal chronicle records an incident from early in the king's reign. It reminds him of a conspiracy to assassinate the king, an attempted murder thwarted by information provided by Mordecai (2:21-23).

6:3-9 The King Takes Counsel

Dialogue with Advisers (3:3-5). The king's conversation with his advisers reveals that the royal administration has not been working as effectively as it should, especially regarding the bestowal of honor in response to meritorious service. In the Persian world, bestowing honor is no small matter, for honor and shame repeatedly function as core values for the culture (Klein: 149-52, 166). The king has dismissed Queen Vashti because she brought shame on him; Haman's rage at Mordecai is prompted by the latter's refusal to honor him. Hence, when the advisers report that in the incident involving Mordecai, "*Nothing has been done for him*" (6:3), the oversight requires a royal response. Mordecai has received no honor for his honorable service to the king.

The king's verbal response is not to order corrective action, but to ask "*Who is in the court,*" in attendance? Again, coincidentally or providentially, Haman has just entered the royal palace. From Haman's dialogue with his family (5:14), the reader knows that he is ready to ask for the execution of Mordecai. Events will take a quite different turn.

Dialogue with Haman (6:6-9). The king begins the dialogue with a seemingly benign request for information on how he might honor someone [*Questions*]. Unfortunately for Haman, the king does not indicate the reason for his request or the favored person. Lacking the correct context within which to understand the question, Haman's self-absorption leads him to draw the wrong conclusion, that the king wants to honor Haman (6:6). Hence, Haman responds by describing the ceremony of honor that he desires for himself.

Haman lays out a grand plan for public recognition of the one to be honored (6:8-9). But in his eagerness to congratulate himself, Haman miscalculates the king's intention and also misspeaks. He places the royal crown not on the head of the honoree, but on the horse (6:8)!

Interpreters have tried to explain or correct Haman's error. Perhaps the *crown* refers to the headdress of the horse. Or perhaps Haman means the horse on which the king rides when the king has the crown on his own head. It is doubtful that such interpretative correction is necessary. The comedy of this situation is obvious: a man's craving for honor causes him to get everything wrong [*Comedy*]. Haman's speech not only puts the royal crown on the horse; it will also force him to bestow honor on his archenemy.

6:10-11 Decision and Implementation

Suddenly, the real situation becomes clear. The king directs Haman to carry out the ceremony *quickly*, not for Haman, but for Mordecai, *the Jew*. For the first time, the narrative indicates that the king knows Mordecai's ethnic identity. We still do not know if the king knows what people are decreed for destruction. Haman has not told the king the identity of the seditious *certain people* he has targeted (3:8). Now Haman ironically stumbles into this shameful situation because the king has not told him till now the identity of one to be honored.

The text does not record Haman's immediate reaction. The narrative's descriptive reticence invites the reader's own reaction in identifying with Haman. Hebrew narrative often requires more reader participation than contemporary writing, where generally the reactions and emotions of the characters are spelled out in more detail *[Characteristics of Hebrew Narrative]*. What is Haman's reaction when he realizes that he has completely misread the situation? Can the king "see" the miscalculation in Haman's face?

Haman carries out the instructions of the king. He clothes his enemy in royal robes and proclaims in the city center: *"Thus it shall be done for the man whom the king wishes to honor."*

6:12 Concluding Note

Although the narrator does not tell us about Haman's initial reaction, we learn about his emotions when he returns home after the parade of honor for Mordecai. He runs to his house in *mourning, . . . his head covered in shame*. Now Haman is in mourning and Mordecai is clothed in royal dress—the reverse of an earlier time when Haman dined leisurely with the king (3:15) and Mordecai walked the streets dressed in sackcloth (4:1).

The Advice from Haman's Wife 6:13

This episode concludes in the same locale as the previous unit, with Haman at his house, listening to the advice of his wife, Zeresh, and friends/advisers. Earlier, their advice pleased Haman (5:14). We are not told Haman's reaction to these words of Zeresh. We can suspect he was much less pleased.

Haman's wife Zeresh informs him, *"If Mordecai . . . is of the Jewish people, you will not prevail against him, but will surely fall before him"* (6:13). It remains unclear what prompts these words from Zeresh. Haman has earlier told her of Mordecai's Jewish identity (5:13). At that time she advised him to seek the king's permission to execute Mordecai. Suddenly, as Haman's fortunes have shifted into reverse, his wife has joined the new direction, because Haman cannot prevail over one *of the Jewish people.*

Perhaps, as some interpreters suggest, Zeresh gives voice to the confidence of the Diaspora Jews: Judaism will not be destroyed by the dispersion that has made Jews a minority in many, often hostile, communities throughout the Persian and later the Greek and Roman worlds *[Diaspora].*

To some degree the story of Esther appears to ground that Diaspora confidence in the promise expressed by the Oracle of Balaam (Num. 24). The narrator has already told the reader that Haman's lineage goes back to Amalek (3:1, notes). The Oracle of Balaam assured following generations that, in the end, the descendants of Amalek would not prevail: "First among the nations was Amalek, but its end is to perish forever" (Num. 24:20).

The words of Zeresh reinforce the inevitability of Haman's demise. The narrator does not tell us of Haman's reaction to these words from family and friends. It must feel to Haman that almost everyone has turned against him. They have.

THE TEXT IN BIBLICAL CONTEXT

Irony and Divine Intervention

Though the literary device of irony pervades the entire narrative of Esther *[Comedy],* in this episode irony becomes explicit. Haman's catastrophe provides a classic case of a situation in which the results of an action are exactly the opposite of the actor's intention. Throughout the story, Haman measures each step he takes for its contribution to increasing his own importance and/or destroying those who refuse to honor him. His collapse comes at the moment of his greatest pride.

At the queen's invitation, he joins the royal couple for dinner. Following that, Haman receives prideful endorsement by his family and friends. However, in a humiliating reversal, Haman is forced to walk through the central square of the city, leading the royal horse, in a parade of honor for the one person who has refused to honor and respect him.

The account of Haman's disaster in the text we are following does not detail the cause of the reversal. However, other biblical narratives and poetry bear witness to God as the author of such reversals. In the Christian church, the passage in Luke's Gospel known as Mary's Magnificat expresses through poetry reversal initiated by divine intervention:

He has shown strength with his arm;
> he has scattered the proud in the thoughts of their hearts.
He has brought down the powerful from their thrones,
> and lifted up the lowly;
he has filled the hungry with good things,
> and sent the rich away empty. (Luke 1:51-53)

This recognition of God's role in the reversal of the arrogant also found expression in the poetry of the prophet Obadiah:

Your proud heart has deceived you,
> you that live in the clefts of the rock,
> whose dwelling is in the heights.
You say in your heart,
> "Who will bring me down to the ground?"
Though you soar aloft like the eagle,
> though your nest is set among the stars,
> from there I will bring you down,
>> says the Lord. (Obad. 3–4)

Irony often serves as a literary device of hope for the oppressed. Through story and song, oppressed people envision a Haman-like reversal that would bring the powerful down from their "thrones" so that the lowly might have food, clothing, and safety. Trusting in the justice of God, the oppressed anticipate the day of the Lord's reversal. Apocalyptic literature, displayed in the latter chapters of Daniel and in the book of Revelation, serves as a dramatic portrayal of such hope.

In the Christian tradition, the passion narrative of Jesus' death serves as the central story of divine irony. According to the Gospel accounts, religious and political leaders had long sought to destroy Jesus (Matt. 12:9-14). With his arrest, they found the opportunity they had been seeking (Matt. 27:1). The narratives report that these enemies of Jesus had to overcome the reluctance of Pilate (Matt. 27:24). They appeared to succeed, and Jesus was executed. However, "on the third day," in spite of extraordinary efforts to assure that Jesus' death would be the end of the story, women who went to the tomb discovered that Jesus was not there. An angel said, "He has been raised" (Matt. 27:62—28:6). Ironically, the very action intended to kill Jesus and end his movement, produced exactly the opposite outcome.

One biblical speech that neatly expresses irony initiated by divine intervention comes from words of Joseph in Genesis 50. Upon meeting his brothers in Egypt, Joseph interpreted the events that nearly ended his life: "You intended to harm me, but God intended it for good to accomplish what is now being done, the saving of many lives" (Gen. 50:20, NIV).

THE TEXT IN THE LIFE OF THE CHURCH
A Haughty Spirit

In a saying widely quoted in the church and culture, the sage declared, "Pride goes before destruction, and a haughty spirit before a fall" (Prov. 16:18). This episode of Haman's miscalculation provides a perfect example.

History—social, political, and religious—provides more illustrations than one would wish. Pride, with its inherent disdain for dissent, has long plagued the church. In the sixteenth century, the power of the Roman Catholic Church and the supremacy of the papacy had only occasionally been challenged. The church responded to such challenges with violent contempt. In response to the abuses of the church's prideful power, Martin Luther, a German monk, priest, and professor, posted a list of ninety-five theses on the door of the Castle Church in Wittenberg. This academic action proved the catalyst that felled the "haughty spirit" of the Roman Church. Destructive pride, however, is not limited to the sixteenth-century church centered in Rome. A haughty spirit has repeatedly rent the garment of the Christian church in every land and age.

Aware of the proverbial truth, "Pride goes before destruction," the believers church communities have sought to avoid not only pride, but any appearance of pride. The wisdom saying they have tried to embody comes from the Beatitudes: "Blessed are the meek, for they will inherit the earth" (Matt. 5:5). One can hear aversion to even the suggestion of pride in the believers church lore about servant saints who, in going about their work in service of others, were almost fearful lest their work be recognized publicly. Under no circumstances would these saints claim importance for their own talents and abilities.

Kenneth Morse tells a version of a story ascribed to various saints in Brethren, Mennonite, and Quaker circles. According to Morse, Rufus Bucher encountered a young man who handed him a pamphlet entitled, "Brother, Are You Saved?" Bucher agreed that it was an important question, but he disclaimed any ability to answer fairly: "I might be prejudiced in my own behalf. You'd better go . . . and ask . . . the hardware merchant, what he thinks about it. Or you might go to the . . . grocer or to one of my neighbors. . . . While there, you might ask my wife and children. I'll be ready to let their answers stand as my own" (Morse: no. 53).

It is possible for Christian communities to become preoccupied with humility, turning it into a prideful virtue. Demonstrating humility can become a test of Christian discipleship, with the appearance of pride serving as a sign of unfaithfulness. In that regard, one notes the dilemma of the plain dress expected in Mennonite and Dunkard communities until early in the twentieth century. On one hand, advocates for plain dress worried lest the change to popular dress would cause members to take pride in outward appearances. On the other hand, plain dress served as a sign, sometimes carried in a prideful way, that they were different. The plain folk intended to live as faithful, humble servants, not "conformed to this world" like some others (Rom. 12:2).

Esther 6:14—7:10

Episode 4
Esther's Second Intervention

PREVIEW

This episode provides the climax to the conflict between Haman and Mordecai, a conflict that requires Esther's intervention (4:8-14). Esther's strategy has developed slowly. She has cautiously approached the king (5:1-2). Although King Ahasuerus received Esther graciously, indeed enthusiastically, she has not immediately asked for relief from the decree of genocide against the Jews. Instead, she has requested a banquet, inviting only the king and Haman to dine with her (5:4).

At the dinner, the king has presented Esther with another opportunity to reveal her request. Again, Esther chose not to do so, but to ask for yet another banquet with the same guest list. Esther has promised to disclose at this second dinner the petition that has prompted her approach to the king. As we shall see, Esther's deliberate strategy will succeed in focusing the king's rage against his previously trusted adviser, Haman.

Adele Berlin (2002:69) reminds us not to overlook the comic elements in this episode. We have seen in a drama almost equal parts comedy and tragedy. To a considerable extent, the comic actions of the king have generated the tragic elements in the story. In the banquet scene in chapter 7, readers may overlook the comic dimensions, focusing only on the more sobering elements, such as Esther's silence at Haman's plea for mercy, a silence that results in his execution. Yet at this dinner we find the same comic king, one who extravagantly offers to give away half the kingdom, who reacts with rage in confusing situations, who misreads circumstances, and who always relies on the advice of others to figure out what to do.

OUTLINE
Introductory Note, 6:14—7:1

The Banquet, 7:2-9
    7:2-4   The Petition
        The King's Offer, 7:2
        Esther's Request, 7:3-4
    7:5-6   The Response
        Response of the King, 7:5
        Accusation by Esther, 7:6a
        Reaction of Haman, 7:6b
    7:7-9   The Decision
        Actions of the King and Haman, 7:7-8
        Advice of Harbona, 7:9a
        The King's Command, 7:9b

Concluding Note, 7:10

EXPLANATORY NOTES

Introductory Note 6:14—7:1

The narrative transition in 6:14 allows chapters 6 and 7 to dissolve into one another (Clines, 1984a: 310). For that reason, some commentaries include 6:14 with the previous episode. Even while the discussion continues at Haman's house, royal officials have arrived and *hurried* Haman off to the second banquet given by Esther. The narrative structure in which the banquet episode invades Haman's family meeting adds urgency to the word *hurry*.

The narrative introduces this banquet in a way similar to the previous dinner for three (5:5). In both cases, Haman is brought *quickly*, and *the king and Haman came to the banquet* together (5:5; 7:1). Because Haman has been snatched from a family discussion anticipating his doom, this banquet has an increased air of danger missing even from the first dinner.

The Banquet 7:2-9

7:2-4 The Petition

The king opens the dinner conversation with the same offer to Esther he has issued twice before (7:2; 5:3, 6). This offer, *"even to half of my kingdom,"* exhibits comic extravagance. One wonders what the king would do if Esther would accept his offer. The story might end quite differently. As readers, we know that Esther's mission is something other than half the royal realm. But will she request yet another dinner?

This time Esther's response to the king's offer takes a new turn. She begins by politely appealing to the king's interest in and desire for Esther herself: *"If I have won your favor"* (7:3). On the basis of the king's bond with her, the queen requests the preservation of her own life *"and the lives of my people."*

According to Levenson (101), Esther's request reflects a common pattern in such petitions. As Israel prepared to enter the Promised Land, God refused to accompany the stubborn refugees across the Jordan (Exod. 33). As leader, Moses sought to intervene on behalf of the people. In his petition, Moses based his petition on God's special relationship to Moses himself. Moses sought to translate that personal bond into favor for the people: "Now if I have found favor in your sight. . . . Consider too that this nation is your people" (33:13). Moses succeeded. God granted his petition.

Esther explains her people's plight to Ahasuerus, using language taken from the decree of destruction: *destroyed, killed, annihilated* (3:13//7:4). The queen insists that she would not be bothering the king if the decree had mandated merely slavery: *"I would have held my peace."*

That much of Esther's speech is clear. But the next phrase is less clear. Frequently, translations continue with an expanded reason similar to the NIV: *"because no such distress [slavery] would justify disturbing the king."* Other scholars, however, have sought to account for the word *enemy* (tsar), which appears in Esther's speech here (paralleled in 7:6). Hence, according to the NRSV, Esther suggests that no *enemy* can pay enough to compensate for the king's loss (of the queen?).

In either case, Esther has a two-fold agenda. She must define the offense in a way that excludes the king from guilt. At the same time she seeks to identify the offense as treason against the king, the exact offense Haman used to obtain the edict of annihilation (3:8). The king then follows with the question *"Who is this person?"* (7:5). Esther names the *enemy* (7:6).

7:5-6 The Response

The king has responded to Esther's petition as one ignorant of the whole situation: *"Who and where is this person?"* The king may lack key pieces of information: the fact that Esther is a Jew and/or that the Jews are the *certain people* condemned by the royal decree obtained by Haman. Both facts are known by others inside and outside the palace. Of course, Ahasuerus may have just forgotten or may never have put all the pieces together. In any case, the king's apparent ignorance does not reflect well on his royal competence.

Esther's response drops all the polite deference that previously has characterized her speech to the king. In words abrupt and emotional, Esther identifies the adversary as *"an archenemy, this evil Haman"* (7:6, EFR). Esther's entire strategy has been aimed at this emotional moment: she names the king's senior adviser as evil.

Immediately terror strikes Haman (7:6b). He knows that things have not gone well since he came to the palace early that morning. He has been forced to implement a ceremony honoring his adversary, Mordecai (6:10-13). However, he, Haman, is still the chief adviser to the king. He alone possesses the royal stamp (3:10, 12). Yet suddenly the queen names him *enemy* and *evil*.

The king has appointed Haman to power and has taken his advice without question. For the king to grant the queen's request, he would have to switch sides in a bitter palace conflict. The deadly conflict has pitted Mordecai against Haman. Haman has used the king to gain the advantage; now Mordecai has countered with the queen. This conflict has been obvious to everyone except the king, who on one hand has granted Haman's decree of destruction against Mordecai and the other Jews, and on the other hand has directed Haman to carry out a parade of honor for *the Jew Mordecai*. Ahasuerus can no longer avoid the conflict through ignorance or incompetence. The king must decide.

7:7-9 The Decision

Not surprisingly, perhaps, the king rises and leaves the room (7:7). Like Mordecai before him, Haman turns to the queen for help, recognizing that now he faces destruction.

As common in Hebrew narrative, the description of this scene omits many details *[Characteristics]*. We know nothing about Esther's reaction to all of this. For the moment, she once again becomes a passive figure. Furthermore, we do not know what the king is thinking or deciding while walking in the palace garden. Readers often assume, as does Haman, that the king's anger has led him to turn against his chief adviser. Perhaps, but we do not know.

Whatever the king may have decided is suddenly preempted by what he sees upon his return. The king discovers Haman on the couch with the queen! The narrator tells us that Haman is pleading with the queen to spare his life. But the king misreads the situation and concludes that Haman is sexually assaulting Queen Esther, a capital offense. This assumption prompts King Ahasuerus to denounce Haman. Haman *turns white* (7:8, EFR).

The last phrase has frequently been translated as *"They covered Haman's face"* (7:8, NRSV, NIV). Such a reading is partly influenced by the practice, in some cultures, of covering a condemned criminal's face. Here that is not likely the case (Klein: 169). Levenson (100) points to the probability that one consonant has been dropped from a Hebrew word. Restoring that letter, r, replaces *khapu* with *khaperu, blanched*.

Faced with a decision, again King Ahasuerus acts not at his own initiative, but on the advice of an adviser (cf. 1:21; 3:11; 6:6, 10). Harbona informs the king that Haman has constructed a gallows for the execution of Mordecai. The king then orders that Haman be executed on the very gallows/stake the condemned man has constructed for his own enemy (5:14, notes; 7:9).

Concluding Note 7:10

Haman's death ends his life in a way ancient sages warned: "Whoever digs a pit will fall into it, and a stone will come back on the one who starts it rolling" (Prov. 26:27). Haman has constructed an elaborate plot to destroy the Jews and to execute Mordecai. Instead, this enemy of the Jews is executed on the very device he has created to destroy his antagonist, fulfilling poetic justice.

While Haman's fortunes have been completely reversed, the king continues to behave in much the same way as when the story opened. Queen Vashti's disobedience enraged the king. His advisers counseled him to dismiss the queen and to inform the entire realm (1:13-20). Implementing their advice calmed the king's anger (2:1). Executing Haman, on the advice of Harbona, once again calms the king's rage. Little has changed with the king.

The tension that has driven the story has been largely resolved. The conflict between Mordecai and Haman has threatened to destroy all the Jews in the Persian Empire. Unable to handle the danger himself, Mordecai has turned to Esther (chap. 4). She has reluctantly taken on her benefactor's problem and succeeded in removing the threat through a series of patient but dangerous maneuvers. Esther's

Esther 6:14—7:10

strategy has depended on the blind ambition of Haman and the comic incompetence of Ahasuerus. Both prove to be true.

THE TEXT IN BIBLICAL CONTEXT

Proverbs and Esther

The sages of ancient Israel regularly expressed in poetry their observation that an act carries with it a predictable consequence. They discerned such predictability not just in the natural world, in operations we sometimes call the laws of nature. They suggested that the same predictable sequence of act-consequence applies to morality: the wise and foolish, the righteous and the wicked. Hence, a righteous person can expect to receive the fruit of her goodness. In like manner, a wicked person would receive what he deserved. This "natural" justice seemed to the sages written into the order of everyday life.

Some two-line proverbs give voice to this natural-justice morality:

The wage of the righteous leads to life,
  the gain of the wicked to sin. (Prov. 10:16)

The righteous will never be removed,
  but the wicked will not remain in the land. (10:30)

The integrity of the upright guides them,
  but the crookedness of the treacherous destroys them. (11:3)

The righteousness of the blameless saves them,
  but the treacherous are taken captive by their own schemes. (11:6)

The righteous are delivered from trouble,
  and the wicked get into it instead. (11:8)

The wicked are overthrown and are no more,
  but the house of the righteous will stand. (12:7)

Even though the sages observed this natural relationship between act and consequence, they did not assign this to a law of nature. A philosophical understanding of "natural law" has developed more recently in Western thought. These ancient sages were quite clear that God's ongoing and active presence stands behind this system of natural justice.

The apostle Paul employed this wisdom theology when encouraging the Corinthian Christians to give generously, as they had promised (2 Cor. 9). He suggested that his image as a leader depended on their generosity (9:3-4). Then the apostle used an agricultural image to insist that there is a direct relationship between philanthropy and future well-being: "The point is this: the one who sows sparingly will also reap sparingly, and the one who sows bountifully will also reap bountifully" (9:6). Paul, like the biblical sages before him, understood that this connection between good act and well-being was grounded not in "natural law," but in divine justice: "[God] who supplies seed to the sower and bread for food will supply and multiply your seed for sowing and increase the harvest of your righteousness" (9:10).

This wisdom understanding of natural justice, however, could not explain the experience of Job. He vigorously debated his friends over just this "theology" of natural justice. Eliphaz repeated to Job the observation of ancient sages that life can be explained by the "law" of natural justice: "Think now, who that was innocent ever perished? Or where were the upright cut off?" (Job 4:7).

Job raged against that conclusion, insisting instead that he was innocent. God was out to get him, and he, Job, could do nothing about it: "[God] snatches away; who can stop him? Who will say to him, 'What are you doing?'" (Job 9:12). In fact, as Job looked about, he saw no natural justice: "Why do the wicked live on, reach old age, and grow mighty in power?" (21:7). It is the innocent who suffer at the hands of the wicked: "From the city the dying groan, and the throat of the wounded cries for help; yet God pays no attention to their prayer" (24:12).

Nor did "natural justice" explain the death of Jesus on a cross, as one of the criminals executed with him recognized: "We indeed have been condemned justly, for we are getting what we deserve for our deeds, but his man has done nothing wrong" (Luke 23:41).

Isaiah recognized that, as true as the wisdom proverb might be, life in all its fullness was far more complex than could be explained by natural justice. Israel learned this while experiencing the Exile in Babylon [Diaspora]. Justice does not always prevail. Thankfully, life cannot be reduced to such a predictable order. By God's grace, sin is not repaid measure for measure. Indeed, by divine design, One has suffered unjustly for the sin of the many: "He was wounded for our transgressions, crushed for our iniquities; upon him was the punishment that made us whole, and by his bruises we are healed" (Isa. 53:5).

THE TEXT IN THE LIFE OF THE CHURCH

Capital Punishment

Though capital punishment was not a matter of debate in this narrative, it remains on the agenda of the Christian church. The end of the twentieth century in the United States has witnessed the return of execution as punishment for a number of crimes involving murder and/or terrorism.

Proponents of capital punishment seldom advocate execution as a deterrent to crime, as was argued in an earlier era. Instead, execution has regained public acceptance as retribution, "an eye for an eye": "If any harm follows, then you shall give life for life, eye for eye, tooth for tooth, hand for hand, foot for foot, burn for burn, wound for wound, stripe for stripe" (Exod. 21:23-24). Although legal statutes in Europe and North America have not incorporated the rest of the ancient law of retaliation, the insistence on requiring "life for life" continues to have many advocates.

As individuals, Christians apparently support the death penalty in a proportion almost equal to that of the general population. In their more considered statements, however, many Christian bodies, including those of the believers church, have opposed execution as the wrong response to crime, even to murder. Sometimes these opponents of capital punishment have argued their case on pragmatic grounds, that any human system of justice is flawed and risks executing an innocent person. In doing so, they express the concern conveyed in the law codes of ancient Israel about the risk of executing an innocent person: "Do not put an innocent or honest person to death, for I will not acquit the guilty" (Exod. 23:7, NIV).

More often, however, the objection of Christians to capital punishment rests on a broad reading of the biblical history and tradition. Vernon Redekop demonstrates that while the law codes in the OT authorize execution for a wide range of religious and family offenses (many of which our society does not even consider a crime), the legal process for approving execution was so stringent as to make execution virtually impossible (Redekop: 13-39).

Furthermore, for many offenses the actual execution was the responsibility of the offender's own family, further deterring capital punishment. The well-known stories of murder in the OT do not result in execution, but in a combination of punishment and mercy: Cain murdering Abel (Gen. 4:1-16), Moses killing the Egyptian (Exod. 2:11-15), David ordering the death of Uriah (2 Sam. 11).

The Gospel narratives portray Jesus as one who denounced evil and condemned iniquity. Nevertheless, the narratives show Jesus returning good for evil, in a creatively reconciling response to criminal violence (Redekop: 63-97). The final response to evil and to the agents of evil rests in God's hands. In response to the evil action that led to his own execution, Jesus offered forgiveness rather than calling for revenge (Luke 23:34).

The mission of the Christian community includes conversion, reconciliation, and restoration rather than revenge, retaliation, and retribution. Everyone abhors and condemns murder. Murder brings unspeakable suffering to the victim and wrenching pain to friends and family. It ignites rage in the community. Nevertheless, retaliating out of that pain and rage only continues violence, whether exacted by the individual or sanctioned by the government. While the murder victim can never be restored to the community, the healing of the community comes not through revenge but through the miracle of costly forgiveness. On rare occasions, God can indeed reach and transform even the one who has committed murder. Should that happen, the guilty one may even participate in the healing of the community.

Scene 3
Resolution and Celebration

Esther 8:1—9:32

Esther 8:1-17
Resolution of the Crisis

PREVIEW

This chapter features reversal—most visibly, a reversal of the fortunes of Mordecai and Haman. Everything that Haman has set in place is reversed by the end of this chapter. Most urgently in need of reversal is the decree authorizing the extermination of the Jews. In fact, that decree of destruction proves the most difficult element to reverse. Earlier in the narrative, Memucan declared that a Persian royal order may not be altered (1:19), a custom that King Ahasuerus reaffirms in 8:8.

While the annihilation edict appears as the critical reversal, other elements of the royal world are reversed in these several verses: the king gives Queen Esther control of the *house of Haman* (8:1), and Mordecai assumes Haman's official position. With that royal position, Mordecai takes possession of the royal signet ring (8:2) and royal robes (8:15). The *blue and white* royal robes reverse the sackcloth and ashes that Mordecai donned after learning about the decree of destruction (4:1).

Esther completes the reversal of the royal order by placing Mordecai over the house of Haman (8:2), a gift the king has previously awarded to her. The struggle for supremacy between the two royal courtiers is over. The carefully crafted scheme of Haman to elevate himself and destroy Mordecai has been completely overturned. Haman is dead, and Mordecai has ascended to the position of prime minister, or vizier, complete with ring, robes, and role.

Esther 8:1-17

OUTLINE

The Promotion of Mordecai, 8:1-2

The Petition of Esther, 8:3-8
    8:3-6   Petition
    8:7-8   Response

The Royal Edict, 8:9-14
    8:9-10   The Writing
    8:11-12   The Purpose
    8:13-14   The Delivery

The Celebration, 8:15-17

EXPLANATORY NOTES

The Promotion of Mordecai 8:1-2

As the story moves toward its conclusion, the narrative returns to quite formal language, including royal titles: *King Ahasuerus* and *Queen Esther*. Haman has exchanged his royal title for one of shame, *enemy of the Jews* (8:1). The narrative first labels Haman as *an enemy of the Jews* in connection with the decree of destruction that Haman has obtained by accusing *a certain people* of subversive activity (3:10, EFR). Queen Esther has declared him an *enemy* in her enraged accusation at the dinner she was giving for the king and Haman (7:6).

Esther has made fully public the relationship between Mordecai and herself, some elements of which have been hidden at least from the king (8:1). As a result, the king promotes Mordecai to the position formerly occupied by his enemy and entrusts into his keeping the royal ring. When Esther gives him control of Haman's *house*, Mordecai is now fully vested with Haman's position, power, and possessions.

The Petition by Esther 8:3-8

Surprisingly, given the sequence of events, Esther resumes a deferential approach to the king that she has employed when the outcome was in doubt (5:2-4). Indeed, her overture to the king at this point appears more solicitous than previously: She *fell at his feet, weeping and pleading* (8:3). Esther's action, however, is not quite the same as before. Clines observes that the use of *fall* does not constitute an act of subservience, but of supplication (Clines, 1984a: 314; cf. 7:7-8).

The intensity of Esther's emotion reflects the fact that this is the petition she has carried from the beginning.

Esther's goal, arising from her verbal exchange with Mordecai (4:9-16), has been to nullify the edict of annihilation against the Jews. She has never asked for the execution of Haman. Instead, at the second dinner, Esther's petition to reverse the edict was interrupted by the king's demand for the name of the offender (7:5). Thereupon, the king has acted on his own anger and the suggestion of Harbona rather than responding to Esther's petition. She has asked only that her life and that of her people be spared (7:3).

Levenson (108) points to poetic repetition in the introduction to Esther's petition:

> If it pleases the king, and
>   if I have won his favor, and
> if the thing seems right before the king, and
>   I have his approval . . . (8:5)

This repetition has the affect of increasing still further the emotional intensity before Esther states the petition itself: *"Let an order be written to revoke the letters devised by Haman."* Unlike when she first voiced her petition (7:3), this time Esther does not ask that her own life be spared. That is no longer in doubt. However, the future of her people still hangs in the balance. This threat to her people is emphasized by the use of poetic parallelism in Esther's speech *[Poetry]*:

> For how can I bear to see the calamity that is coming on my people?
> Or how can I bear to see the destruction of my kindred? (8:6)

King Ahasuerus responds to Esther's petition in characteristic fashion. Whenever the situation requires a decision, the king turns the responsibility over to others, either soliciting their counsel, which he accepts without question (1:13-21; 2:2-4; 6:6), or granting them permission to act as they choose (3:10-11; 7:9). Here again, in words that echo his response to Haman's petition for a decree against *a certain people* (3:11), the king gives Esther permission to *"write as you please with regard to the Jews"* (8:8).

The king assumes no responsibility for Haman's plot resulting in that earlier irrevocable royal decree. Instead, he claims credit for thwarting Haman's evil intention (8:7). Nor will the king take the initiative this time. He tells Esther to do whatever she wants, promising that whatever she directs will be carried out: the new *"edict . . . sealed with the king's ring cannot be revoked"* (8:8).

The Royal Edict 8:9-14

The date mentioned here (Sivan 23, in May-June) places this edict two months and ten days later than Haman's edict authorizing the annihilation (3:12-15). In the first decree, the Jews are objects of the edict; this time, they are included as addressees, and their language is explicitly mentioned as one of the scripts into which the decree is to be translated. This *certain people* earlier accused of treason (3:8-9) has now become visible and celebrated, the only ethnic group mentioned by name.

The new decree, written in the name of King Ahasuerus, is quickly distributed throughout the Persian realm by couriers on horseback. Uncertainty remains concerning the words used to describe the horses employed in this delivery. The terminology is taken by most translations to indicate that these animals have been specially bred for the royal stables: "fast steeds bred from the royal herd" (8:10, NRSV), or "fast horses especially bred for the king" (NIV).

This second decree does not nullify the first; royal tradition apparently forbids that (8:8; cf. 1:19; Dan. 6:8). Instead, it gives the Jews permission to defend themselves, thus setting up a balance of power. Mordecai seemingly expects that this provision for a countering force will deter any attack.

Readers have been most troubled by the fate of *women and children* in this edict. The decree seems to give the Jews permission *to destroy, to kill, and to annihilate* any of the enemy group, including their women and children. Even in a story featuring hyperbole, this offends most listeners.

Some interpreters, while admitting the offense of sanctioning the annihilation of women and children, explain the content of this edict as exactly replicating, and hence countering, Haman's earlier decree. In that decree, the Persians are permitted *to destroy, to kill, and to annihilate all Jews, young and old, women and children* (3:13). In the interest of assured deterrence, the Jews are permitted to do the same.

Clines (1984a: 317), following others, suggests a different translation: *The king allowed the Jews . . . to destroy, to kill and to annihilate any armed force . . . that might attack them, their children and women* (8:11). Such a translation understands *children and women* as potential Jewish victims to be defended rather than as objects of a Jewish counterattack. While this version may sit better with many readers, it does not help those troubled by deterrence grounded in mutual violence, and it rests on tenuous translational assumptions (Fox, 2001:100).

The Celebration 8:15-17

Following the edict mandating the annihilation of the Jews, Haman and King Ahasuerus enjoyed a dinner. Meanwhile, the residents of the capital were *thrown into confusion* (3:15), and Mordecai tore his clothes, putting on sackcloth and ashes (4:1). After the second edict, the response is quite different. Mordecai leaves the presence of the king, wearing royal robes, while *the city of Susa shouted and rejoiced* (8:15). The Jewish population has responded to Haman's initial decree with intense mourning (4:3). An equal and opposite Jewish celebration follows the public announcement of Mordecai's decree (8:16-17).

Verse 17 has perplexed many readers: *Many of the peoples of the countries professed to be Jews, because the fear of the Jews had fallen on them.* Both the translation and the meaning are unclear. A developed practice and procedure for conversion to Judaism likely did not emerge until the teaching of sages or rabbis in the houses of study (synagogues) in the first century B.C. That does not mean that nothing like a "conversion" occurred prior to the first century. Indeed, conversions both of conviction and of convenience may have occurred earlier, such as under the political sponsorship of Jewish military and political leader John Hyrcanus and other Hasmoneans. They were seizing control of Palestine from the Greeks in the late second century B.C. (Ben-Sasson: 219ff.).

The literature available indicates that in the Babylonian and Persian period, the energy of the religious leadership was directed to maintaining the identity of the Jews, rather than converting others to Judaism. Conversion was not discussed. Hence, Moore (1971:82), among others, proposes that the text of 8:17 refers not to religious conversion, but to non-Jews who join themselves to the Jews in the sense of siding with the Jews, out of *fear*, because it has now become dangerous to be anti-Jewish.

THE TEXT IN BIBLICAL CONTEXT

Leadership in a Foreign Land

Narratives portraying the ascendancy of Jews in non-Jewish political contexts appear frequently throughout the Bible and in extrabiblical literature. The story of Joseph provides the prototype of such narratives (Gen. 37–50). As a result of infighting among the sons of Jacob, Joseph was sold into slavery in Egypt. Being blessed by God with unusual administrative skill and supported throughout by divine presence, Joseph rose to leadership first in the household of Potiphar, later in the Egyptian prison where he was held, and finally in the royal government of Egypt. Joseph in Egypt is a story of persecution and struggle, but ultimately of the ascendancy of a Hebrew in a foreign land.

The narrative of Moses in Egypt has a similar motif, yet concludes not with leadership for a foreign land, but in flight from that land (Exod. 1–15). Moses was born in a Hebrew community in Egypt at a time when the Hebrew minority was severely persecuted. His mother, through extraordinary efforts, saved him from a government attempt to destroy all male Hebrew infants. Rescued by Pharaoh's own daughter, Moses was raised in the royal house with his own mother as "wet nurse" and nanny.

Moses' violent rage at the treatment of the Hebrew people by their Egyptian overlords forced him to flee the country. Later, Moses returned to Egypt, assumed leadership of the Hebrew community, and helped them escape Egyptian persecution. Though raised in the royal house of Egypt, Moses never became an official in the Egyptian government as did Joseph. Nevertheless, he went back to confront that government and to demand that they let his people emigrate.

The narratives of the Jewish Diaspora pick up the tradition of Jews who emerged as leaders in a foreign land. Besides Esther and Mordecai, the narratives about Daniel celebrate one who became a major figure in a foreign land. This Jewish exile was able and prepared for government leadership, but his religious piety constantly created tension with the government officials. As a result, Daniel exercised leadership as a sage and royal adviser, rather than as an official in the government. Indeed, according to the accounts, this Jewish sage became so revered that the king fell down and worshiped Daniel (Dan. 2:46).

A second-century B.C. narrative, the Letter of Aristeas, tells how Demetrius, head of the Egyptian royal library, became so attracted to the wisdom of the Jewish writings that he sought to have them translated into Greek (Charlesworth: 7-34). He successfully appealed to the king, Ptolemy II (Philadelphus, 285-247 B.C.), to emancipate all Jews and provide for the translation of the Jewish Scriptures. As with the story of Daniel, this account celebrates not so much how Jewish political leadership emerged in a foreign land, but how non-Jews came to appreciate the wisdom and ethics found in the Jewish Torah. According to this "letter," seventy-two Jewish elders were chosen to make the translation. From this story comes the name *Septuagint* (LXX, 70) for the best-known Greek version of the OT (Letter of Aristeas 1-50, 301-307; in Charlesworth: 12-16, 32-3).

Still another wisdom narrative, one that appears in the writings of several groups in the ancient Near East (seventh to sixth century B.C.), portrays respect for a Jewish figure living in a non-Jewish community. As found in Jewish literature, the story of Ahiqar narrates the tale of a Jewish sage who became a high official in the Assyrian government. This Jew, Ahiqar, however, was betrayed by his adopted son, Nadin, who had him imprisoned and scheduled for execution. Ahiqar's life was spared by the executioner, whose life Ahiqar had saved earlier. A criminal was substituted for Ahiqar, and Ahiqar was hidden by his friend. When Nadin failed to provide the wise counsel needed by the Assyrian king in a dispute with Egypt, Ahiqar was brought out of hiding and restored to his position of eminence (Ahiqar, in Charlesworth: 479-507).

These narratives name and remember heroes of the faith who lived and prospered in foreign lands. They illustrate the determination, wisdom, and piety required to live as strangers in strange lands. Such stories encouraged the displaced people to follow the counsel God gave to Jeremiah: "Seek the welfare of the city where I have sent you into exile, and pray to the Lord on its behalf, for in its welfare you will find your welfare" (Jer. 29:7).

THE TEXT IN THE LIFE OF THE CHURCH

Self-Protective Leadership

Power in the political realm can shift quickly, as happens in this narrative. Such sudden shifts may occur whether the officials have obtained their position by election, inheritance, appointment, or violence. The tenuous character of political power often generates efforts to consolidate and maintain one's position. Some efforts may be Haman-like in their attempt to destroy opposition. Even without such drama, the endeavor to stay in office can turn the attention of an official away from assigned responsibilities, wasting precious energy toward eliminating anyone who might pose a threat. Ironically, such political self-protection usually results in exactly what the officeholder fears, the loss of power, because it calls out a "Mordecai" who organizes to protect his own power, position, or people.

Even though it is popular (and sometimes accurate) to blame the officeholder for distorted self-serving leadership, in North America the electorate often participates in such perversion. North Americans voice their desire for leaders who will put the common good over self-interest. Yet in choosing leaders, they often make their own individual interests the highest priority. Then they wonder where all the

"Hamans" come from, those who conspire to protect their own position at the expense of working for the common good.

Nor are these leadership dynamics limited to the political and economic realm of society. The church frequently turns to 1 Timothy 3:1-13, which describes some of the characteristics needed in leaders. They are to be temperate, sensible, respectable, hospitable, gentle, not quarrelsome. Yet when selecting leaders for their congregation or denomination, members frequently talk about a prospect's position on various theological, ethical, or social issues. They tend to neglect considering the fruit of the Spirit in the leader's life, or characteristics the congregation prefers.

For their part, church pastors, administrators, and teachers often conclude that their position in the church depends less on their spiritual maturity and wisdom, than on their "orthodoxy" on specific issues. That sets up the possibility that leaders will, like Haman, seek to dismiss, demean, or even destroy the opposition. Those destructive actions inevitably mobilize the opposition *to take revenge on their enemies* (8:13).

In such church "wars," all sides, when assembling their support, invoke Christ's name and God's will. In so doing, they frequently emphasize a woe oracle from Jesus, "Woe to you who are laughing now, for you will mourn and weep." But then they often ignore the instruction that follows: "Love your enemies, do good to those who hate you, bless those who curse you, pray for those who abuse you" (Luke 6:25-27).

Esther 9:1-32
Institution of Purim

PREVIEW

As the story draws to a close, the festival of Purim becomes the focus of attention *[Purim]*. In the narrative, Mordecai and Esther not only authorize the (mid-March) festival, but explain why it has become a two-day event (9:26-32). According to the account, the struggle against the *enemies of the Jews* takes a different course in the *citadel of Susa* than in the towns and the villages of Persia. As a result, the villages throughout the realm celebrate Purim on Adar 14, and those living in city of Susa on Adar 15 (9:15-19).

While the festival of Purim likely constitutes the intended focal point of this scene, the eyes of many readers fix on the violence that precedes the authorization of that holiday. Hearing the biblical text on its own terms, however, requires bracketing momentarily any personal response. The destruction of the enemies completes the plot of this story.

The motif of reversal, which has characterized each moment of the resolution, appears as the defining element in this closing scene as well: *On this day the enemies of the Jews had hoped to overpower them, but now the tables were turned and the Jews got the upper hand over those who hated them* (9:1b, NIV). Just as Haman died on the instrument of death that he had constructed for the execution of Mordecai (7:10), so the violence that the enemies of Jews intended turns back on them.

Besides the jarring violence, this concluding chapter presents other difficulties. At a number of places, the sequence of the text reads awkwardly. The reintroduction of the king's offer to grant Esther's petition (9:13) results in her request to execute the sons of Haman, who are earlier reported to be killed (9:10). After Haman is long dead and gone from the story (7:10), his role is summarized again (9:24-26a). As Clines (1984a: 329) notes, 9:26b-28 can be understood as the concluding statement for the book, and yet 9:29-32 resumes the story.

These and other difficult verses in chapter 9 have produced numerous proposals that verses and phrases may have been added later. We cannot know for sure. It is enough to understand that throughout the generations, the festival of Purim has changed both in practice and in its connection with the narrative of Esther. These developments have likely complicated the closing verses of the story.

OUTLINE

The Reversal, 9:1-15
    9:1-4   Basic Statement
    9:5-10   The Destruction
    9:11-13   Dialogue: King and Queen
    9:14-15   Conclusion in Susa

Victory Feasts, 9:16-19
    9:16-17   In the Villages and Towns
    9:18-19   In Susa

Authorization of Purim, 9:20-32
    9:20-23   Letter from Mordecai
    9:24-28   Reason for Purim
    9:29-32   Letter from Esther and Mordecai

EXPLANATORY NOTES

The Reversal 9:1-15

9:1-4 Basic Statement

The theme of reversal that has defined the resolution of the plot becomes explicit here. On the very day in which the enemies of the Jews expect to destroy them, the Jews themselves gain power over their foes (9:2). The crisis has begun with the decree of destruction that Haman obtained. The annihilation of the Jews is set for the thirteen day of the twelfth month (Adar, Feb.-Mar.; 3:13). Resolution has become possible when Esther obtains a counterdecree that provides for Jewish self-defense and the destruction of the enemies (8:11). Finally the tables are turned: the enemies rather than the Jews themselves are destroyed.

As much as the violence catches the readers' attention, the narrator wants us to marvel at the reversal of the Jewish position in Persian society. From being the object of state-sponsored annihilation, now *all the officials of the provinces . . . were supporting the Jews* (9:3). Indeed, the reversal is so complete that *all* the royal officials are now cooperating with the second decree, the one written by Mordecai, rather than Haman's decree, even though the first decree has not been revoked.

The change in Mordecai's position symbolizes what has happened to the whole Jewish people. Mordecai himself has been transformed from a mourner in sackcloth and ashes (4:1), almost sentenced to death (5:14), into a dignitary dressed in royal blue and white (8:15), a powerful royal official whose fearful fame spreads throughout the realm (9:4).

9:5-10 The Destruction

The narrative presents the Jewish destruction of their enemies not with descriptions of battles, but with formalized summary statements. They *struck down all their enemies*, they *destroyed them*, they *did as they pleased to those who hated them* (9:5-6). As printed, the Hebrew text presents the names of ten who are killed (Haman's sons) in two parallel columns (9:7-9), each preceded by a column repeating the word *and*. We do not know the reason for this unusual format. To current readers, the names formatted this way look like a list of those missing or killed in war.

The narrator introduces one phrase that is repeated two more times: *They did not touch the plunder* (9:10, 15-16). Mordecai's royal decree has provided the Jews the right to seize or destroy the goods of their enemies (8:11//3:13), but they have explicitly avoided doing so. Perhaps this refrain, *They did not touch the plunder*, provides another memory echo of the "holy war" conflict between Israel and the Amalekites, ancestors of Haman (cf. 3:1, notes).

As noted in 2:5 and 3:1, by identifying Mordecai as a descendant of Saul's family and Haman as an Amalekite, this narrative connects the conflict between Mordecai and Haman with the memory of an ancient antagonism. That epic conflict was never resolved because Saul disregarded the divine command for annihilation of the Amalekites, choosing to spare the life of Agag, king of the Amalekites. In addition, Saul and his people kept the valuable goods, disobeying the Lord by

Esther 9:1-32   **247**

choosing to destroy only the worthless possessions of the Amalekites (1 Sam. 15:3, 9).

This time Haman, descendant of Agag, and his whole family are destroyed, and no spoils are taken (Esther 9:10). It may be too great a stretch to see the death of Haman and his entire family as the resolution of Saul's disobedience. Nevertheless, this narrative connects the conflict in Persia with the long history of Israel threatened with annihilation by its enemies, a memory that stretches far back in time.

9:11-13 Dialogue: King and Queen

A word from the king to Queen Esther interrupts the report of the reversal in Jewish fortunes. The king's attention is caught not by the deliverance of the Jews but by the "impressive" death toll in the capital city (Fox, 1991:112). He asks Esther for a battle report from other regions of the realm (9:11). Before receiving an answer, however, the king repeats his offer to grant Esther's petition, whatever it might be—essentially the same offer he has made three times before (5:3, 6; 7:2).

Now Esther asks for another day to complete the destruction of the enemies, plus the execution of the sons of Haman (9:13). Many read this latter petition as a request to have bodies of Haman's sons exposed for public display since the narrator reports their execution in 9:10. The text can be read either way, as a request for execution or for exposure.

Readers may prefer a picture of Esther as a heroine kept away from the violence. They are disconcerted by her request to continue the acts of *revenge* (8:13). Though many current readers struggle with the violence of this story, the narrative itself echos poetry from the prophets and psalmists, such as Psalm 92:5-9:

> How great are your works, O LORD!
>   Your thoughts are very deep!
> The dullard cannot know,
>   the stupid cannot understand this:
> though the wicked sprout like grass
>   and all evildoers flourish,
> they are doomed to destruction forever,
>   but you, O LORD, are on high forever.
> For your enemies, O LORD,
>   for your enemies shall perish;
>   all evildoers shall be scattered.

9:14-15 Conclusion in Susa

King Ahasuerus stays in character to the end of the story. Throughout the narrative, he turns to advisers whenever the situation requires a royal decision. Most recently, Harbona, one of the king's eunuchs, provided advice to the king in response to the royal rage against Haman (7:9). The king always follows the advice he receives.

So too, on all previous occasions, he has granted requests from Queen Esther (5:5; 6:14; 8:7-8). Therefore, the reader is not surprised when the narrator reports the king's response to Esther's request this time: *So the king commanded this to be done* (9:14). Ahasuerus authorizes another day to destroy the enemies in Susa, and the sons of Haman are hung.

Victory Feasts 9:16-19

The story of Esther begins with a series of royal banquets (1:1-10). Dinners and feast are featured throughout the narrative. Haman and the king dined after signing and sending out the decree of destruction (3:15). The first two requests from Esther were for royal dinners to be attended by the king, queen, and Haman (5:4, 8). It was at dinner that the king turned on Haman, allegedly for assaulting the queen (7:8). Hence, quite appropriately, the narrative concludes with feasts (9:17, 19).

The first two feasts in the story presented the royal court as excessively ostentatious and the king as impulsive and weak (chap. 1). That royal ineptitude created the near tragedy of Jewish annihilation. The victory feasts by the Jewish communities serve to complete the narrative reversal. With the destruction of their enemies complete, the Jews gather for *feasting and gladness* (9:17). These are not ridiculously extravagant royal banquets, but the joyful victory banquets of a people nearly annihilated by the evil and ineptitude infecting the Persian monarchy.

Esther 9:16-19 provides the basis for Mordecai's later instruction that Purim is to be a two-day festival (9:21). As the Jews struggle against their enemies, the narrator says, events in Susa take a course different from what happens in *villages* and *open towns* of the royal provinces. Hence, the victory banquet occurs on different days in separate parts of the Persian Empire: on Adar 14 in villages and towns, and on Adar 15 in Susa. Notice also the final phrase: *a holiday on which they send gifts of food to one another* (9:19). In his Purim instructions, Mordecai will pick up this element also.

Authorization of Purim 9:20-32

9:20-23 Letter from Mordecai

Chapter 9 concludes with statements authorizing the festival of Purim *[Purim]*. This passage provides an *etiology* for the holiday: in narrative form, it explains Purim's origin for future generations. Question: "Why do we observe Purim?" Answer: "Because Mordecai and Esther instructed that these days be kept by all Jews, *year by year*, in remembrance of a time *when the Jews gained relief from their enemies*" (9:21-22; cf. Exod. 12:26-27; Deut. 6:20-25; Josh. 4).

The authorization begins with a letter from Mordecai. He instructs all Jews to keep Adar 14-15 as a holiday *year by year* (9:21). In connection with these dates, Levenson (126) insists that what Purim celebrates is not the battles and the violence. If that were the case, the festival would be Adar 13-14. Instead, Purim is in remembrance of *the days on which the Jews gained relief from their enemies*. Notice also that the gift-giving mentioned in 9:19 is expanded in Mordecai's instruction to include *presents to the poor* (9:22).

The narrator follows the report of Mordecai's letter with the observation that the Jews have already begun to do what Mordecai instructs. Now, as instructed by Mordecai, Purim will become an annual holiday. This remark contains an admonition to future generations that they should follow this example and continue to celebrate Purim.

9:24-28 Reason for Purim

While the intention of the entire unit has been etiology, answering questions about reasons for the holiday, verses 24-28 set forth an explanation for the name *Purim*. The narrator rehearses enough of the story to remind the readers that Haman cast *the Pur*, translated to mean *the lot* (9:24; cf. 3:7). The narrator then becomes explicit with the etiology: *Therefore these days are called Purim, from the word Pur* (9:26).

Nevertheless, one obvious question remains unanswered: Why is the plural form of the noun used? *Purim* is plural, but Haman cast *Pur*, one lot (9:24). Nowhere in the narrative do we find the plural, except as the name of the holiday. Furthermore, the word *Pur* is used only once in the story (3:7). There it is accompanied, for the sake of clarification, by the Hebrew word for lot *(goral)*.

This wording has led many scholars to suggest that the holiday of Purim was not originally connected with the narrative of Esther. Perhaps the Jewish community took over another holiday, connecting it with Esther and thus transforming it into a celebration of a time when *the Jews gained relief from their enemies*. The Christian communities have accomplished a similar transformation of December 25. However, no one has convincingly identified a holiday that might serve as a forerunner of Purim.

The precise history of the festival and the term, Purim, is still more difficult to unravel. The earliest reference outside of Esther itself to the festival associated with this story is found in the 2 Maccabees, a book found in the Greek Septuagint text, but not the Hebrew Bible. In 2 Maccabees the festival is called *the day of Mordecai* (15:36). While scholars may not uncover the earliest history of this festival, the narrative of Esther intends to provide explicit and persuasive authorization for this Jewish holiday for all future generations (9:28).

With 9:26b-28, the narrative moves from authorizing Purim (9:21) to mandating its observance: *These days should be remembered and kept throughout every generation, in every family, province, and city; and these days of Purim should never fall into disuse among the Jews* (9:28). Alongside Hanukkah, Purim is one of two Jewish holidays that lack the authority of Moses *[Purim]*. It seems probable that Purim had trouble gaining widespread acceptance, perhaps because its authorization lies outside the Torah.

9:29-32 Letter from Esther and Mordecai

Although the statement mandating the institution of Purim provides a natural and firm conclusion, the narrative is resumed with a letter from Queen Esther, *along with the Jew Mordecai*. According to the narrator, this letter repeats the instruction to keep Purim. The emphasis on writing strengthens the mandate to observe Purim: *written authority, it was recorded in writing* (9:29, 32).

This second letter adds an element to the previous authorization of the holiday. Purim is to include *fasts* and *lamentations* (9:31) as well as *gladness and feasting* (9:22). This incorporates the fast reported in Esther 4 into the remembrance evoked by Purim. From beginning to end, the book features numerous banquets and feasts; yet it actually hinges its drama on an occasion of lamentation and fast. Mordecai appears publicly in intense lamentation because of Haman's edict of annihilation of the Jews (4:1). Esther calls the whole community to fast as she approaches the king in order to save her people (4:16). According to the regulations fixed and recorded by command of Queen Esther, Purim is to have rituals of fasting and lamenting as well as feasting and gladness.

Epilogue

Ahasuerus and Mordecai

Esther 10:1-3

EXPLANATORY NOTES

In the epilogue, the scene suddenly changes. From the authorization of Purim grounded in letters by Mordecai and Esther, the narrative shifts to the action of the king: *Ahasuerus laid tribute on the land* (10:1). We see a disconnect between 10:1-3 and the previous chapter. Also, these verses do not appear in some other ancient editions of the story of Esther. Hence, many scholars conclude that 10:1-3 was added by a later Jewish community.

Whether that be the origin or not, Moore observes that this epilogue returns us to the opening scene (Moore, 1971:100). There we saw King Ahasuerus acting in all his royal authority to throw an extravagant banquet (1:1-9). In this epilogue, King Ahasuerus again exerts his royal authority, this time to levy taxes not only on the land, but also on the islands.

One thing has changed: Mordecai the Jew stands beside Ahasuerus, next in rank (10:3). The Jewish community, which has come so close to extermination, now has Mordecai standing next to the king. This powerful man is popular because *he sought the good of his people*. The pogrom in Persia that nearly destroyed the Jewish people would not be repeated as long as Mordecai *interceded for the welfare of all his descendants*.

Esther 10:1-3

THE TEXT IN BIBLICAL CONTEXT

Listening to Rage and Terror

The violence, in which the Jews inflict measure for intended measure, except for not taking plunder, seems especially jarring to contemporary ears at one point. Esther suddenly petitions the king for a continuation of the war against the enemies and retribution against Haman's family (9:13). Current horror at state-sponsored mass murder, such as in the Holocaust and in "ethnic cleansing," reinforces the conclusion that Esther 9 stands outside anything to be taken as normative for Christians. Occasionally Christians handle this dichotomy by relegating chapter 9 to the "old order" or "dispensation," replaced by Jesus' command to "love your enemies" (Matt. 5:44). This makes the chapter irrelevant except as a negative witness, a testimony to what one must not believe.

The biblical context of this material, however, gives us reason to pause and reflect further. The narrative does not contain scenes of battles and strategies for annihilation, but formal statements: *No one could withstand them* (9:2). *The Jews struck down all their enemies* (9:5). *The Jews killed and destroyed five hundred people* (9:6). *[They] killed seventy-five thousand of those who hated them* (9:16).

As mentioned in the notes (on 9:11-13), this language, announcing the destruction of the enemies, echoes throughout the pages of the Bible and even into the NT. Poems and stories of reversal, with victims becoming victors, appear throughout the biblical narrative from Miriam (Exod. 15) to Mary (Luke 1). The mighty and powerful threaten the weak and weary. Through an unexpected and dramatic reversal, the powerful "horse and rider [are] thrown into the sea" (Exod. 15:21), and the "lowly" are "lifted up" (Luke 1:52).

Jeremiah, one of the prophetic poets of Israel, unleashed a series of oracles against enemy nations. Concerning Egypt, Jeremiah proclaims:

> That day is the day of the Lord God of hosts,
>   a day of retribution,
>   to gain vindication from his foes.
> The sword shall devour and be sated,
>   and drink its fill of their blood. (Jer. 46:10)

Rather than military language, Isaiah uses metaphors from agriculture and nature to picture the reversal that will give Israel rest from its enemies:

> Now, I will make of you a threshing sledge,
>   sharp, new, and having teeth;
> you shall thresh the mountains and crush them,
>   and you shall make the hills like chaff.
> You shall winnow them and the wind shall carry them away,
>   and the tempest shall scatter them.
> Then you shall rejoice in the LORD;
>   in the Holy One of Israel you shall glory. (Isa. 41:15-16)

Jeremiah and Isaiah reflect the long prophetic tradition of expressing, in anticipation and in thanks, the joy of Miriam at the sea, when she saw the mighty army of Pharaoh destroyed by the divinely controlled walls of water.

It is not just Miriam, the prophets, and the psalmists who rejoice that the mighty are or will be destroyed, and that the people of faith will have rest from their enemies. Mary reclaims that tradition in her song known as the Magnificat:

> The Mighty One has done great things for me,
>   and holy is his name.
> His mercy is for those who fear him,
>   from generation to generation.
> He has shown strength with his arm;
>   he has scattered the proud in the thoughts of their hearts.
> He has brought down the powerful from their thrones,
>   and lifted up the lowly;
> he has filled the hungry with good things,
>   and sent the rich away empty. (Luke 1:49-53)

The motif of reversal—"many who are first will be last, and the last will be first" (Matt. 19:30)—lies at the heart of the good news (gospel) for those who are oppressed. Readers will do well not to dismiss poems and narratives, like Esther, that picture this world turned upside down. That will include even the violent scenes in which the enemies are destroyed so that the oppressed can gain *relief from their enemies* (Esther 9:22). Listening to the rage and terror of those narratives will carry the reader to the depth of the misery God has seen and the cry of agony God has heard (Exod. 3:7).

Jesus spoke a new word to that intense anguish, a word absolutely committed to release the captives:

> But I say to you that listen:
> Love your enemies,
>   do good to those who hate you,
> bless those who curse you,
>   pray for those who abuse you. (Luke 6:27-28)

Esther 10:1-3

THE TEXT IN THE LIFE OF THE CHURCH

Living in the World

The final moment of the narrative of Esther pictures Ahasuerus, the king of Persia, and Mordecai, the Jew, standing together (10:3). Levenson (133-4) expresses the importance of that picture for the Jewish community:

> The scene with which . . . Esther closes is one for which Jewish communities in the Diaspora have always longed: Jews living in harmony and mutual goodwill with the Gentile majority, under Jewish leaders who are respected and admired by the rulers, yet who are openly identified with the Jewish community.

Many Christians would share a similar vision and hope as well—many but not all.

Christians have differed in their ways of understanding the relationship between the church and the institutions of society, including the government. Some share a vision similar to that articulated by Jon Levenson: Christians working with non-Christians in harmony and mutual goodwill, each respected and admired by the others, and openly identified with their own faith communities. They hear this vision of harmony and mutual respect reflected in the idyllic picture of the messianic age portrayed in Isaiah 11:6-9:

> The wolf shall live with the lamb,
>   the leopard shall lie down with the kid,
> the calf and the lion and fatling together,
>   and a little child shall lead them. . . .
> They will not hurt or destroy
>   on all my holy mountain;
> for the earth will be full of the knowledge of the LORD
>   as the waters cover the sea.

Others do not picture the messianic era as an age characterized by religious as well as ethnic diversity. Instead, they expect a day when all will live in a society that has become universally Christian. A similar hope is carried by many in Islam, Judaism, and other religious traditions, hope for a day when their particular religious faith will have become universal. They would read the vision in Isaiah 11, not as a time of different religious communities living and working together, but of a single faith, worshiping one God in the same way. Many Christians find this hope of the triumph of the Christian faith reflected in the poetry of Revelation 11:15:

> The kingdom of the world has become the kingdom of our Lord
> and of his Messiah (Christ),
> and he will reign forever and ever.

Still others expect constant antagonism between the faith community, called apart from the world, and the institutions of society, including business and government. This perspective—reflected explicitly in the Amish, Old Order Brethren, and some especially traditional Mennonite groups—insists that the church should remain as separate from the world as possible. The "world" is sinful, and God has called the faithful to live as a separate people, holy to the Lord. They hear this call to separation in the language of 1 Peter 2:8b-9:

> They stumble because they disobey the word, as they were destined to do. But you are a chosen race, a royal priesthood, a holy nation, God's own people, in order that you may proclaim the mighty acts of him who called you out of darkness into his marvelous light.

Certainly one can find many variations on these perspectives, as well as on other views of the relationship between the Christian community and the institutions of society. Not all would see the closing scene of Esther as a model or as idyllic, with the Gentile Ahasuerus and the Jew Mordecai living in harmony and mutual goodwill. Most Christians and Jews, however, do prefer that picture over the violent antagonism that sets one against the other, each plotting and praying for the annihilation of the other.

Outline of Esther

Scene 1: Tension in the Royal Court	**1:1—3:6**
Episode 1: Conflict in the Royal Family	1:1—2:20
Deposing of Vashti	1:1-22
Introduction	1:1
Chronicle of the Banquets	1:2-9
The King	1:2-8
The Queen	1:9
Disobedience and Its Consequences	1:10-22
Disobedience of Vashti	1:10-12
Consequences	1:13-22
Consultation with Advisers	1:13-20
Royal Edict	1:21-22
Selection of Esther	2:1-20
Introductory Comment	2:1
Proposed Selection Process	2:2-4
Proposal by Royal Advisers	2:2-4a
King's Acceptance	2:4b
Introduction of Mordecai and Esther	2:5-7
Selection of a Queen	2:8-17
Gathering the Candidates	2:8-11
The Standard Procedure	2:12-14
Selection of Esther	2:15-17
Concluding Banquet	2:18
Concluding Comment	2:19-20
Episode 2: Conflict Among the Royal Courtiers	2:21—3:6

Conspiracy Against the King	2:21-23
Conflict Between Courtiers	3:1-6

Scene 2: Action and Counteraction — 3:7—7:10

Episode 1: Haman Versus Mordecai	3:7—4:17
Plot of Haman	3:7-15
Casting the Lot (Pur)	3:7
Speech to the King	3:8-9
Description of Danger	3:8
Request	3:9
Response of the King	3:10-11
Issuing an Edict	3:12-15a
Concluding Note	3:15b
Response of Mordecai	4:1-17
Ritual of Mourning	4:1-3
Response of Esther	4:4-5
Mission of Hathach	4:6-16
Inquiry and Report	4:6-9
Dialogue: Esther and Mordecai	4:10-16
Concluding Note	4:17
Episode 2: Esther's First Intervention	5:1-14
Intervention by Esther	5:1-8
The Approach	5:1-2
The Dialogue	5:3-5a
The Banquet	5:5b-8
Decision by Haman	5:9-14
The Problem	5:9-10a
The Counsel	5:10b-14a
The Response	5:14b
Episode 3: Royal Decree Honoring Mordecai	6:1-13
The Bestowal of Honor by the King	6:1-12
Introductory Note	6:1-2
The King Takes Counsel	6:3-9
Dialogue with Advisers	6:3-5
Dialogue with Haman	6:6-9
Decision and Implementation	6:10-11
Concluding Note	6:12
The Advice from Haman's Wife	6:13
Episode 4: Esther's Second Intervention	6:14—7:10
Introductory Note	6:14—7:1
The Banquet	7:2-9
The Petition	7:2-4

Outline of Esther

The King's Offer	7:2
Esther's Request	7:3-4
The Response	7:5-6
Response of the King	7:5
Accusation by Esther	7:6a
Reaction of Haman	7:6b
The Decision	7:7-9
Actions of the King and Haman	7:7-8
Advice of Harbona	7:9a
The King's Command	7:9b
Concluding Note	7:10

Scene 3: Resolution and Celebration   8:1—9:32

Resolution of the Crisis	8:1-17
The Promotion of Mordecai	8:1-2
The Petition of Esther	8:3-8
Petition	8:3-6
Response	8:7-8
The Royal Edict	8:9-14
The Writing	8:9-10
The Purpose	8:11-12
The Delivery	8:13-14
The Celebration	8:15-17
Institution of Purim	9:1-32
The Reversal	9:1-15
Basic Statement	9:1-4
The Destruction	9:5-10
Dialogue: King and Queen	9:11-13
Conclusion in Susa	9:14-15
Victory Feasts	9:16-19
In the Villages and Towns	9:16-17
In Susa	9:18-19
Authorization of Purim	9:20-32
Letter from Mordecai	9:20-23
Reason for Purim	9:24-28
Letter from Esther and Mordecai	9:29-32

Epilogue: Ahasuerus and Mordecai   10:1-3

Essays

CHARACTERISTICS OF HEBREW NARRATIVE From the stories of childhood to the memories of adulthood, narrative prose accompanies one throughout life. Each person relives the past and dreams about the future in story form. Christians employ narrative to pass on the faith tradition and to introduce themselves and their church. While everyone uses other prose forms such as instruction, exhortation, and letter, nothing captures the listeners attention more than story. Narrative is so familiar that most individuals pay little attention to the literary characteristics that make prose a narrative.

Since this commentary covers mostly narrative texts, it is important for readers to understand the narrative style of the ancient Near East in general and of ancient Israel in particular. Some of the most familiar elements of narrative, such as plot, are discussed in other essays [Narrative Structure; Novella; Short Story]. Here the focus is on elements that distinguish Hebrew narrative style from the narratives in our culture. None of the elements discussed below are completely foreign to our stories, but they mark some of the distinctive features of Hebrew stories: description, direct speech, understatement, and repetition.

Description. Narratives combine description (narration) with dialogue (direct speech) to portray people in particular times, places, and situations (Coats, 1983:4). The narrator may provide long descriptions of people, places, or action. However, most biblical narratives feature only brief descriptions. The biblical narrator frequently uses only a single word or two to characterize a person. The reader might learn the family lineage to which the individual belongs (son or daughter of) or a brief word about a character's physical, emotional, or spiritual situation. One frequently finds words like "old," "beautiful," "angry," and "good," but seldom more than that.

The listener is almost never given enough information to form a complete picture of the characters or to know more than one aspect of their personality. The brevity of biblical description might cause one to pass over the words. Yet that single descriptive word represents an element the narrator considers important for understanding the characters and the ensuing action.

Description of places and action is often equally brief. In fact, description of place may be completely missing or exist only in the mention of a geographical area such as a town or even a country. Readers of contemporary narratives have become used to vivid description of action as a prominent feature in storytelling. That is seldom done in Hebrew narratives. Instead, the listener finds the action in biblical narratives described in brief, almost summary, fashion, even though it appears that the whole narrative has been pointing to that action.

Adele Berlin notes that the story of Esther does use extensive narrative description, unusual for biblical narrative (Berlin, 2001: xxv-xxvi). The reader receives the story as told by the narrator, much more so than many biblical stories. Berlin notes the extensive use of indirect speech, that is the narrator tells us what the characters said to one another, as well as the description of people, places and things. This has the affect of distancing the reader from the events of the story. Whereas the brief descriptive comments of Ruth and Jonah calls the reader into the story to fill in the descriptive "gaps" the narrator has left open, the extensive use of description in Esther enables the reader to be a more passive onlooker.

Direct Speech. In Hebrew narratives, direct speech plays a primary role and usually is more central than description (Alter, 1981:63-87). Often much of the narrative description serves mainly to tie together or bridge between different speeches. Hence, readers must carefully attend to speeches made by the different characters. Often those speeches provide access to what is going on between people and also within the individual. A biblical speech can provide information about the topic addressed and also insight into the speaker's character. Because of the brevity of description, these insights come as subtle impressions. Other people reading the same speech might understand the character differently, especially since often the narrator has not told us how we are expected to understand the individual.

Therefore, it is important to pay attention to the way a person speaks as well as to the context and content of what is said. A long speech might be set next to a short one. Gentle language of one speaker may contrast with harsh words of another, or flowery speech with earthy language. For the most part, readers are not told whether to laugh or cry but, with careful listening to speech, may discover a suitable response. One frequently finds it more difficult to see humor than sadness expressed in the Hebrew narratives. North American readers lack much of the context, information, and skill needed to recognize humor in the ancient texts *[Comedy]*.

Understatement. Hebrew narratives present the personality of the characters with a light touch. As noted above *(Description),* only a single word may serve to introduce us to the individual. This minimal description, perhaps mentioning only one feature, provides the character with an aura of mystery, inviting listeners to fill in the picture (Berlin, 1983:137). The readers immediately become active participants in the story, making decisions and drawing conclusions. They can decide whether Boaz has his eye on Ruth all along or is "captured" by Naomi's plan. They can determine whether Ahasuerus is an able monarch victimized by an evil adviser, or a weak king controlled by whoever speaks last.

Readers find more than personality understated in Hebrew narrative. Information that contemporary readers expect is frequently not there at all.

Apparently the narrator is content to let such information go unstated, such as the location of Jonah when God speaks to him (Jon. 1). On occasion, this "missing" information was obvious to the "first" audience, so the writer omits it. This may be true for the marriage customs necessary to better understand the situation of Ruth and Boaz (Ruth 4). At other times, the information is withheld only to be given to us later in the story. The story of the repentance and deliverance of Nineveh is over (Jon. 3) before we learn the reason for Jonah's initial refusal to go (Jon. 4).

Finally, some obvious "gaps" seem to have been intentionally left by the narrator (Alter, 1981:114-30; Sternberg: 186-229). Filling these gaps requires readers to participate more actively in the drama. They find themselves needing to decide about the personality of a character and drawing their own conclusion about the motives for an action. Hence, one feels drawn into the story by narrative moments that require a reader's decision, a moment in which more than one option is possible. In any case, the presence of understatement as an important element of Hebrew narrative style reaches out to the listener, making one an active participant in the story and not just a passive reader.

Repetition. Repetition, sometimes redundant to modern ears, plays a key role in ancient Hebrew narrative. In English translation, occasionally key words appear over and over in a story. The reader of Ruth can quickly spot the word *glean* repeated in chapter 2 and *redeem* in Ruth 4, because most translations have not used English synonyms to translate the same Hebrew word. In the Hebrew of Ruth 1, however, the word *šub (return)* appears several times. But the use of synonyms in English versions (such as *go back*) means that readers of the story in English will not notice how often certain words are repeated.

Repetition exists not only with single words, but also with phrases repeated in a speech or narration, or even spoken in speech and mirrored in the narration. Often a phrase is repeated with synonyms rather than in the original expression. At times, such changes in wording will betray important nuances. Other times, these synonymous phrases reflect the two-part sentence familiar from Hebrew poetry *[Poetry]*.

As an important literary device in Hebrew narrative, repetition may result from its deep roots in oral storytelling (Olrik: 132-3). Even if the short stories and novellas have originated as written narrative, they were intended to be read aloud. In oral storytelling, repetition can function as thread to carry the narrative along, keeping the listener on the chosen path. At other times, the repeated word or phrase has a more important role, perhaps conveying a central thrust of the story. Such may be the case for the words *great* and *evil* throughout the story of Jonah. Finally, repetition using parallel phrasing may serve to emphasize and reinforce a particular circumstance or situation or to mark the beginning and ending of narrative units. Repetition of phrases relate to time frequently mark such beginning or end points, e.g., "after these things," Esther 2:1; 3:1.

A little practice in working with a few of the literary devices distinctive to Hebrew narrative can greatly increase a reader's ability to interpret the stories. But most important, such exploration enables the stories to come alive as readers are drawn into the drama as participants. The best understanding of narrative comes not by remaining outside and analyzing, but by joining the story and living with the characters.

Essays

CHARACTER TYPES IN HEBREW NARRATIVE Adele Berlin (1983: 32-3) draws our attention to three different character types in Hebrew narrative: full characters, flat characters, and agents, playing a single role or function.

Full Characters. The narratives develop full characters in some depth. These persons have names, emotions, and opinions as well as actions. The personality of such characters can develop and change in the course of the story, or at least the reader sees different dimensions of the individual's character. Ruth, Jonah, and Esther are all portrayed in some depth throughout the course of these short stories.

Sometimes the different dimensions of a full character emerge as they interact with other characters in the drama. For example, the reader understands more and more of Jonah as he interacts with God. Other times, depth of character emerges in different situations. Ruth's strength becomes visible as she seeks to solve the family food crisis and then the lack of an heir. The political skill of Esther matures as she assumes responsibility to avoid the approaching catastrophe. Full characters can be known and understood at some depth through the narrative. That understanding prompts a depth response in the reader: sympathy, identification, antipathy.

Flat Characters. The narrator presents a more limited view of flat characters. In the narrative, they are subordinate to the full characters. The reader learns little about their personality and almost nothing about their emotions. What is visible is frequently stereotyped and predictable. Flat characters do not affect the trajectory of the plot except as they relate to the main characters. Generally they appear in *a specific role,* such as a queen or king, an enemy, or a mother. In the story of Esther, Vashti appears only briefly as the first queen. She acts to throw a party and to disobey the king. Then Vashti disappears from the narrative. Haman appears throughout the story, but he acts always and predictably as an enemy of the Jews.

Agents are functional characters who act only in a single scene and carry out a specific assignment. We know nothing of the person except the action. Frequently the character remains nameless. In the story of Jonah, the role of the unnamed king of Nineveh is limited to an act of contrition and a prayer of repentance. In Esther, we find several agents: Hegai, the royal eunuch, in charge of the women of the palace; Hatach, the messenger between Esther and Mordecai; and named or unnamed royal advisers to the king and Haman.

Berlin (1983:32-33) observes that while one can identify these three character types in biblical narrative, the lines between the types are permeable and open to discussion. Perhaps enough is known about Haman to classify him as a full character. What about Boaz and Mordecai? Are they full or flat characters? The reader knows little about their personality or emotions, but they are not as stereotyped as Haman. On the other hand, neither of them are as fully developed as Ruth and Esther. Whether or not these types of characters can always be neatly defined, this typology calls our attention to the way in which each narrative beckons some characters forward while leaving others in the background.

COMEDY: HUMOR, IRONY, AND SATIRE Currently the word *comedy* is used in at least two ways. On one hand, it designates a specific genre of literature, characteristically concluding with a happy ending. On the other hand, comedy refers to a situation, in life or story, that prompts laughter.

Comedy, as a genre of literature, swings upward at the end, reintegrating the hero into a rightful place in society (Exum and Whedbee: 8). A tragedy is exactly the opposite. It ends with the hero fallen, either because of a personal flaw or an inability to overcome an evil.

A comedy may or may not inspire laughter in the readers. Even if we laugh at certain moments in the comedy, we do not laugh at the comedy as a whole. Comedy as a genre of literature is a serious work (Lehmann: 100). Northrop Frye defines the Bible as a whole as comedy (Frye, 1963:455). All the tragic elements of the biblical story are eventually taken up in resurrection, thus ending in salvation rather than disaster.

Indeed, a good comedy starts with one of the many available dangers or threats in life. The manner of portraying that danger may or may not elicit the reader's laughter. However, a story becomes a comedy when the threatening element in life is overcome, thus creating a new future (Lehmann: 104). As such, comedy can generate hope in subsequent readers whose present situation similarly threatens their future. Comedy affirms that in life, harmony is more enduring than alienation, and well-being is more basic than nonbeing.

Humor depends on the listener's perspective. To see the humor, the reader must understand the situation portrayed. Everyone has difficulty understanding the humor of another culture or even a different generation. Humor usually walks a narrow ledge between tears and laughter. What prompts laughter in one person, may offend or even hurt another. What may elicit laughter one moment, may cause pain in the same person at another time.

Laughter generally arises from incongruity. Lehmann reminds us that "comedy did not invent incongruity" but discovered it in life (Lehmann: 111). Individuals speak and act in absurd ways that exceed even the most imaginative storyteller. Life's incongruities become occasions for laughter when the story lets us view a situation with the narrator's eye. At its best, humor can be a great teacher, helping us identify inappropriate responses and actions that will inevitably bring trouble. Laughter can free us to change and lay aside behavior that is habitual but self-defeating (Ackerman, 1981:244). In addition, laughter can enable us to set "disasters" behind us and accept our own faults and foibles.

Stories that prompt laughter may also hurt. They can demean another person or group by placing the reader in a superior position: wise rather than foolish, smart rather than stupid, beautiful rather than ugly. Such humor makes fun of other people, usually because they look, speak, or act differently. We often try to distinguish good and bad humor by differentiating between laughing at another person and laughing with another. However, if the other one is an object of laughter, the line between *at* and *with* becomes nearly invisible.

Current readers overlook most of the laughter-producing situations in biblical stories. This happens in part because the humor in the Bible fits a people long ago and far away. We do not see some of the laughable incongruities in the texts unless someone points them out. Humor that must be explained seldom produces laughter.

There is yet another reason why we miss some of the humor present in biblical narratives. Unlike humor in the North American culture, biblical humor is often a matter of understatement instead of exaggeration. The humor of exaggeration appears in both Jonah and Esther: the excessive feasts in Esther, and the great fish in Jonah. Ruth is more typical of biblical narratives because it presents humor with a subtle touch: Boaz looks at all the workers in his fields and notices one person! We know little about the nature of ancient Hebrew oral and literary humor (Gunn: 126). Likely even the most informed biblical readers miss much of what ancient listeners would have found funny.

Adele Berlin insists that our inability to recognize and appreciate humor in biblical narrative has been especially problematic in the story of Esther (2001:xviii-xxii). She notes that in Esther the comic elements are not just incidental, included to provoke laughter, but are the essence of the book. Aspects of the book have concerned readers (e.g. the violence, absence of the divine name) become less troubling if one recognizes that throughout this story features exaggerations, incredible coincidences, comic misunderstandings, and outrageous situations.

Because the Bible is our sacred book, some feel that humor undercuts the serious intent of the Bible. For most Christians, however, that attitude has been replaced by the realization that laughter and the sacred can work together seriously.

Irony is one comedic device used by ancient as well as modern storytellers and writers. It depends explicitly on incongruity and misunderstanding. Words spoken in irony usually mean the exact opposite of their obvious and customary use. Skillful use of irony requires listeners to decide if the narrative really intends the word as irony (Good: 14-26). Irony is a favorite literary device of the "underclasses." Because the reader cannot be certain if it is ironic or direct speech, the speaker can voice anger at an oppressor without being caught.

Similarly, ironic actions in a story produce the opposite of their expected result. As such, irony woven into the plot of a story informs the readers that in life the best-laid plans usually do go astray. Generally, irony identifies experiences in life that go awry, turning out worse than expected. In Esther, Haman's path to destruction presents an obvious example of irony. Life situations that turn out better than anticipated are celebrated as good fortune or grace rather than irony.

Satire is militant irony (Holbert: 60-66). Satire uses exaggeration and caricature as its weapons. The characters are made to look ridiculous in their actions and attitudes. According to Frye, satire without any humor dissolves into invective (Frye, 1957:224). Frequently the line between those two is difficult to identify. The ridicule of the villain lengthens the distance between the audience and the characters. In irony, the listener can frequently say, "I am like that. Things like that happen to me." In satire, the reader who identifies with the offending character experiences humiliation and shame. Satire intends to belittle and demean.

In Hebrew short stories, we find frequent use of humor, including irony. Jonah, Ruth, and Esther furnish many examples. Satire is another matter. Some scholars suggest that the narrator in Esther uses satire in portraying Haman and Ahasuerus, and in Jonah in depicting the prophet. Remember that satire turns a character into a villain. While the narrator may intend for us to look on Haman as a villain, the same cannot likely be said about Jonah and probably not Ahasuerus.

THE DIASPORA In the last half of the eighth century B.C., the Assyrian kingdom began a successful military expansion westward from central

Mesopotamia to Syria and Palestine. Eventually the Assyrians reached Israel and under Sargon II conquered the capital city of Samaria, 721-720. Sargon reorganized the region as an Assyrian province. As a part of that reorganization, many of the Israelites were displaced and moved elsewhere in Assyria. Other population groups moved into the cities, villages, and countryside (2 Kings 17). This began what has come to be called the dispersion of the Jews, the Diaspora.

A little more than a century later, the Babylonian conquest of Jerusalem made the Diaspora a reality not only for the people of northern Palestine, but for the south as well. With the subjection of Jerusalem in 597 and its fall in 586, the population of Judah was scattered south to Egypt, north to Asia Minor, and east to Babylon and perhaps beyond (2 Kings 24–25).

This dispersion left the Israelites without a political or religious center and resulted in a transformation of the people's identity. Perhaps the most significant change was the emergence of their religious identity as a people of the Book. While no one can trace the exact history of the formation of the Torah, scholars recognize how important it was that the Torah was emerging as the central element in the Jewish people's identity. The Bible (Tanak: Law, Prophets, and Writings of the OT) was variously interpreted but came to be held in common throughout the distant cities and regions of the Babylonian, Persian, Greek, and Roman empires. It served to establish and maintain the faith and practice of the Jewish people.

While the Torah may have been the most crucial element in maintaining the identity of the dispersed people, it was not the only factor. The Jews nourished what is often called an ethnic identity, a sense of peoplehood based on remembered heritage and family connections. This ethnic identity, more than religion, plays a role in the narrative of Esther. There Esther is described as orphaned and subsequently brought up by her *cousin* Mordecai (2:7). Esther always refers to the Jews as a people without mentioning distinct religious practices, especially in the Hebrew version of the story.

Whether living as a distinct ethnic people or with religious identity or both, the Diaspora Jews never lost the sense that they were dispersed. They expected to be regathered in Jerusalem one day.

THE INTERPRETING COMMUNITY OF FAITH Throughout history the Christian church has entrusted the interpretation of Scripture to various individuals or groups. The Roman Catholic Church has looked to the priests, bishops, and members of the Catholic orders for an authorized interpretation. These clergy depend on traditional Catholic doctrine for interpretive direction. The papacy has remained the guardian of true doctrine. While traditional doctrine in Roman Catholicism establishes interpretive parameters, it allows Catholic scholars a great deal of freedom to study the Bible and creatively explore its narratives, poetry, and accounts.

The Reformed Protestant tradition has emphasized the role of scholars to "rightly" interpret the Word of God (2 Tim. 2:15). While traditional creeds may play a role, these academics in the Reformed tradition have insisted that the Bible, as carefully interpreted, should take precedence over traditional church doctrine in Christian faith and action. This perspective, grounded in its commitment to an educated clergy who interpret the Bible within the congregation, was responsible for founding most of the earliest seminaries and divinity schools in North America.

The believers church approaches biblical study differently from either the Roman or Reformed tradition. Although valuing both traditional doctrine and educated scholars, these groups have lifted up the importance of the individual believer and the faith community in biblical interpretation. The Pietistic heritage has encouraged the individual to read the Bible, prayerfully expecting the Holy Spirit's presence to give meaning and message. Pietism has recognized the interpretive role of each believer, whether one was an academic, a member of the clergy, or a lay member.

The Anabaptist heritage has reminded the individual that each one must always be in conversation with the believing community to validate the meaning and message of the Bible. The Anabaptists have talked about the Spirit's presence where two or three (or more) gather to study the Bible and pray (cf. Matt. 18:19-20; Acts 15:28).

The believers church tradition has recognized that the process of biblical interpretation is never complete. Therefore, neither creedal doctrine nor academic commentary can finally determine the interpretation of Scripture. Each generation is entrusted with the Bible and charged with the responsibility to prayerfully and carefully interpret the text for its time, respectful of tradition and attentive to the Spirit. This has made believers church groups rather reluctant to write commentary, remembering that, in the past, commentary has often been used to codify a single interpretation that was then used to criticize and even to persecute dissenters.

The absence of a single orthodox interpretation, however, has never meant that all interpretations are equally true and beneficial. Interpretation can destroy as well as construct. Christian history, from ancient times until this day, illustrates the frequency with which individuals and communities can use an interpretation of the Bible to initiate violence, authorize slavery, or justify discrimination. Individuals are not free to define the meaning of a biblical text apart from the church that transmitted the Bible (Bird: 63). For that reason the believers church tradition encourages all voices in the community, past and present, to offer their best understanding, creating a conversation within the interpreting community. Out of that conversation concerning the Bible's meaning and message, the believers church community anticipates a transformed people rather than a single orthodox interpretation.

Hence, the believers church tradition rejoices in the variety of interpretive possibilities presented by biblical narrative and poetry. It runs counter to the believers church tradition to expect elders, clergy, or scholars to identify a single meaning and message of the text. In the believers church tradition, the Bible is to be studied and discussed, prayed and lived, so that God's new word will be heard through this ancient, inspired canon.

JONAH AND HISTORICAL ANALYSIS Historians have long insisted that history provides the best vehicle for understanding and interpreting a biblical text. If we identify when the text was written, by whom, and to whom, we gain crucial insight into the Bible's message. After clarifying the message of the text through historical analysis, the interpreter can relate that identified message to a contemporary setting.

This interpretative process of using history has been influential and valuable for much of the biblical literature. It has enabled readers to listen to the prophets in their own time as they struggled to be heard in the din of events that often dulled the ears of the ancient listeners. Such historical investigation has enabled interpreters to understand the law codes as they functioned in different cultural, economic, and political eras.

Nevertheless, scholars have recognized that some biblical literature cannot be easily identified as the product of a certain time and location. Foremost in this regard has been the book of Psalms. A few of the psalms can be reasonably located in time and place, such as the psalm of the Babylonian Exile (Ps. 137). However, we cannot know the history of most psalms. Efforts to reconstruct a history of the biblical psalms—whether by dating poetic language, historical allusions, or authorship—have proved impossible and the interpretative results unsatisfying.

Scholars have encountered the same difficulty in trying to date the narrative of Jonah. Attempts to date the book of Jonah have ranged all the way from the reign of Jereboam II in Samaria (ca. 785-750 B.C.) to the postexilic era of Ezra and Nehemiah (fifth century B.C.) or even much later. To determine the date of a biblical narrative, scholars use various historical tools: dating the Hebrew language used, identifying "historical" allusions in the text, and deciding the historical era in which the narrative best fits. The results for Jonah have not yielded a satisfactory conclusion.

This historical discussion itself is not problematic. The difficulty comes when the interpretation of Jonah is built on a tentative historical reconstruction. Working from different historical results, scholars have come to disparate conclusions about the intention of the book. Hence, depending on the date chosen for the book's origin and its subsequent editing, the message of Jonah is said variously to be the prophet's fear of appearing as a false prophet, an explanation for the fall of Samaria to Assyria, the necessity of repentance, the freedom of God's mercy, opposition to religious exclusivism, or something else.

The lack of success in firmly rooting Jonah in one specific historical era, has prompted other scholars to explore this narrative as Hebrew literature without direct reference to a presumed date of origin. To be sure, the importance of history is not disregarded. However, literary analysis focuses on the nature and character of ancient Hebrew literature, rather than on the date of origin of any particular narrative or poem. In a literary approach, the distinctiveness of this ancient literature requires that interpreters attend to its special characteristics *[Characteristics of Hebrew Narrative].*

While literary approaches to the book have identified many of the same interpretative possibilities for Jonah as proposed by historical analysis, literary analysts do not expect to discover a single message. By their very nature, narratives and poetry are creative and generative. It becomes the responsibility of the faith community to listen to the interpretive possibilities revealed by a careful literary and historical reading of the text, and to discuss the implications for faith and action.

KHESED: UNCOMMON AND FAITHFUL ACTION Few words in the Hebrew Bible have attracted more attention and study than *khesed*. Several books and many articles have explored this word especially since Nelson Glueck called attention to its importance in 1927 (English ed., 1967). Glueck claimed that *khesed* is one of the Bible's weighty words, prescribing responsible ethical conduct within the community of faith. According to Glueck, *khesed* specifies assistance given as a duty or obligation to those in need. In ancient Israel, it was a virtue prompted by distinctively religious obligation. As such, *khesed* fulfills the demands of justice and righteousness toward God and toward the poor and needy. However, *khesed* is not conduct that is confined to human actors. In the Bible, God also does *khesed,* acting to bring aid and salvation to the people through divine strength and power (Glueck: 54-55, 68, 102).

By connecting *khesed* so closely to a legal covenant, Glueck chose to emphasize the obligatory character of the word. Katherine Sakenfeld observes that the earlier biblical traditions do not make *khesed* a legal obligation. She insists instead that *khesed* has a distinctively voluntary character. *Khesed* describes assistance different from and perhaps beyond what civil and religious law requires. While *khesed* has no legal force, Sakenfeld points to the expectation that one who can give assistance will do so. This expectation might be grounded in reciprocal assistance (helping someone in return for aid received) or in a close family or community relationship that made such assistance part of the ethical norms of ancient Israel. She further observes that *khesed* does not refer to everyday acts of kindness. The one doing *khesed* acts to assist an endangered person, providing emergency assistance for those unable to help themselves (Sakenfeld, 1978:44-5, 78-82).

Sakenfeld also helps us understand the *khesed* of God. The term expresses God's active assistance both for individuals and for the community. The Bible tells us that God may act in *khesed* based on prior divine promise, in response to repentance, or as an act of divine grace and forgiveness (Sakenfeld, 1978:147-50). Although the biblical tradition affirms God's commitment to *khesed*, the texts never lose sight of the fact that such action is grounded in divine freedom, not in obligation. Nevertheless, Psalm 136 appropriately reinforces the affirmation, "The *khesed* of the LORD endures forever." Nature declares and history illustrates the powerful presence of God's help and protection—divine *khesed.*

Along with words such as "compassion" *(rakham)* and "mercy" *(khanan)*, *khesed* came to define the very ground of life within community and with God. *Khesed* is an act that preserves and promotes life (Zobel: 51). *Khesed* urges us to act out of opportunity and strength to assist those suffering and oppressed. One acts in *khesed* out of relational responsibility, but also for God's sake.

Most English Bibles use *kind* or *kindness* to translate *khesed* (Ruth 1:8 and 2:20, NRSV, NIV, NASV). However, versions use other words such as *loyalty,* in hope of providing the best nuance for *khesed* in a given text (Ruth 3:10, NRSV). Much of the time the translator is caught with no good English equivalent to the Hebrew word *khesed*. Hence, we are left with translations such as *kind* and *loyal,* which are not adequate. One wishes for an English word that conveys more strength and drama to define *khesed*, the act of promoting life in an emergency situation.

KINSHIP MARRIAGE Deuteronomy 25:5-10 addresses a crisis in the family arising when one of the sons dies without male offspring. The widow of the deceased was not to be sent outside the family to be married. Instead, her husband's brother was to take her as wife into his household. The brother would then act as a surrogate husband and father in place of his deceased brother. The firstborn (presumably a son) would be legally the son of his mother and her deceased first husband. Scholars call this custom levirate marriage, taken from the Latin *levir,* meaning "husband's brother."

Kinship or levirate marriage served several functions. The specific purpose mentioned in Deuteronomy 25 involved the household or family name of the deceased. The son of this kinship marriage preserved the name and family line of his deceased "father." Likely this meant more than simple perpetuation of a name. It also kept the property of the deceased in the immediate family. It also provided security for the widow, keeping her from poverty and prostitution or being married outside the family.

The directives regarding this practice in Deuteronomy also note occasions when the brother-in-law might refuse his kinship responsibility. In that case, in a ceremony of shame, the widow was to remove the sandal from the foot of the offending brother-in-law and spit in his face. Henceforth, the offending family would carry a shameful name: "the house of him whose sandal was pulled off" (Deut. 25:10). The fact that Deuteronomy provides a ceremony of shame rather than other legal sanctions, suggests that kinship marriage may have remained largely a matter of custom rather than law (Thompson: 88-9). Leviticus prohibits a man from marrying or having sexual relations with his brother's wife (Lev. 18:16; 20:21). Leviticus does not mention an exception for kinship marriage with a deceased brother's wife who lacks a son.

The Genesis 38 narrative featuring Tamar and Judah shows this kinship marriage in practice. Judah's eldest son, Er, was married to Tamar. After Er died, it was his brother Onan's responsibility to provide a son for Er. Onan refused and subsequently died, and Judah neglected to assign this responsibility to his son Shelah, fearing that he also might die. Tamar felt forced into a position of deceiving Judah himself into making her pregnant and thus performing the levirate duty. This narrative may suggest that the practice of kinship marriage varied greatly in different times and places. It appears that Judah did not actually marry Tamar, but he recognized that he had fathered a child for his deceased son and kept Tamar and her twin sons in the family (Coats, 1972:463-4).

The story of Ruth describes what may be another variation on the kinship marriage custom (Niditch, 1985:452). Ruth's husband, Mahlon, has no surviving brother, and as Boaz declares, Ruth is free to marry anyone (Ruth 3:10). However, in the legal case witnessed by the Bethlehem village elders, Boaz announces that he intends to take Ruth as his wife for the express purpose of providing an heir for Ruth's late husband (4:10). In this narrative, the kinship marriage responsibility seems to belong not just to brothers living together (Deut. 25:5), but also (if a brother is lacking) to the *redeemer* (Ruth 4:14, NASB), the *next-of-kin* responsible to insure that family property not be lost because of debt *[Redeemer/Go'el]*. In still another twist to this custom, the son born to Ruth and Boaz becomes not the son of Mahlon and Ruth, but the son of Naomi, Mahlon's mother! (Ruth 4:17).

MOAB Moab was a high plateau and hill country located on the east side of the Dead Sea, a land now part of Jordan. Although archaeologists have uncovered few large towns and villages on this plateau, they have ancient evidence of extensive production of grain in the area, primarily barley and wheat (Hubbard, 1988a: 85-7). The language of Moab belongs to the Semitic family that also includes Hebrew. Scholars know less of the history of Moab than they would like, and the Hebrew traditions about Moab influence the tone of negative associations with the name in ancient Israel.

According to Genesis 18–19, it was the decadence and disaster of Sodom

Essays

that gave birth to Moab. God directed Lot, Abraham's separated nephew (Gen. 13), to flee from Sodom with his family (Gen. 19). After considerable argument, they did leave, but the reluctance of Lot's wife resulted in her death. The tragedy closes with Lot and his daughters living in a cave. The two daughters decided that because they had no opportunity to marry, they would become pregnant by their father. After dulling his judgment with alcohol, the women in their turn lay with their father. The son born of the incest by Lot's eldest daughter was Moab, claimed as the ancestor of the Moabites.

A second narrative about the antagonism between Moab and Israel comes from Israel's stories of its sojourn in the wilderness. Balak, the king of Moab, decided that he must stop the horde of Israelites about to journey through his land (Num. 22–24). So he sent for a Babylonian diviner, Balaam, and requested that he place a curse on these dreaded people.

Balak's verbal assault against Israel failed due to divine intervention. However, Israel's sojourn in Moab, as narrated in Numbers 25, further fueled the antagonism in Israel's memory. The problem then was not Moab's king but "the women of Moab" (Num. 25:1), who brought with them another religion. This violation of Israel's faith provoked divine wrath. God's anger led to the death of "twenty-four thousand" (Num. 25:3-9).

Yet another narrative tells of the hostility between Israel and Moab. This one comes from traditions of the time *when the judges ruled* (Ruth 1:1). Eglon, a Moabite ruler, defeated the Israelites and took possession of the "city of palms," probably Jericho (Judg. 3:12-30). Israel later sent tribute to Eglon, using a left-handed Benjaminite by the name of Ehud. By deceit, Ehud convinced Eglon to dismiss his guards. Alone with the king, Ehud stabbed Eglon, burying his whole weapon in the fat of the obese king (3:22). Ehud returned home and led an attack against the now leaderless Moabites.

Israel's stories about Moab included a founding son conceived in incest, a fearful king unable to buy a curse on Israel, seductive women leading Israelite men astray, and a stupid king so fat the sword of his death is buried in him—stories heavy with satire and anger *[Comedy, Irony, and Satire]*. This attitude toward Moab was likely reinforced by the disqualification of Moabites declared in Deuteronomic law: "No Ammonite or Moabite shall be admitted to the assembly of the LORD. Even to the tenth generation, none of their descendants shall be admitted" (Deut. 23:3-5).

NARRATIVE STRUCTURE The narrators of Hebrew literature had at their disposal a wide variety of ways in which they could organize their narratives. Most of these modes of organizing are familiar to us.

Sequence of Events. For example, a narrator often uses a manner of presentation that includes a sequence of events. This sequencing enables the reader to move easily with the characters through the plot. At times, however, the narrator wants to let us observe events or conversations that occur simultaneously. In that case, the readers are taken from scene to scene without a sense of sequence. On such occasions, the narrator will usually tell us that one thing happened at the same time as the other. In Esther 6:4, for example, the narrator tells us that Haman enters the palace court while the king is in conversation with his servants. In Esther 1:9, however, we may presume that the queen's banquet happens at the same time as the king's, but the narrator does not explicitly say that.

Narrative Sequence: Still other methods of organizing narrative material are obvious and familiar. Folk literature exhibits a simple and familiar narrative sequence. The narrative begins with a problem or tension. It may be established by the clash between characters, as occurs at the opening of Esther, or a statement such as the one opening the story of Ruth: *There was a famine in the land* (1:1). Various kinds of plans, action, or interventions follow from this problem. These lead eventually to a resolution of the tension. In the book of Jonah, we find two tensions at the beginning: God's dispute with Nineveh, and Jonah's clash with God. The former is resolved at the end of Jonah 3. The clash between God and Jonah extends the plot to chapter 4, which closes with an incomplete resolution. Thus we see that narrative sequence produces a pattern of problem→action→resolution.

Journey Sequence. This is another form of Hebrew narrative flow. The narrator may choose to follow the journey of the main character or characters. Certainly, such an organization includes a time sequencing of the material. Yet time is really secondary to progress of the trip. Hence, the narrative may begin with preparations for departure, followed by the journey itself, and then arrival at the intended destination (Ruth 1:6-22). Often we do not know how much time elapses from the beginning to the end of the journey. The progress of the journey rather than movement of times is most important.

Chiasm is one distinctive organizational method, occurring occasionally in Hebrew literature. In literature with a chiastic organization, the opening element and the closing element are parallel (like brackets or bookends) in clearly discernible ways, such as in content or function. The next element in the unit then parallels the next to last. This balancing continues until arriving at the central section of the literary unit. That central element in the chiastic structure stands alone. Symbolizing chiastic parallelism with letters looks something like this A, B, C, D, C^1, B^1, A^1. Chiastic literature may have any number of such sections. The only requirement is that each one is balanced by another, except for the center one.

No doubt chiasm functions as an important literary device, shaping both poetry and narrative literature in the Hebrew Bible. We can see it in the structure of Ruth 2. Yet we may have trouble identifying the presence of chiasm in any particular piece of literature because it is foreign to our own literary style. Hence, we can easily overlook chiasm and miss one of the narrator's important guides to the center of the narrative. The opposite temptation is also found among interpreters, to "discover" a chiastic pattern by forcing sections to balance one another when they probably do not.

It is most important for us to test different possibilities of identifying the organizational structure of the literature. Such recognition of narrative structure increases our ability to look at the story through all the lenses the narrator provides.

NARRATOR For the most part, a biblical story is told from the perspective of a third person, a narrator who stands outside the drama itself. Sometimes this narrator tells the story from the position of a single observer, watching the drama from above. More frequently, the narrator moves about from place to place, looking over the shoulder of different characters as well as reporting the silent thoughts and feelings of the individuals (Berlin, 1983:43-82).

We have become so accustomed to stories told by such an unnamed and omniscient narrator that we seldom observe how such a literary device guides the listener. The narrator leads us through the plot of the story by reporting certain dialogue, thoughts, and action, but not others, and by describing the selected characters, but only in limited ways *[Characteristics of Hebrew Narrative]*. Occasionally the narrator includes an evaluative comment or adjective that directs the reader to view the events in a certain way. By featuring the names, thoughts, or words of specific characters, the narrator places a character in the foreground. Other characters are relegated to secondary roles, sometimes operating in a stereotypical manner to contrast with the main characters, or performing a specific function necessary to the plot *[Character Types in Hebrew Narrative]*.

Since the narrator guides the listeners through the drama, we need to notice carefully the narrator's conceptual point of view (Longman: 106-7). That viewpoint provides access to one theological perspective available in the narrative. We seldom find the narrator explicit about that perspective, but from hints, suggestions, and evaluative comments, we can identify the point of view. Besides giving us the narrator's conceptual perspective, careful observation enables us to discern the characters toward whom the narrator feels sympathy or antagonism. Such discernment frees us to imagine the drama through other points of view than the one provided by the narrator. We can wonder about the perspective of characters relegated to the background.

By moving freely from place to place and from character to character in the drama, the narrator allows considerable freedom for the listener. The reader is not limited to a single point of view. Hence, the story does not come to us as a flat, one-dimensional narrative. Instead, it has multidimensional depth within which we are free to move, observe, and discern (Berlin, 1983:44-5).

In this multidimensional presentation, we often have available not only the narrator's point of view, but also that of specific characters. The story of Jonah is built around the contrasting perspectives of the two major characters, God and Jonah. For most of the narrative, the narrator makes us onlookers as the plot unfolds. Suddenly in the last episode (Jon. 4), the perspective shifts and we see the events more directly through the eyes of Jonah and God. In Esther 6, we find a scene in which the narrator provides us the perspective of Ahasuerus and Haman at the same time. From the point of view of the narrator, who stands above them both, the limited perspectives of Ahasuerus and Haman turn the scene into a comedy.

The variety of perspectives portrayed in Hebrew narrative provides color and depth to the stories. It makes the reader of such narratives an active participant (Berlin, 1983:82). We can reread the narratives many times, each time standing in the shoes of a different character. This permits us to differ from the narrator's evaluation of an action or decision. God has entrusted these narratives to us, allowing us the freedom to live in them and learn from them. It often seems that God has trusted us with more interpretative freedom than we allow ourselves and considerably more than we usually permit to others.

NINEVEH Nineveh lay far to the north and east of ancient Israel. This city, on the east bank of the Tigris River, a few miles south of the (Ararat) mountain foothills, became the capital of Assyria with the ascension of the Assyrian monarch Sennacherib in 705 B.C. Although an ancient city, rebuilt several times, Nineveh reached its greatest size and importance as the capital of the Assyrian Empire. Its glory was relatively short-lived; less than a hundred years later, the Assyrian empire fell to the Babylonians and the Medes. Nineveh fell with it in 612.

Nineveh, the capital of Assyria in the century when Judah felt violently oppressed by Assyrian control, became the object of Judah's hatred. Nahum's prophetic judgment oracle is directed entirely against Nineveh. With unrestrained glee, Nahum celebrated the fall of Nineveh. Of course, Nineveh was a distant city that few people in Judah had ever visited. We do not find mention of the city in the biblical texts before Sennacherib (2 Kings 19:36), except in the list of Assyrian cities found in the table of Nations (Gen. 10:11-12).

Direct Assyrian domination of Israel came with the army of Tiglath-pileser III (744-727; 2 Kings 15). For several years Israel maintained a vassal relationship with Assyria, paying taxes (tribute) as demanded. The Israelite king Pekah (740-732) tried to change that. He allied the country with the Syrian King Rezin II against Assyria. This brought Assyrian wrath against the whole area. Syria was conquered and parts of Israel were annexed as separate Assyrian provinces (2 Kings 16).

From the royal annals of Tiglath-pileser III, we read his claim to have placed Hoshea on the throne of Israel, following what he alleged was a popular revolt (Pritchard: 284). At first Hoshea duly paid the taxes levied by Assyria. However, upon the death of Tiglath-pileser III, he joined an anti-Assyrian coalition against Shalmaneser V (727-722; 2 Kings 17). This brought Assyria back more violently than ever. The siege of the Israelite capital of Samaria began about 725. It resulted in Samaria's capture and destruction in 722/721 B.C., perhaps after Sargon II (721-705 B.C.E.) had ascended to Assyrian throne.

With the fall of Samaria, the northern kingdom (Israel) ceased to exist, exposing the southern (Judah) to Assyrian control more directly than before. With the death of Sargon II, Judah's king, Hezekiah (715-686) decided he too would renounce allegiance to Assyria. This brought the army of the new Assyrian king, Sennacherib (795-681), against Judah. Jerusalem survived this and subsequent Assyrian attacks. Several factors seem to have contributed to Assyria's failure to take Jerusalem. Hezekiah built a water tunnel that protected Jerusalem's water supply inside the city walls. The king also attempted temporarily to appease Sennacherib with money. But apparently more crucial, an epidemic struck the Assyrian troops, which the biblical account celebrates as divine deliverance (cf. 2 Kings 18–20 and a history of ancient Israel, such as Shanks: 131-6). Even though Jerusalem did not fall, the rest of Judah was devastated by the Assyrian army. Archaeological investigations at the fortress of Lachish provide one example of the destruction of Judah by the Assyrian army.

Israel and Judah experienced Assyria as a ruthless aggressor and an oppressive colonial power. Such an assessment is verified by the artistic remains preserved from the Assyrian Empire. War dominates Assyrian art. The murals characteristically portray the king as a victorious warrior. Battle scenes of slaughter fill out the picture. The scenes feature various ways in which the Assyrian army tortured the defeated enemy: dismemberment, burning, flaying. Nahum's vehement rage against Nineveh reflects the Israel and Judah's experience with the violent superpower to its northeast. The opening words in Jonah (1:2) speak about the wickedness of the Ninevites. Ancient listeners to the story of Jonah would carry in their memory the horror stories of Assyrian oppression and occupation.

NOVELLA The term *novella* means "little novel." This term groups together narratives longer than short stories and shorter than novels. A biblical novella displays the characteristics of all biblical narratives *[Characteristics of Hebrew Narrative; Character Types in Hebrew Narrative; Narrator]*, especially those of a short story *[Short Story]*. Like a short story, the aesthetic dimensions of narrative plot are more central to a novella than reporting the data of history. Similarly, it is more important that the novella maintain its narrative integrity than that it conform to particular tenets of "orthodox" theology. That is not to say that a novella lacks any concern for historical data or theology. However, efforts to force such a narrative to conform to specific data and ideas will misconstrue the nature of the literature, diverting attention from the story's truth and beauty.

A novella differs from a short story in significant ways. A novella is longer, as we can see by comparing Ruth and Jonah with the biblical novellas about Esther and Joseph (Gen. 37–50). Partly because of the greater length, a novella can involve more characters and develop them in more complex ways. Indeed, one of the primary distinctions between the biblical short story and the novella concerns the development of character in the narrative. While the short story reveals or illustrates the character of the hero, in the novella there is space to develop the character in new directions. Thus Joseph reassures his brothers of his continuing love and care for them (Gen. 50), showing that he is no longer the person who earlier tattled on them, arrogantly proclaiming his superiority (Gen. 37).

The length of the novella permits more complex development of plot as well. Subplots frequently appear and are resolved as a part of the complication or resolution of the dominant plot. A character can enter the drama, play a significant role in one of these subplots, and then disappear. In the Joseph novella, Potiphar's wife (Gen. 39), the royal steward, and the baker (Gen. 40–41) appear and leave. Each of their stories is completed in a brief episode. Yet in a novella, each episode contributes to the complication and/or resolution of the main plot. These auxiliary characters and subplots are seldom fully developed in the novella, but they make for a more complex narrative than is found in the biblical short story.

As noted, the Joseph narrative and the story of Esther constitute the most familiar examples of the biblical novella. Judith and Tobit, narratives found in the Roman Catholic canon and the Protestant Apocrypha, provide additional examples of novellas. It would be well for those in the Protestant tradition to read Tobit and Judith.

THE PERSIAN EMPIRE A Persian royal son Cyrus II took control of Media and Persia in a military coup against his grandfather and political master, Astyages, king of the Medes (about 550 B.C.). From his home territory just east of the Persian Gulf, Cyrus launched a successful military campaign, taking over a region stretching from Asia Minor (now Turkey) to the eastern section of (present-day) India. The key event for biblical history in the Persian conquest involves the defeat of the Babylonian army by Cyrus and the surrender of their capital city, Babylon, in 539.

The Samaritans and the Jews, after living first under the rule of the Assyrians, then under the Babylonians, now found themselves as residents of the Persian Empire. The Samaritans and the Jews, forcibly dispersed by the armies of Assyria and Babylon *[Diaspora]*, experienced the Persians as much more benevolent in their attitudes and actions. In an edict attributed to Cyrus (Ezra 1:2-4; 2 Chr. 36:23), the Persian monarch permitted all exiles to return to their home territory and resume their religious practices. The returning refugees did not dare to establish independent political states, but they could rebuild their religious sanctuaries and shrines. From 539 to 516, some Jews did return to the Palestine. Under the leadership of Zerubbabel, Nehemiah, and Ezra, they established a community in Jerusalem and built a new temple.

The biblical books of Chronicles, Nehemiah, and Ezra provide scholars some understanding of life in Palestine in the Persian period. We know less about the many Jews who continued to live dispersed throughout the Persian cities. The biblical narratives of Esther and Daniel 1–6 retell stories that were passed on concerning those Diaspora Jews *[Diaspora]*, but they provide only brief snapshots. Hence, we can say little about the life of Jews living dispersed throughout the region in the fifth and fourth centuries B.C.

The Persian Empire controlled the region for over two centuries, until the rise of the Greek Empire under the leadership of Alexander of Macedonia. Alexander the Great crossed into Asia Minor in the spring of 334 B.C. and defeated a Persian army. In subsequent battles against the Persians (334-330), Alexander completed the conquest of Persia. With that, the political and cultural center shifted from the east (Persia) to the west (Greece/Macedonia).

POETRY The division between poetry and prose exists more clearly in modern literature than in the Hebrew writings of the Bible. Nevertheless, we can identify literature that displays the character of narrative *[Characteristics of Hebrew Narrative]* and designate it as prose. Other literature, written with a terse two-part sentence style, we recognize as biblical poetry (Kugel, 1985:804). Although the two-part sentence style can be found scattered about in narrative, scholars generally agree that its presence indicates a poetic element present in the prose. Some literature, such as the Psalms, Proverbs, and much of the prophetic material, is mostly poetic.

Historically, the two-part sentence structure of Hebrew poetry has been called *parallelism*. Robert Lowth proposed that the two-part parallel unit was the most characteristic element in Hebrew biblical poetry. Lowth observed that often the second line repeats the first line, either with synonyms or antonyms. Lowth's theory of parallelism worked fairly well when the second line of the poetic couplet displayed a synonymous or antithetical relationship to the first. Frequently, however, the relationship between the two lines appears more complex than synonymous and antithetical parallelism can describe.

Current research into Hebrew poetry remains indebted to Robert Lowth for describing the two-part sentence structure. Yet his terminology, *parallelism*, unduly prejudiced the discussion of the relationship between the two lines (Kugel, 1981; Alter, 1985). Instead, James Kugel proposes that we speak about a second line asserting, strengthening, or otherwise completing the thought in the first line (Kugel, 1985:804). In each poetic unit, the interpreter must investigate the way in which the second line completes or even extends the thought of the first.

For example, in Jonah 2:5 the second line reasserts but also extends in a new direction the image portrayed in the first:

The waters closed in over me,
    the deep surrounded me.

In the first line, the word *waters* is the common term for a large body of water. In the second line, the word *deep* pushes the picture in a new direction. The *deep* is not ordinary water, not even deep water, but the primordial cosmic sea. The poet feels ominously engulfed by the waters of chaos. Therefore, as we read the two-part poetic line, we must carefully discern not only the repetition that might be present but also the way the second line develops the poetic picture. By using the term *parallelism*, we may lose some of the richness available in the pictures painted by Hebrew poetry.

The terseness and free style of the two-line sentence of Hebrew poetry makes a poem difficult to read and translate. Modern translations of biblical poetry may therefore differ dramatically from one another. Israel's poets had a large vocabulary and did not follow the same grammatical "rules" generally observed by their prose counterparts. Nevertheless, the attentive reader is richly rewarded by the terse and yet free style of biblical poetry that paints pictures and stimulates images.

PURIM According to the rabbinical writings, Purim is to be a two-day festival held on Adar 14-15 (usually mid-March, depending on the lunar calendar). A day of fast precedes these two days of celebration. On Purim, the Jewish community gathers to hear the reading of the story of Esther. Custom dictates that the reading can be interrupted by listener response: cheers for Mordecai and Esther, and especially with shouts denouncing Haman. In many Jewish congregations, the listeners even employ noisemakers and shouts to drown out the reader every time Haman's name is read, causing the whole event to take on a joyful carnival atmosphere. The service concludes with blessings for Esther and Mordecai, usually adjourning to food and fun in celebration of every occasion when the Jews have persisted against enemies seeking to destroy them. In addition to joyful celebration, Purim also includes the distribution of provisions to those in need (Esther 9:22).

The festival is named for the word *Pur* used for casting lots in the Hebrew book of Esther (3:7; 9:24). Actually, the word *Pur* is not Hebrew, so the narrator follows it with the Hebrew word for lot, *goral*. The plural, *Purim*, appears in the book only as the name of the festival (9:26-32). This has prompted scholars to explore the possibility that the celebration originated as a non-Jewish festival that Judaism took over and adapted to serve as a holiday to remember this story. Although there are many proposals to this effect, none have proved convincing enough to gain general acceptance.

Purim shares one thing in common with Hanukkah. Both festivals receive their biblical authorization in writings outside of the books of Moses (Gen.—Deut.). Most major Jewish feasts and sacred days claim the authority of Moses, both through stories, as with Passover (Exod. 12), and religious calendars (as in Exod. 23; 34; Deut. 16; Lev. 23). The feast of Hanukkah, however, celebrates rededication of the temple (164 B.C.) following the Maccabean revolt against the Hellenistic (Seleucid) empire, part of Alexander the Great's legacy. Perhaps to win support for these two non-Mosaic festivals, the narratives about each repeatedly insist and instruct Jews concerning the celebration of the festival (Esther 9:26-32; Addition F in the Apocrypha, 10:4—11:1; 2 Macc. 1:1—2:18; 1 Macc. 4:41-59; cf. John 10:22, "festival of the Dedication," or Hanukkah).

QUESTIONS Questions play a wide range of roles in everyday speech. Speakers use questions to request, argue, and admonish, among other assignments. Questions perform several functions in biblical speech. As we read Hebrew narrative, we need carefully to examine speeches that feature questions. Often we can learn much about the mood, feelings, and intention of a speaker by recognizing the character of a question.

Frequently Hebrew narrative provides only indirect access to a character's interior thoughts, feelings, and mood *[Characteristics of Hebrew Narrative]*. The narrator expects the reader to detect each character's mood and/or personality through indirect indicators. Of course, the easiest way to determine a speaker's feelings is to have the speaker or narrator tell us directly. That happens occasionally in biblical narrative. Thus we learn that Naomi is bitter (Ruth 1:20), and that the sailors are terrified (Jon. 1:5). But many more times, we readers must discover for ourselves the mood, motivation, and intention of a narrative character (Alter, 1981:117). Knowledge about the purpose and aim of various kinds of questions can help us do that (Hyman, 1983:17-25).

In the Bible, the common interrogative usually simply asks for information. Nothing need lie behind it other than a situation in which one character has information that the other wants. Perhaps Boaz wants no more than information when, awaking in the dark of the night and finding a woman, asks, "Who are you?" However, there may be more to his question than that. Though obtaining data can be important, a character in a story may want information to gain an advantage. That only becomes clear in the context of the narrative itself. Nevertheless, many questions carry little more than a request for information.

A second kind of question, familiar to most of us, is the rhetorical question. Rhetorical questions use the interrogative form to make a statement. In other words, they are intended as statements, though disguised as questions. Hence, a rhetorical question makes room for only one answer. The "correct" answer is obvious in the literary context. For example, after an almost endless battle between Job and his friends over the nature of God, the LORD finally enters the debate. God addresses Job with a long series of rhetorical questions: "Who determined [the earth's] measurements? . . . Who shut in the sea with doors when it burst out from the womb?" (Job 38:5, 8). The rhetorical questions clearly have a declarative intention, frequently conveying irritation if not anger. Yet rhetorical questions are defined not so much by their intention as by the required answer.

A third category of questions is defined by their intention. These questions are designed to entrap, accuse, teach, or express emotions (Hyman, 1983:17-25). It may be helpful to separate these intentions into different categories. But they all have one element in common. The recognition of the question's intention frequently rests in the discernment of the reader. For example, on one occasion Jesus' enemies asked him a question that on the surface could be a simple request for information. But the narrator tells us ahead of time that they were really trying to accuse Jesus: "In the law Moses commanded us to stone such women. Now what do you say?" (John 8:5).

Other questions carry in them an implicit accusation, whether or not the narrator makes that explicit. God addressed Cain with such a question: "Where is your brother Abel?" (Gen. 4:9). It is not likely that God needed information from Cain. In fact, Cain answers God with another question, which also has an accusatory tone: "Am I my brother's keeper?" (4:9). The reader will discover in biblical narratives other questions that may or may not be intended as accusatory (such as Gen. 3:9; Mark 5:30).

Frequently the Gospels report Jesus using didactic questions, designed to teach. For example, Jesus told the temple leaders about two sons. One of them promised to carry out the instruction of his father, but did not. The other objected and even refused to obey, but eventually complied. Jesus then asked, "Which of the two did the will of his father?" (Matt. 21:31). Jesus used their answer to teach them more about the character of God's reign.

Any scheme of classification certainly oversimplifies the variety of questions found in biblical literature. The role of each question needs to be examined for its distinctiveness as well as its genre. However, conscious awareness of different kinds of questions will help us interpret texts. Sometimes correct discernment of the type of a spoken question will provide a key to understanding an entire text or story. At other times, such analysis will enable a narrative character to come alive to a reader in new ways. In any case, questions themselves often provide considerable information.

REDEEMER/GO'EL The function of *redeemer (go'el)* in ancient Israel arose from the strong tradition of family solidarity. Family in Israel involved not only parents and children, but also an extended family, the "house of the father," and perhaps even the family of families *(mišpakhah)*, which many call a clan (Gottwald: 285-318). This family solidarity required that the strong in the family come to the aid of distressed members in matters of justice and debt. For example, if a person was killed or injured, it was the responsibility of a family member to make sure that justice was done. In this legal function of the redeemer, the Hebrew *go'el* is often translated "avenger" (Num. 35:19-27, NRSV, NIV).

Another function of the redeemer happened when a family member would fall into debt. Such debt might be caused by illness that prevented the individual from earning a living for the family, or by other misfortune, such as drought or pestilence that destroyed the crops. The unfortunate family member might then be forced to sell the property to obtain food or even sell oneself into debtor slavery. It was the responsibility of the related redeemer to buy the land back and also to buy out the individual's service contract (Lev. 25:25-54).

The texts about the custom do not specify only one in the extended family to assume the responsibility to be redeemer. Leviticus 25:48-49 names the enslaved person's brother, uncle, or cousin as a possible redeemer, then goes on to designate "anyone of their family who is of their own flesh." Folks who managed to recover economically could redeem themselves (Lev. 25:49).

No one knows how well the system worked in behalf of the poor family members. The responsibility of redemption was to be exercised promptly when a need arose. Apparently Jeremiah redeemed some family property in his home town of Anathoth even before it was sold. However, no one quickly stepped forward to assist Naomi when she returned to Bethlehem impoverished (Ruth 1:20-21; 4:3). Some suggest the *next-of-kin* (NRSV) chose not to step forward because the land would eventually come his way at the death of the childless widow (LaCocque, 1990:97). He chose not to spend his money in spite of Naomi's destitute situation until his hand was forced by Boaz. Boaz announced that he would act as *redeemer* and buy the land back into the family if the nearest of kin did not act as custom required (NIV, *kins-*

man-redeemer: 2:20; 3:9, 12; 4:1, 3, 6, 8, 14. NASB, 4:14, *redeemer).*

Obviously, this practice of redemption to assist poor members of the extended family provided an analogy for language about God's action on behalf of the poor. God became the one who functioned as redeemer, rescuing Israel from the hands of its enemies (Mic. 4:10). The one without any access to help could turn to God, asking for God, the Redeemer, to intervene (Ps. 119:154; Ringgren, 1980:353). Psalm 72:4, 14 assigns to the king the role of redeemer in Israel, making sure justice is provided for the poor and deliverance for those oppressed. It is not surprising, then, that the redeemer—*go'el* role became central to the messianic vocation (Luke 24:21).

SHORT STORY Short stories constitute one of the most familiar narrative forms *[Characteristics of Hebrew Narrative].* In our culture we experience short story in oral, written, and visual form. Scholars differ on the origin of the short story in ancient Israel. Some maintain that the short story originated in written form, distinguishing short story from the tale, which seems to have been passed from generation to generation in oral form before it was written. Regardless of its origin, the biblical short story was written to be read aloud. Most people listened to the story, perhaps beginning as children. Most ancient listeners never learned to read. Only recently has reading become the dominant mode of experiencing the short stories of the Bible.

We can easily recognize a biblical short story because in many ways it is similar to the short story in contemporary culture. The Greek philosopher Aristotle (384-322 B.C.) identified plot as one of the primary marks of the short story (*Complete Works,* 2329f.). He noted that the plot moves through a story segment, in which the problem becomes complicated and the tension increases. Finally comes the moment when the hero's fortune changes. That leads to the resolution, or denouement, and finally the end of the short story.

Familiarity with the story plot in general may lead readers to overlook the importance of identifying the movement of the distinctive plot in each biblical short story. In reading biblical narratives, even the most familiar ones, we will increase our understanding if we take time to chart the flow of the story from the beginning tension to the moment when the story reaches its crest and begins to resolve or relax. The individual pieces of the story need to be understood in relationship to that flow. Removing a segment of the story and treating it apart from its place in the plot can lead to misinterpretation.

Length constitutes a second obvious feature of the biblical short story. Such a narrative can be read in a single sitting. Nevertheless, a short story is longer than narratives often called tales (such as about Cain and Abel in Gen. 4, or the Tower of Babel in Gen. 11), brief accounts that can be read in a few minutes.

The short story involves only a few characters, frequently one or two figures. There may be other people in the story, but they have momentary or background roles *[Character Types in Hebrew Narrative].* Unlike the longer novella *[Novella],* the short story tends to reveal rather than develop the character of the hero or heroes of the narrative (Humphreys: 92). The outward circumstances of the hero may change so that we understand the person better at the conclusion of the story, but only rarely will there be change in the basic character of the individual.

All biblical narratives have elements of history, aesthetics, and theology

(Sternberg). Different narratives feature one of these elements more than the others. Some narratives intend to convey public events and thus feature that historical data prominently (as in the narratives of David rising to the throne, and Solomon after him; 1–2 Sam.; 1 Kings 1-11). Other narratives are dominated by theological issues, seeking directly to address the nature and character of God (God's contests with Pharaoh, Exod. 7–12, and with Baal, 1 Kings 18). A short story is a narrative that features the aesthetic. Although it certainly is not without theological and historical concern, its plot attends first of all to the flow of tension and resolution, rather than accommodating the expectations of historical data. God enters into the action as the drama requires rather than as theological orthodoxy might insist. The biblical short story wants to keep listeners interested in the drama rather than to inform them about data or correct the reader's theology.

A biblical short story has a message. It seeks to be persuasive, but not in declaratory ways. It wants the reader first to be involved, and second to be informed. Hence, with each new reading, the listener may hear a different word from the text. Obviously, the narrative is not free to mean all things to all people. Yet if one carefully invests oneself in the narrative, the message happens through the reader's involvement in the short story.

TWELVE PROPHETS The Hebrew Bible is called Tanak, an acronym for its three parts handed down to us: *Torah*/Law/Pentateuch, *Nevi'im*/Prophets, and *Ketubim*/Writings. The Torah includes the first five books: Genesis to Deuteronomy. In Jewish tradition, those five books constitute the heart of the sacred writings, and to some extent the rest of the Hebrew canon is considered commentary on the Torah.

The second part of the Hebrew Bible is called the Prophets. Tradition has divided the prophets into two parts and eight scrolls. The Former Prophets include Joshua, Judges, Samuel, and Kings; the Latter Prophets are Isaiah, Jeremiah, Ezekiel, and the Book of the Twelve. We do not know the exact meaning of "former" and "latter." The terms may simply indicate which books come before the others in the Hebrew Bible.

The third part to the Hebrew canon is designated the Writings. This section includes all the rest of the books, beginning with Psalms and concluding with 2 Chronicles (Luke 24:44 names this part "Psalms," the opening and longest book in the group).

The Christian tradition has adopted a sequence of biblical books different from the three-part Hebrew text. This division, which likely reflected a different Hebraic tradition, became popular in the Christian church through the use of a Greek translation, the Septuagint (Childs: 667). This translation of the Hebrew text used a four-part division of the canon: the Pentateuch (Gen. to Deut.), the historical narratives (Josh. to Esther), Psalms and Wisdom (Job to Song of Solomon), and the Prophets (Isa., Jer.–Lam., Ezek., Dan., and the Book of the Twelve).

In spite of the different books variously included in both the Jewish and Christian canon, both traditions have treated the Book of the Twelve as a single entity. While the number and list of prophets included in the twelve has been consistent, the sequence of the twelve has varied (Dyck, 1986:222). Nevertheless, the Jewish, Protestant, and Catholic canon currently employ the same sequence: Hosea, Joel, Amos, Obadiah, Jonah, Micah, Nahum, Habakkuk, Zephaniah, Haggai, Zechariah, and Malachi.

The formal designation of these as the Book of the Twelve books goes back at least into the second century B.C. Sirach 49:10 says,

> As for the twelve prophets,
> may their bones flower again from the tomb
> since they have comforted Jacob
> and redeemed him in faith and hope. (JB)

Individually, these twelve illustrate the variety of prophetic activity in ancient Israel. Together they witness to the vitality of that tradition, from the Assyrian domination over Israel and Judah in the eighth century, and on to the Persian control of Judah and Samaria in the fifth century B.C.

VILLAGE FARMING Cultivation of crops and herding flocks constituted the basic village economy in the hill country of Palestine. Villages were located near a supply of fresh water, a well, spring, or a reliable stream. The villagers generally built their homes close together, often arranging the houses with the water supply at or near the center of the town. The open area around the well served as a gathering place for the community. Most Palestinian villages lacked walls. However, some of the larger towns did have surrounding walls to protect them from bandits and discourage military attack. A primary gathering place in towns with protective walls was the open area just inside *the gate* (Ruth 4:1-12).

The fields for the village included the tillable soil lying around and near the town. These fields belonged to specific families in the village and were passed on from generation to generation. For the most part, the fields were unfenced, designated by the name of the family and marked with boundary stones.

There seems to be little evidence of irrigation. Instead, the farmers depended on rainfall to water their crops. The uncertain nature of the rainfall made drought the primary worry of the village farm family. The varieties of crops cultivated by the village farmers depended on the availability of water. The two most important grain crops were wheat and barley. While wheat may have been the preferred grain, barley proved the most drought resistant and seems to have been planted most in the southern hill country.

The planting season in most villages began in late fall, to take advantage of the winter rains. The barley was usually ready for harvest in mid to late April, followed by the wheat harvest later in May. The harvesting was done by hand, using a sickle with a blade made early of flint and then later of iron. The harvester would grab the grain stalks by hand and cut them off close to the ground. Apparently the stalks were then laid in piles, to be tied up in bundles and carried to the threshing place. At the threshing floor, the stalks were beaten with sticks or trampled by work animals, perhaps dragging a sledge or some instrument (cf. 2 Sam. 24:22). The loosened grain was then winnowed, allowing the wind to blow away the dust and chaff so that relatively clean kernels of barley or wheat could be gathered into baskets or bags (cf. Ps. 1:4).

The poor in the village had no fields to cultivate. Crop failure, illness, accident, or death could cause a family to lose possession of their fields. If the fields had to be sold to pay off family debts, the family would be reduced to life as landless poor. This might force the family to move to a place where they could find food and maybe resume farming. Certain groups in the town usually had no tillable land. These included the widows (generally women who had lost their husbands and had no children), orphans (young children without parents), and aliens (people who had moved to the village from another area or country). These landless villagers were often at risk of disease from malnutrition.

The poor in the village could acquire food by gleaning, gathering the grain that had broken off and fallen during the harvesting work. Hebrew custom prohibited an owner from gleaning the field after harvesting, even directing the owner not to go back and pick up overlooked stalks of grain (Deut. 24:19-21). In some traditions, the owner was supposed to leave the odd patches of grain at the edges or corners of the field so there might be some for the poor, the widow, the orphan, and the alien to glean (Lev. 19:9-10). One suspects such gleaning usually provided only a meager food supply. In fact, the whole village agricultural economy, especially in lean years, produced little more than the families themselves needed to eat.

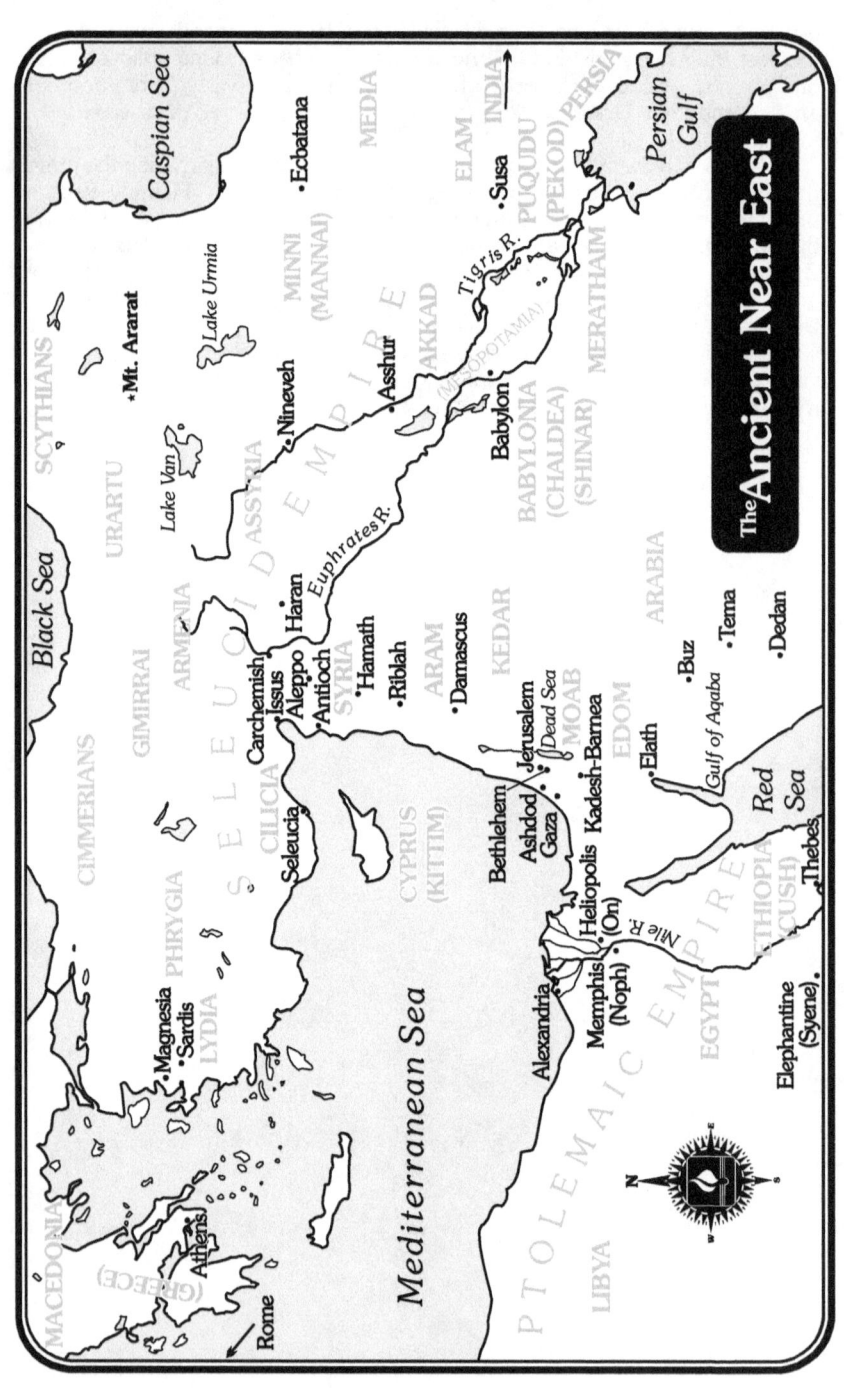

Bibliography

Ackerman, James S.
   1981   "Satire and Symbolism in the Song of Jonah." In *Traditions in Transformation*. Ed. B. Halpern and J. D. Levenson. Winona Lake, Ind.: Eisenbrauns.
   1987   "Jonah." In *The Literary Guide to the Bible*. Ed. R. Alter and F. Kermode. Cambridge, Mass.: Harvard Univ. Press.

Alter, Robert
   1981   *The Art of Biblical Narrative*. New York: Basic Books.
   1985   *The Art of Biblical Poetry*. New York: Basic Books.

Aristotle
   1984   *The Complete Works of Aristotle*. Rev. Oxford translation. Ed. Jonathan Barnes. Princeton, N.J.: Princeton University Press.

Bal, Mieke
   1987   *Lethal Love: Feminist Literary Readings of Biblical Love Stories*. Bloomington, Ind.: Indiana Univ. Press.
   1993   "Heroism and Proper Names, or the Fruits of Analogy." In *A Feminist Companion to Ruth*, 42-69. Ed. A. Brenner. Sheffield, England: Sheffield Academic Press.

Baly, Dennis
   1985   "Bethlehem." In *Harper's Bible Dictionary*. San Francisco: Harper & Row.

Bankson, Marjory Z.
   1987   *Seasons of Friendship: Naomi and Ruth as a Pattern*. San Diego, Calif.: LuraMedia.

Beal, Timothy K.
   1995   "Tracing Esther's Beginnings." In *A Feminist Compaion to Esther, Judith, and Susanna*. Ed. A. Brenner. Sheffield: Sheffield Academic Press.

Beattie, D. R. G.
   1971   "*Kethibh* and Qere in Ruth 4:5." *Vetus Testamentum* 21:490-4.

1974 "The Book of Ruth as Evidence of Israelite Legal Practice." *Vetus Testamentum* 24:251-67.
1977 *Jewish Exegesis of the Book of Ruth*. JSOTSup, 2. Sheffield, England: Sheffield University.
1978a "Ruth III." *Journal for the Study of the Old Testament* 5:39-48.
1978b "Redemption in Ruth, and Related Matters: A Response to Jack M. Sasson." *Journal for the Study of the Old Testament* 5:65-8.
1987 "Ruth 2:7." *Zeitschrift für die alttestamentliche Wissenschaft* 99:422-3.

Beckwith, Roger
1985 *The Old Testament Canon of the New Testament Church and Its Background in Early Judaism*. Grand Rapids: Eerdmans.

Bellis, Alice Ogden
1994 *Helpmates, Harlots and Heroes: Women's Stories in the Hebrew Bible*. Louisville: Westminster John Knox.

Ben-Amos, D., ed.
1976 *Folklore Genres*. Austin: Univ. of Texas Press.

Ben-Sasson, H. H., ed.
1976 *A History of the Jewish People*. Cambridge: Harvard Univ. Press.

Berg, Sandra B.
1979 *The Book of Esther: Motifs, Themes and Structure*. Missoula, Mont.: Scholars Press.
1980 "After the Exile: God and History in the Books of Chronicles and Esther." In *The Divine Helmsman*. Ed. J. L. Crenshaw and S. Sandmel. New York: Ktav.

Berlin, Adele
1983 *Poetics and Interpretation of Biblical Narrative*. Bible and Literature Series. Sheffield, England: Almond Press.
1988 "Ruth." In *Harper's Bible Commentary*. San Francisco: Harper & Row.
2001 *Esther*. The JPS Bible Commentary. Philadelphia: Jewish Publication Society.

Bickerman, Elias
1967 *Four Strange Books of the Bible*. New York: Schocken Books.

Bird, Phyllis
1974 "Images of Women in the Old Testament." In *Religion and Sexism*, 41-8. Ed. R. R. Ruether. New York: Simon & Schuster.

Bos, Johanna W. H.
1986 *Ruth, Esther, Jonah*. Atlanta: John Knox.
1988 "Out of the Shadows: Genesis 38; Judges 4:14-22; Ruth 3." *Semeia* 42:37-67.

Bowers, R. H.
1971 *The Legend of Jonah*. The Hague: Martinus Nijhott.

Brenner, Athalya
1983 "Naomi and Ruth." *Vetus Testamentum* 33:385-97.
1985 *The Israelite Woman*. The Biblical Seminar. Sheffield, England: JSOT Press.
1993 "Naomi and Ruth." In *A Feminist Companion to Ruth*, 71-84. Ed. A. Brenner. Sheffield, England: Sheffield Academic Press.

1989 *The Israelite Woman: Social Role and Literary Type in Biblical Narrative.* Sheffield: JSOT Press.
1994 "Who's Afraid of Feminist Criticism? Who's Afraid of Biblical Humor? The Case of the Obtuse Foreign Ruler in the Hebrew Bible." *Journal for the Study of the Old Testament* 63:38-55.
1995 "Looking at Esther Through the Looking Glass." In *A Feminist Companion to Esther, Judith, and Susanna.* Ed. A. Brenner. Sheffield: Sheffield Academic Press.

Brenner, A., and F. van Dijk-Hemmes
1993 *On Gendering Texts: Female and Male Voices in the Hebrew Bible.* Leiden: Brill, 1993.

Brueggemann, Walter
1988 *Israel's Praise: Doxology Against Idolatry and Ideology.* Philadelphia: Fortress.

Burrows, Millar
"The Literary Category of the Book of Jonah." In *Translating and Understanding the Old Testament: Essays in Honor of H. G. May,* 80-107. Nashville: Abingdon.

Bush, Frederick W.
1996 *Ruth, Esther.* Word Biblical Commentary. Waco, Tex.: Word Books.

Callanan, Maggie, and Patricia Kelley
1997 *Final Gifts: Understanding the Special Awareness, Needs and Communications of the Dying.* Reprint. New York: Bantam Books.

Calvin, John
1950 *Commentaries on the Twelve Minor Prophets.* Vol. 3. Tr. J. Owen. Grand Rapids: Eerdmans.

Campbell, E. F.
1974 "The Hebrew Short Story: A Study of Ruth." *A Light Unto My Path,* 83-101. Ed. H. N. Bream et al. Philadelphia: Temple Univ. Press.
1975 *Ruth.* Anchor Bible. Garden City, N.Y.: Doubleday & Co.
1990 "Naomi, Boaz, and Ruth: Complexities Within Simplicity." *Judaism* 35:290-7.

Ceresko, Anthony J.
1990 "Jonah." In *The New Jerome Biblical Commentary.* Ed. R. E. Brown. Englewood Cliffs, N.J.: Prentice Hall.

Charlesworth, James H., ed.
1985 *The Old Testament Pseudepigrapha.* Vol. 2. New York: Doubleday.

Childs, Brevard S.
1979 *Introduction to the Old Testament as Scripture.* Philadelphia: Fortress.

Clements, R. E.
1975 "The Purpose of the Book of Jonah." In *Congress Volume: Edinburgh, 1974.* Vetus Testamentum Supplement, 28. Leiden: Brill.

Clines, D. J. A.
1984 *The Esther Scroll: The Story of the Story.* Sheffield: JSOT Press.

    1984a *Ezra, Nehemiah, and Esther.* New Century Bible. Grand Rapids: Eerdmans.
    1990 "Reading Esther from Left to Right: Contemporary Strategies for Reading a Biblical Text." In *The Bible in Three Dimensions.* Ed. D. J. A. Clines et al. Sheffield: JSOTSup Press.
    1991 "In Quest of the Historical Mordecai." *Vetus Testamentum* 41:129-36.

Coats, George W.
    1972 "Widow's rights: a crux in the structure of Genesis 38," *Catholic Biblical Quarterly* 24:461-466.
    1983 *Genesis.* Forms of Old Testament Literature. Grand Rapids: Eerdmans.

Craghan, John
    1982 *Esther, Judith, Tobit, Jonah, Ruth.* Wilmington, Del.: Michael Glazier.

Cundall, A. E., and L. Morris
    1968 *Judges, Ruth.* Chicago: InterVarsity Press.

De Troyer, Kristin
    1995 "An Oriental Beauty Parlour: An Analysis of Esther 2.8-18." In *A Feminist Companion to Esther, Judith, and Susanna.* Ed. A. Brenner. Sheffield: Sheffield Academic Press.

Dorothy, Charles V.
    1996 *The Books of Esther: Structure, Genre and Textual Integrity.* Ann Arbor, Mich.: UMI Dissertation Service.

Durnbaugh, Donald F.
    1967 *The Brethren in Colonial America.* Elgin, Ill.: Brethren Press.
    1986 *European Origins of the Brethren.* Elgin, Ill.: Brethren Press.

Dyck, Elmer
    1986 "Canon and Interpretation: Recent Canonical Approaches and the Book of Jonah." Ph.D. diss. McGill Univ., Montreal.
    1990 "Jonah Among the Prophets." *Journal of the Evangelical Theology Society* 33:63-73.

Eagleton, Terry
    1990 "J. L. Austin and the Book of Jonah," in *The Book and the Text: The Bible and Literary Theory*, R. Schwartz, ed. Cambridge, Mass.: Basil Blackwell.

Eller, David
    1986 "Social Outreach." In *Church of the Brethren: Yesterday and Today.* Ed. D. F. Durnbaugh. Elgin, Ill.: Brethren Press.

Ellul, Jacques
    1971 *The Judgment of Jonah.* Grand Rapids: Eerdmans.

Exum, J. Cheryl, and J. W. Whedbee
    1984 "Isaac, Samson, and Saul: Reflections on the Comic and Tragic Visions." *Semeia* 32:5-40.

Farmer, Kathleen A. R.
    1998 "The Book of Ruth" In *The New Interpreters Bible, Vol. II.* Nashville: Abingdon Press.

Fewell, Donna N., and David M. Gunn
    1988 "A Son Is Born to Naomi." *Journal for the Study of the Old Testament* 40:99-108.

1989 "Boaz, Pillar of Society." *Journal for the Study of the Old Testament* 45:45-59.
1990 *Compromising Redemption: Relating Characters in the Book of Ruth*. Louisville: Westminster John Knox.

Fox, Michael V.
1990 *Redaction of the Books of Esther*. Atlanta: Scholars Press.
2001 *Character and Ideology in the Book of Esther*. Second Edition. Grand Rapids, Mich.: Wm. B. Eerdmans Publishing Co.

Freedman, David Noel
1990 "Did God Play a Dirty Trick on Jonah at the End?" *Bible Review* 6:26-31.

Fretheim, Terence E.
1977 *The Message of Jonah*. Minneapolis: Augsburg.
1988 "Jonah." In *Harper's Bible Commentary*. San Francisco: Harper & Row.

Frye, Northrop
1957 *Anatomy of Criticism*. Princeton, N.J.: Princeton Univ. Press.
1963 *Fables of Identity*. New York: Harcourt, Brace, & World.
1982 *The Great Code*. London: Ark.

Gardner, Richard
1991 *Matthew*. Believers Church Bible Commentary. Scottdale, Pa.: Herald Press.

Gerleman, Gillis
1960 *Ruth*. Biblischer Kommentar Altes Testamentum, XVIII. Neukirchen: Neukirchener Verlag.

Glueck, Nelson
1967 *Khesed in the Bible*. Cincinnati: Hebrew Union College Press.

Good, E. M.
1965 *Irony in the Old Testament*. Philadelphia: Westminster.

Gordon, Cyrus H.
1962 "Tarshish." In *Interpreter's Dictionary of the Bible*, vol. R-Z. Nashville: Abingdon.

Gottwald, Norman
1979 *The Tribes of Yahweh: A Sociology of the Religion of Liberated Israel, 1250-1050*. Maryknoll, N.Y.: Orbis Books.
1985 *The Hebrew Bible: A Socio-literary Introduction*. Philadelphia: Fortress Press.

Graber, J. D.
1957 "Anabaptism Expressed in Missions and Social Service." In *The Recovery of the Anabaptist Vision*, 152-66. Ed. G. F. Hersberger. Scottdale, Pa.: Herald Press.

Gray, John
1986 *Joshua, Judges, Ruth*. New Century Bible Commentary. Grand Rapids: Eerdmans.

Green, Barbara
1982 "The Plot of the Biblical Story of Ruth." *Journal for the Study of the Old Testament* 23:55-68.

Gunkel, Herrmann
1912 "Jonabuch." In *Die Religion in Geschicte und Gegenwart, III*: 638-43. Tübingen: J. C. B. Mohr.

Gunn, David M.
    1984   "The Anatomy of Divine Comedy: On Reading the Bible as Comedy and Tragedy." *Semeia* 32:115-29.
Gunn, David M., and Danna Nolan Fewell
    1993   *Narrative in the Hebrew Bible.* Oxford: Oxford Univ. Press.
Hals, Ronald
    1969   *The Theology of the Book of Ruth.* Philadelphia: Fortress.
Hammer, Reuven
    1986   "Two Approaches to the Problem of Suffering." *Judaism* 35:300-5.
Hauser, A. J.
    1985   "Jonah: In Pursuit of the Dove." *Journal of Biblical Literature* 104:21-37.
Heinemann, Karl, ed.
    1900   *Goethes Werke,* Bd. 4. Leipzig: Bibliographisches Institut.
Heschel, Abraham J.
    1962   *The Prophets.* 2 vols. New York: Harper Torchbooks.
Holbert, John C.
    1981   "'Deliverance Belongs to Yahweh!' Satire in the Book of Jonah." *Journal for the Study of the Old Testament* 21:59-81.
Hongisto, Lief
    1985   "Literary Structure and Theology in the Book of Ruth," *Andrews University Studies* 23:19-28.
Hubbard, Robert L.
    1988a   *The Book of Ruth.* New International Commentary on the Old Testament. Grand Rapids: Eerdmans.
    1988b   "Ruth 4:17: A New Solution." *Vetus Testamentum* 38:293-301.
Humphreys, W. Lee
    1985   "Novella." In *Saga, Legend, Tale, Novella, Fable.* Ed. G. W. Coats. Sheffield, England: JSOT Press.
Hyman, Ronald T.
    1983   "Questions and the Book of Ruth." *Hebrew Studies* 24:17-25.
    1984   "Questions and Changing Identity in the Book of Ruth." *Union Seminary Quarterly Review* 39:189-201.
Klein, Lillian R
    1995   "Honor and Shame in Esther." In *A Feminist Companion to Esther, Judith, and Susanna.* Ed. A. Brenner. Sheffield: Sheffield Academic Press.
Knight, G. A. F., and F. W. Golka
    1988   *Revelation of God.* International Theological Commentary. Grand Rapids: Eerdmans.
Kugel, James L.
    1981   *The Idea of Biblical Poetry.* New Haven: Yale Univ. Press.
    1985   "Poetry." In *Harper's Bible Dictionary.* San Francisco: Harper & Row.
Jouon, P.
    1953   *Ruth.* Rome: Pontifical Biblical Institute.
LaCocque, André
    1990   *The Feminine Unconventional: Four Subversive Figures in Israel's Tradition.* Minneapolis: Augsburg Fortress.

Bibliography

LaCocque, André, and Pierre-Emmanuel LaCocque
   1981   *The Jonah Complex*. Atlanta: John Knox.
   1990   *Jonah: A Psycho-Religious Approach to the Prophet*. Columbia, S.C.: Univ. of South Carolina Press.

Laffey, Alice L.
   1990   "Ruth." In *The New Jerome Biblical Commentary*. Englewood Cliffs, N.J.: Prentice Hall.

Landes, George M.
   1967   "The Kerygma of the Book of Jonah." *Interpretation* 21:3-31.
   1972   "Review of Jacques Ellul, *The Judgment of Jonah*." *Interpretation* 26:98-9.
   1976   "Jonah." In *The Interpreter's Dictionary of the Bible*, Suppl. vol.: 488-91.
   1978   "Jonah: A Masal?" In *Israelite Wisdom: Essays in Honor of Samuel Terrien*. Missoula, Mont.: Scholars Press.
   1982   "Linguistic Criteria and the Book of Jonah." *Eretz-Israel* 16:147-70.

Lehmann, Benjamin
   1981   "Comedy and Laughter." In *Comedy: Meaning and Form*. Ed. R. Corrigan. New York: Harper & Row.

Levenson, Jon D.
   1997   *Esther*. Louisville: Westminster John Knox.

Limburg, James
   1988   *Hosea-Micah*. Interpretation. Atlanta: John Knox.
   1990   "Jonah and the Whale Through the Eyes of Artists." *Bible Review* 6:18-26.
   1993   *Jonah*. Old Testament Library. Louisville: Westminster John Knox.

Longman, Tremper
   1987   *Literary Approaches to Biblical Interpretation*. Grand Rapids: Zondervan.

Lowth, Robert
   1816   *Lectures on the Sacred Poetry of the Hebrews*. London: Ogles, Duncan, and Cochran.

Luther, Martin
   1974   "Lectures on the Minor Prophets." In *Luther's Works*, vol. 19. Saint Louis, Mo.: Concordia Publishing House.

Magonet, Jonathan
   1983   *Form and Meaning: Studies in Literary Techniques in the Book of Jonah*. Bible and Literature Series. Sheffield, England: Almond Press.

McGee, J. Vernon
   1988   *Ruth and Esther: Women of Faith*. Nashville: Thomas Nelson.

Melville, Herman
   1957   *Moby Dick*. New York: Holt, Rinehart & Winston.

Menno Simons
   1984   *The Complete Writings of Menno Simons*. Trans. Leonard Verduin. Ed. J. C. Wenger. Scottdale, Pa.: Herald Press.

Meyers, Carol
   1988   *Discovering Eve: Ancient Israelite Women in Context*. Oxford: Oxford Univ. Press.
   1993   "Returning Home: Ruth 1:8 and the Gendering of the Book of

Ruth." In *A Feminist Companion to Ruth*, 85-114. Ed. A. Brenner. Sheffield, England: Sheffield Academic Press.
1999 "Women of the Neighborhood." In *Ruth and Esther*. Ed. A. Brenner. Sheffield, England: Sheffield Academic Press.

Miles, John A.
1974 "Laughing at the Bible: Jonah as Parody." *Jewish Quarterly Review* 65:168-81.

Milne, Pamela J.
1986 "Folk Tales and Fairy Tales: An Evaluation of Two Proppian Analyses of Biblical Narratives." *Journal for the Study of the Old Testament* 34:35-60.

Moore, C. H.
1971 *Esther*. Anchor Bible, 7B. New York: Doubleday.
1977 *Daniel, Esther, and Jeremiah: The Additions*. Anchor Bible, 44. Garden City: Doubleday.

Morse, Kenneth I.
1997 *Preaching in a Tavern*. Elgin, Ill.: Brethren Press.

Murphy, Roland
1981 *Wisdom Literature: Job, Proverbs, Ruth, Canticles, Ecclesiastes, Esther*. Forms of O.T. Literature. Grand Rapids: Eerdmans.

Niditch, Susan
1985 "Legends of Wise Heros and Heroines." In *The Hebrew Bible and Its Modern Interpreters*. Ed. D. Knight and G. Tucker. Chico, Calif.: Scholars Press.
1987 "Esther: Folklore, Wisdom, Feminism, and Authority." In *Underdogs and Tricksters: A Prelude to Biblical Folklore*. San Francisco: Harper & Row.

Niditch, Susan, and R. Doran
1977 "The Success Story of the Wise Courtier: A Formal Approach." *Journal of Biblical Literature* 96:179-93.

Nielsen, Kirsten
1985 "Le choix contre le droit dans le livre de Ruth." *Vetus Testamentum* 35:201-12.
1997 *Ruth: A Commentary*. Trans. Edward Broadbridge. Louisville: Westminster John Knox.

Olrik, Axel
1965 "Epic Laws of Folk Narrative." In *The Study of Folklore*. Ed. A. Dundes. Englewood Cliffs, N.J.: Prentice Hall.

Payne, Robin
1989 "The Prophet Jonah: Reluctant Messenger and Intercessor." *Expository Times* 100:131-4.

Phillips, Anthony
1980 "Uncovering the Father's Skirt." *Vetus Testamentum* 30:38-42.
1986 "The Book of Ruth—Deception and Shame." *Journal of Jewish Studies* 37:1-17.

Prickett, Stephen
1996 *Origins of Narrative*. Cambridge: Cambridge Univ. Press.

Pritchard, J. B.
1958 *The Ancient Near East: An anthology of texts and pictures*. Princeton, N.J.: Princeton University Press.

Rad, Gerhard von
  1965 *Old Testament Theology*, vol. 2. New York: Harper & Row.
Rayburn, Carole A.
  1982 "Three Women from Moab." In *Spinning a Sacred Yarn*. New York: Pilgrim Press.
Redekop, Vernon W.
  1990 *A Life for a Life: The Death Penalty on Trial.* Scottdale, Pa.: Herald Press.
Ringgren, Helmer
  "Esther and Purim." In *Studies in the book of Esther.* Ed. C. A. Moore. New York: Ktav.
Ringgren, Helmer
  1980 *Israelite Religion*, translated by David Green. Philadelphia, PA: Fortress.
Ringgren, Helmer, and O. Kaiser
  1981 *Das Hohe Lied, Klageleider, Das Buch Esther.* Das Alte Testament Deutsch. Göttingen: Vandenhoeck & Ruprecht.
Sakenfeld, Katherine Doob
  1978 *The Meaning of Khesed in the Hebrew Bible: A New Inquiry.* Missoula, Mont.: Scholars Press.
  1985 *Faithfulness in Action: Loyalty in Biblical Perspective.* Philadelphia: Fortress.
  1999 *Ruth.* Louisville: Westminster John Knox Press.
Sasson, Jack M.
  1978a "Ruth III: A Response." *Journal for the Study of the Old Testament* 5:49-51.
  1978b "The Issue of *Géullah* in Ruth." *Journal for the Study of Old Testament* 5:52-64.
  1987 "Ruth." In *The Literary Guide to the Bible.* Ed. R. Alter and F. Kermode. Cambridge, Mass.: Harvard Univ. Press.
  1989 *Ruth: A New Translation.* 2nd ed. Baltimore: Johns Hopkins Univ. Press.
Shanks, Hershel, ed.
  1988 *Ancient Israel: A Short History from Abraham to the Roman Destruction of the Temple.* Englewood Cliffs, N.J.: Prentice Hall.
Simon, Uriel
  1999 *Jonah.* The JPS Bible Commentary. Philadelphia: Jewish Publication Society.
Snyder, Graydon
  1985 *Ante Pacem: Archaeological Evidence of Church Life Before Constantine.* Macon, Ga.: Mercer Press.
Sternberg, Meir
  1985 *The Poetics of Biblical Narrative.* Bloomington, Ind.: Indiana Univ. Press.
Stoffer, Dale R.
  1989 *Background and Development of Brethren Doctrines, 1650-1987.* Philadelphia: Brethren Encyclopedia, Inc.
Stuart, Douglas
  1987 *Hosea-Jonah.* Word Biblical Commentary, 31. Waco, Tex.: Word Books.

Talmon, S.
   1963 "Wisdom in the Book of Esther." *Vetus Testamentum* 13:419-55.
Thompson, T., and D. Thompson
   1968 "Some Legal Problems in the Book of Ruth." *Vetus Testamentum* 18:79-99.
Trible, Phyllis
   1963 "Studies in the Book of Jonah." Ph.D. diss. Columbia Univ.
   1976 "Two Women in a Man's World: A Reading of the Book of Ruth." *Soundings* 49:251-79.
   1978 *God and the Rhetoric of Sexuality*. Overtures to Biblical Theology. Philadelphia: Fortress.
   1994 *Rhetorical Criticism: Context, Method and the Book of Jonah*. Minneapolis: Augsburg Fortress.
   1996 *The Book of Jonah*. New Interpreter's Bible, 7. Nashville: Abingdon.
Troyer. *See* De Troyer
Vawter, Bruce
   1983 *Job and Jonah*. New York: Paulist Press.
Von Rad   *See* Rad, Gerhard von
Waard, Jan de, and Eugene Nida
   1973 *A Translator's Handbook on the Book of Ruth*. New York: United Bible Societies.
Westermann, Claus
   1967 *Basic Forms of Prophetic Speech*. Philadelphia: Westminster.
   1978 *Blessing in the Bible and the Life of the Church*. Philadelphia: Fortress.
   1979 *What Does the Old Testament Say About God?* Atlanta: John Knox.
   1989 *The Living Psalms*. Grand Rapids: Eerdmans.
White, Sidnie Ann
   1989 "Esther: A Feminine Model for Jewish Diaspora." In *Gender and Difference in Ancient Israel*. Ed. P. Day. Minneapolis: Fortress.
   1992 "Esther." In *The Women's Bible Commentary*. Ed. C. A. Newsome et al. Louisville: Westminster John Knox.
Wolff, Hans W.
   1959 "Jonahbuch." In *Die Religion in Geschichte und Gegenwart*, 3. Tübingen: J. C. B. Mohr.
   1986 *Obadiah and Jonah*. Minneapolis: Augsburg.
Wyler, Bea
   1995 "Esther: The Incomplete Emancipation of a Queen." In *A Feminist Companion to Esther, Judith, and Susanna*. Ed. A. Brenner. Sheffield: Sheffield Academic Press.
Zobel, Hans-Jurgen
   1986 "Khesed." In *Theological Dictionary of the Old Testament*, vol. 5. Ed. Botterweck and Ringgren. Grand Rapids: Eerdmans.
Zucker, David J.
   1995 "Jonah's Journey." *Judaism* 44:362-8.

Selected Resources

For further study of these narratives, you may consult (1) books on the nature, character, and interpretation of OT narrative; and (2) commentaries and studies on Ruth, Jonah, and Esther.

Old Testament Narrative

Alter, Robert. *The Art of Biblical Narrative*. New York: Basic Books, 1981. Provides readers with an understanding of certain distinctive and easily recognized characteristics that mark Hebrew narrative. Readers can see for themselves how biblical narratives are similar and different from contemporary narratives.

Berlin, Adele. *Poetics and Interpretation of Biblical Narrative*. Bible and Literature Series. Sheffield, England: Almond Press, 1983. Has a well-written study of the artistic character of biblical narrative. Berlin provides a way into biblical narrative that invites readers to move through analysis into interpretation.

Kugel, James. *The Idea of Biblical Poetry*. New Haven, Conn.: Yale University Press, 1981. Takes the reader through the long history of appreciating the aesthetics of biblical poetry. Like Alter and Berlin, Kugel uses little technical jargon but gives clear and careful help to reading and enjoying Hebrew poetry.

Kugel, James, and Rowan Greer. *Early Biblical Interpretation*. Library of Early Christianity. Philadelphia: Westminister, 1986. Early in the present era, the Jewish and Christian communities took parallel but different paths as they read the Old Testament. Kugel and Greer help us understand the formation and direction of those two interpretative traditions.

Commentaries and Studies

Berlin, Adele. *Esther.* The JPS Bible Commentary, Philadelphia: The Jewish Publication Society, 2001. Provides excellent observations concerning the distinctive character of the narrative style in Esther. Her conclusions about the use of humor in Esther may change the feel of the story for some who have been troubled by the book.

Bush, Frederick W. *Ruth, Esther*. Word Biblical Commentary. Waco, Tex.: Word Books, 1996. A thorough but readable commentary on both Ruth and Esther. More than is possible in this and other recent commentaries, Bush's study presents the conclusions of many different scholars regarding issues of text and interpretation.

Clines, David J. A. *Ezra, Nehemiah, and Esther.* New Century Bible. Grand Rapids: Eerdmans, 1984. Presents a careful commentary on Esther by one of the leading figures in narrative interpretation. As Clines writes, he keeps a focus on the use of the Bible in preaching and teaching.

Farmer, Kathleen A. Robertson. *The Book of Ruth.* New Interpreters Bible, Volume 2. Nashville: Abingdon, 1998. This excellent commentary elaborates further the narrative's use of key words and word plays to carry the story and point to mean. She provides carefully written observations on the importance of the story for Christian faith and practice.

Levenson, Jon D. *Esther.* Old Testament Library. Louisville: Westminster John Knox, 1997. Demonstrates the extent to which Jewish and Christian interpretations again walk together. His commentary enriches the Christian community by incorporating insights from the rich Jewish heritage.

Limburg, James. *Jonah.* Old Testament Library. Louisville: Westminster John Knox Press, 1993. Provides a valuable resource for those preaching and teaching Jonah. Limburg makes use not only of the written interpretative tradition, but also of the Jonah as interpreted through Christian art.

Nielsen, Kirsten. *Ruth: A Commentary.* Old Testament Library. Louisville: Westminster John Knox, 1997. Helps readers interpret Ruth not only as a distinctive narrative, but also in relationship to other biblical stories. For example, she carefully carries out an interpretive conversation between the stories of Ruth and of Tamar, the daughter-in-law of Judah (Gen. 38).

Trible, Phyllis. *The Book of Jonah.* New Interpreter's Bible, 7. Nashville: Abingdon, 1996. Provides valuable analytical and interpretative comments for preacher and teacher. Trible characteristically suggests new interpretive possibilities for this narrative while remaining in conversation with other scholars.

Index of Ancient Sources

(Except for a book in its own commentary section)

OT TEXTS
Alpha Text (Greek)
.................163, 165
Septuagint (Greek)
..18, 162-64, 177, 179
Tanak (Hebrew Bible)
....................18, 281
Masoretic Text (Hebrew)
..18, 162-65, 177, 281

OLD TESTAMENT
Genesis
1–50 277
2:17 216
2:21 116
3:9 279
4 280
4:1-16 233
4:9 278
8:6-12 106
10:11-12 274
11 280
12:1-20 31
12:10 30
13 271
14:18-20 120
15:6 141
15:12 116
16:6 108
18:1-18 20
18–19 270-71
19 ....17, 20, 271
19:1-3 20
19:25 141
19:29 141
19:30-38 65
19:36-37 29
19:37 21
20:1-18 120
20:11 120
21:2 82
21:2-3 84
23:7 195
26:1 30
26:1-11 31
27:25-36 188
27:29 ....195, 204
27:34 204
29:32 84
29:32-35 85
30:1-24 85
30:24 84
31:20 108
32:18 47
34 208
35:16 29
35:19 29
37 275
37–50 ....161, 188, 240-41, 275
38 .....74, 85-86, 208, 270
38:1-30 65-66
38:27-30 74
39 275
39:6-20 188
39:10 196
39:14 117
40–41 275
41:40 188
41:42 203
42:5 30
43:14 207
47:20-21 167
50 ....223, 275
50:20 ....17, 223-24

Exodus
1–15 241
1–40 277
1:16 117
2:11-15 233
2:15 108
2:23-24 53
3:7 254
3:11 108
3:12 209
4:14-17 135
4:18 135
4:24-26 135
5:22-23 136
6:1-8 135
7–11 165
7–12 281
12 ....165, 277
12:14 165
12:26-27 249
14:11 117

14:31 141	27:8-11 30	4:11-12 189
15 253	35:19-27 279	4:14 189
15:20 75		
15:21 253	**Deuteronomy**	**1 Samuel**
17 194	1–34 277	1–31 18
18 120	5:16 208	1:14 82
20:5 36	6:20-25 249	1:20 82
20:12 208	10:17-19 43	2:1-10 128
21:23-24 233	13 208	2:21 36
21:24-25 193-94	15:1-18 53	4:9 117
22:21 20	15:7-8 54	9:2 216
22:22-24 43	16 .... 208, 277	10:1 216
22:25-27 53	18:22 98	14:11 117
23 277	19:8-13 119	15 194
23:7 233	19:16-21 194	15:3 246-47
23:10-11 66	21:1-9 119	15:8 194
23:11 53	23:3 17	15:9 246-47
32:34 36	23:3-5 271	16–31 281
33 228	24:19-21 283	16:1-13 28
33:13 228	25:5 270	17:12 28
34 277	25:5-10 269-70	24:4 60
34:6 149	25:10 270	27:1 216
	25:19 194	30:13 47
Leviticus	29:23 141	
1–27 277		**2 Samuel**
16:29-34 142	**Joshua**	1–24 281
16:30 142	1–24 .... 27, 161	3 215
18:16 270	2 .... 86, 120, 196	11 .. 87, 190, 208, 233
19:9-10 .... 53, 283	2:3 197	13 208
20:21 270	4 249	19:24 205
23 277	6:22-25 197	19:28 205
23:5 203-204	19:15 28	21:1 30
23:39-43 151		21:1-14 31
25 .... 54, 66-67	**Judges**	21:9 215
25:2-7 .... 53, 66	1–21 .... 18, 27, 161	21:14 31
25:8-10 71	3:12-30 271	24:22 282
25:25-34 .... 53, 279	4:21 .... 60, 116	
25:48-49 ... 62-63, 67, 279	6–8 190	**1 Kings**
	6:15 108	1–11 281
Numbers	4–5 17	1 87
1–36 277	4–5 75	1:31 195
14:18 149	11 190	14:19 219
21–25 21	13–16 190	17–19 109
22–24 .... 120, 271	14–16 17	17:8-10 105
24 222	19–21 .... 17, 28	17:9-10 106-108
24:13 120		18 .... 121, 281
24:20 .... 194, 222	**Ruth**	18–19 75
25 .... 21, 271	1–3 208	18:1-40 31
25:1 .... 59, 271	2:10 189	18:2 30
25:3-9 271	3:9 189	19:4 150
	3:11 189	20:31-32 204

Index of Ancient Sources

21 75
21:27-28 204

2 Kings
6:24-30 31
6:25 30
8:1-6 71
11 75
14:25-26 106
15 274
16 274
17 274
18–20 274
18:37 204
19:36 274
22:14-29 75
24 185
24–25 ... 108-109, 266
24:4 119
25 185

1 Chronicles
2:19-20 29
2:4-15 74
3:16 185

2 Chronicles
36:23 276

Ezra
1–10 .... 98, 268
1:1 179-80
1:2 117
1:2-4 276
4:14-15 219
9–11 20

Nehemiah
1–13 .... 98, 268
5:1 205
8:13-18 151
9:1 204
9:17 149
9:31 149

Esther
1–12 27
2:12-13 58
4:3 142
4:16 142
9:31 142

Job
1–42 40-41
1 40
1:1 150
1:1-22 40
1:8 150
3 150
4:7 232
9:12 232
21:7 232
24:12 232
38:5 278
38:8 278

Psalms
1–150 .... 121, 268
1:4 282
6:5 109
9:12 53
10:17-18 53
21:9 125
22 42
22:1 42
22:1-21 42
22:6-7 42
22:16-18 42
27:14 280
29:5-9 247
30:9 109
34:10 217
41 125
42 125
72 53
72:4 280
82 53
82:2-8 53
86:15 149
88:10 109
89:8-9 121
92:5-9 247
103:8 149
111:4 149
115:3 119
116 125
118 125
119:154 280
124 125
135:6 119
137 268
137:4 108
139:8 109
145:8 149

Proverbs
1–31 75
5:3 59
7:5 59
10:16 231
10:30 231
11:3 231
11:6 231
11:8 231
12:7 231
16:18 224
22:14 59
26:27 230

Ecclesiastes
1–12 18
6:12 206

Song of Solomon
1–8 .... 18, 75
5:7 59

Isaiah
1:23 53
6:10 154
11:6-9 255
21:7 125
41:15-16 254
45:1-2 179
53:5 232

Jeremiah
1:6 108
18:7-8 138-39,
                          143-44
29:7 242
29:10 179
26:10-15 119
29:23 206
34:8-17 67
36:5-10 142-43
36:6 142
36:7 143
36:9 142
36:23-26 143
46:10 253
49:18 141
50:40 141

Index of Ancient Sources

Lamentations
1–5 18

Ezekiel
14:14 106
14:20 106
28:3 106

Daniel
1:3-7 189
2:37 117
2:46 241
3 .... 189, 194
3:30 189
6 .... 178, 189
6:1 176
6:2 180
6:7 180
6:28 189
9:1 176

Book of the 12 Prophets 281-82

Hosea
11:9 154

Joel
1:1 105
1:2-4 142
1:13-14 142
2:13 149-50

Amos
4:1 53
7:3 143
7:6 143

Obadiah
3–4 223

Jonah
1:2 274
2:5 276-77
3:5-6 204
3:9 206

Micah
4:10 280
5:2 29

Nahum
1:3 149
3:19 154

Zechariah
7:3-7 142

NEW TESTAMENT
Matthew
1 65
1:1-17 86
1:18-25 .... 86, 208
1:21 209
1:25 84
2:1-23 86
4:18-22 109
5:5 224
5:44 253
8:25 122
11:19 87
12:18 88
12:38-42 144-45
12:39 106
12:40-41 95
12:9-14 .... 153, 223
16:4 144
18:15-20 12
18:19-20 267
19:30 254
20:1-16 155
21:31 279
25:23 88
25:40 155
26:20-25 216
27:1 223
27:11 197
27:24 .... 197, 223
27:62-66 223
28:1-6 223

Mark
1:16-20 109
5:30 279
6:23 213
10:27 97
10:43-45 87
14:17-21 216
15:34 42

Luke
1 .... 128, 253

1:26-56 208
1:49-53 254
1:51-53 222-23
1:52 253
1:57-63 85
2 165
2:5 208
6:25-27 243
6:27-28 254
11:29-32 144-45
11:32 145
17:4 146
22:21-23 216
23:34 233
23:41 232
24:21 280
24:44 281

John
8:5 278
10:22 277
11:48 197
11:48-50 181
13:21-30 216

Acts
10:22 120
15 198
15:28 267
19 197
21–22 197
23–24 197
28:16 197

Romans
3:23 77
5:6-11 154
8:28 17
8:39 190
12:2 225
15:26 54

1 Corinthians
14:29 11

2 Corinthians
5:17 76
9 231
9:3-4 231
9:6 232
9:10 232

Index of Ancient Sources

Galatians
2:10 54
4:4 209
5:22-23 130

Ephesians
1:10 209

Philippians
2:7 88

Colossians
1:24 41

1 Thessalonians
5:16 41

2 Thessalonians
3:1-13 243

2 Timothy
2:15 266

Hebrews
9 189-90
10:9-10 197
13:2 20

1 Peter
2:8-9 256
2:10 188

2 Peter
1:20 11

1 John
4:7-12 154

Revelation
1–22 162
4–10 154
11:15 255-56

APOCRYPHA
Daniel
13:61 194

Esther, Additions to
1:5 177
1:11 177
1:22 179

6:1 219
10:4-13 277
11:1 277
13:1-7 163
13:12 206
13:12-13 195
13:15 163
13–14 206
14:18-19 163
16:1-24 163

1 Maccabees
4:41-59 277

2 Maccabees
1:1-64 277
2:1-18 277

Sirach/Ecclesiasticus
44–50 189-90
49:10 282

Susanna
61 194

PSEUDEPIGRAPHA
Ahiqar, Letter of ... 242
Aristeas, Letter of
1-50 241
301-307 241

OTHER SOURCES
Aristotle 280
Assyrian art 274
Augustine of Hippo
 162
Tiglath-pileser III,
Annals of 274

The Author

Eugene F. Roop is president of Bethany Theological Seminary, Richmond, Indiana, and also Wieand Professor of Biblical Studies. He has taught there since 1977, after teaching at Earlham School of Religion in 1970-77. He is an ordained minister in the Church of the Brethren and has pastored churches in Indiana, Maryland, and Pennsylvania.

Roop is known for his disciplined yet devotional approach to Bible study, his transparent spiritual and prayer life, and his commitment to the Christian faith. This commentary is an expression of his lifelong enjoyment and study of biblical narrative.

He brings to his teaching and writing a deep commitment to the Bible as central to the teaching and preaching ministry of the congregation. His articles have appeared in various religious publications, and his books include *Genesis* (in the BCBC series), *Let the Rivers Run, Heard in Our Land,* and (with others) *A Declaration on Peace.*

After studying at Manchester College (B.S.), Roop earned further degrees at Bethany Theological Seminary (M.Div.), and Claremont Graduate University (Ph.D.). Through various programs, he also studied as a postgraduate in the USA and the UK. He has served extensively on boards and agencies for the community and for the church—congregational, district, and denominational.

Roop and his wife, Delora Mishler Roop, are members of the Richmond Church of the Brethren. They have two children and three grandchildren.

"The strength of the Anabaptist hermeneutic is its sensitivity to the human elements of the biblical text and the practical implications of the biblical message for believers today. In both regards, Eugene Roop's work on Ruth, Jonah and Esther is outstanding. Combining the best of recent scholarship with a high regard for the authority of Scripture, Roop makes us all grateful that these three short books have been preserved in the canon for our inspiration and edification." —*Daniel I. Block, John R. Sampey Professor of Old Testament Interpretation, The Southern Baptist Theological Seminary, Louisville, Kentucky*

"The editors of this handsome series did well to select Eugene Roop to interpret these three exquisite biblical narratives, for Roop is precisely the kind of sensitive and discerning commentator who attends to the literature in all its artistic depth and subtlety. Roop is well grounded in good interpretive method, and here uses his competence to write in clear and accessible ways that lets the text draw close to Church readers. Roop has a sense of the powerful theological intentionality of these texts, but like the texts themselves, lets that intentionality surface gently and playfully, showing restraint about things hidden, delight in things teasing, sobriety in truth affirmed, exactly how the Church may engage the Bible." —*Walter Brueggemann, Columbia Theological Seminary, Decatur, Georgia*

"A well-informed, reliable guide to three often-missed biblical books. Highly commended as a user-friendly tool for pastors and teachers. The church needs to hear these books, and this book gives them an understandable voice." —*Robert L. Hubbard Jr., North Park Theological Seminary, Chicago, Illinois*

"Eugene Roop shows awareness of those in the church who will read this volume as a means of understanding the Bible's relevance for their life and faith in the church. He has succeeded in giving due diligence both to the various intricacies of the text along with its meaning, but also he has taken careful steps to show its application for the community of the faithful who will benefit from the biblical message. Congratulations on achieving this important balance! This commentary could well serve as a model to other scholars on how to combine good biblical scholarship with a highly readable and practical approach to the biblical text. This is a commentary for the whole church and I highly recommend it!" —*Lee M. McDonald, Acadia Divinity College, Wolfville, Nova Scotia*

"Eugene Roop has written a very readable and informative commentary on the biblical books of Ruth, Jonah and Esther. The volume demonstrates that Roop is thoroughly acquainted with contemporary and traditional scholarship on these three books. A particular strength is the attention given to what he refers to as "weighty words" and the internal structures of the narratives. Roop's Christian commitments are in evidence when he engages puzzling theological matters such as the absence of God in the book of Esther. All three books are appropriately treated as narratives and examined as such."
—*Wilma Bailey, Christian Theological Seminary, Indianapolis, Indiana*

www.ingramcontent.com/pod-product-compliance
Lightning Source LLC
Chambersburg PA
CBHW020639230426
43665CB00008B/238